WORLD CUP
The Argentina Story

WORLD CUP

The Argentina Story
by David Miller of the *Daily Express*

FREDERICK WARNE

Acknowledgements

Of the 16 finalists in the World Cup I was able to see 12, and 14 of the 38 matches. All the rest I saw on television—some, thanks to the Buenos Aires press centre, several times!—but I am obviously indebted to many colleagues for information passed on in the international 'brokerage' which is central to every World Cup or Olympics. In particular I would like to thank the following for assistance: Francisco Bengolea and Carlos Fletcher (Argentina), Mick Michels (Belgium), Hans Henningsen and José Werneck (Brazil), Svend Nielsen (Denmark), Rene Court (FIFA), Patrick Mahé, Roland Mesmeur and Robert Nataf (France), Marc Serné and Joop van der Berg (Holland), Massimo Della Pergola (Italy), Nissim Kivity (Israel), Ian Archer, Rodger Baillie, Alex Cameron and Allan Herron (Scotland), Pedro Escartin (Spain), Hans Blickendorfer, Ulrich Kaiser, Dr Wilfried Gerhardt and Ulfert Schroeder (West Germany), and from England, among many, David Lacey (*The Guardian*), Brian Glanville and Rob Hughes (*The Sunday Times*), Hugh McIlvanney (*Observer*), Harry Miller (*Daily Mirror*), James Mossop (*Sunday Express*) and Jeff Powell (*Daily Mail*).

Copyright owners of the photographs are as follows:

Associated Press pages 8, 11, 12, 16, 18 (right), 38 (all), 39, 41 (both), 48, 49, 52, 60, 61, 63, 66, 74, 76, 78, 87, 88, 90, 96, 98, 100, 105, 106, 108, 111, 112, 113, 116, 122, 123, 131, 137, 146 (inset), 151, 153, 156 (both), 162, 168, 170; Keystone Press Agency pages 22, 23, 24, 27, 29 (both), 31, 33, 34, 37, 43, 63 (inset), 64, 70 (inset), 72; Popperphoto title page, pages 9, 15, 17, 18 (left), 99, 101, 104, 119, 124, 126, 127, 129, 134, 138, 139, 140, 142, 145, 146, 150, 158 (both), 159, 160, 165, 167; Syndication International colour photographs 1–13, pages 50, 51, 54, 59, 65, 68, 70, 80, 81, 82, 93, 106 (inset), 154.

With 13 colour photographs and 100 black and white photographs

Stop Press, Chapter 4, page 70

On September 5 1978 it was announced that Don Revie, former England manager, had asked the Football Association for a hearing regarding his indefinite suspension from all football for breach of contract, having in August served his writ for libel against the *Daily Mirror*.

Contents

Foreword by Sir Stanley Rous, CBE

Honorary President and former President of FIFA 1961–74

The author is fully qualified to write a detailed report of the FIFA World Cup in 1978. I first met him when he was a schoolboy at Charterhouse, one of Britain's oldest soccer schools, attending a summer coaching course for prominent boys. Later I saw him playing for Cambridge against Oxford, and for Pegasus, the combined Universities club which became famous by twice winning the FA Amateur Cup.

As a writer on sports generally, and football in particular, he became well known with *The Daily Telegraph* and *Sunday Telegraph*, and since 1973 he has been a leading authority on football for the *Daily Express*. This book is the third he has written on World Cup tournaments. In 1966 he contributed to the Football Association official report of the tournament, and in 1970 and 1974 he was commissioned by the FA and the West German FA to write comprehensive reports of the World Cups in Mexico and Germany.

Although England regrettably did not compete in Argentina in 1978, David Miller has given extensive coverage of their unsuccessful qualifying matches, and of the entire campaign of Scotland. He is so knowledgeable about the players, managers, administrators and the referees that every outstanding incident before, during and after the games is expertly recorded. I hope readers will turn these pages over and over again to recall the skilful football which will long live in the memory of all participants and spectators.

Stanley Rous
London, July 1978

CHAPTER ONE

Triumphant Hosts

The eleventh World Cup, a whirlpool of colour, emotion and controversy, was fascinating most of all because it provoked a torrent of questions, the answers to all of which will be agreed by no two players, managers, administrators or journalists. Certainly there were no great teams such as Hungary, Uruguay and Brazil in the period 1954–70, while Holland had fallen slightly from their own plateau of shimmering elegance which should have gained them the title in 1974. There were no great players, if by great we mean those super-players of whom there have been barely half a dozen since the Second World War: Di Stefano, who never played in the World Cup Finals, Schiaffino, Puskas, Pele, Bobby Charlton, George Best (who also never played in the finals) and Cruyff. Another was Josef Bozsik, illustrious colleague of Puskas in 1954, whose early death, together with that of Real Madrid's revered president, Santiago Bernabeu, was a sad prelude to the finals.

Mercifully, Argentina was free for the duration of the tournament of the political violence we had all feared throughout the previous two years, and the controversies were all confined to football. Were Argentina, the triumphant hosts, given the World Cup by an Italian referee's incompetence? Would the risk-all, adventurous tactics of Cesar Menotti have succeeded anywhere but at home in Argentina? Were Holland, ruthless though they may at times have been, robbed? Were the referees as uniformly weak as was suggested? Were Brazil, steadily improving after an abysmal opening, just too late to regain their title? Were France, eliminated in the First Round, the most gifted team of all? Had Italy *genuinely* changed their defensive mentality under Enzo Bearzot? Were Scotland mad, or merely mismanaged by Ally MacLeod? Were managers, indeed, controlling events, or controlled by them? Is West Germany's leadership in international soccer at an end, following their failure to beat Tunisia and defeat by Austria? Is Afro-Asia *really* on the threshold of international soccer equality? Is FIFA wise even to contemplate a 24-nation final tournament in Spain in 1982? Is football better or worse than it was four, eight, 20 years ago? Was the 1978 World Cup a 'feast of football' stage-managed with panache by the host nation, or a farrago of financially and politically motivated, vested interests—a juggernaut in which FIFA sometimes seems no longer to have control of the steering or the brakes?

Ten days before the finals, Hungary were England's guests in London for a friendly match. Their manager, Lajos Baroti, is a father figure in the game: now 63, a handsome, white-haired man who has been national manager, off and on, since the 1958 finals in Sweden, the most experienced of all the men in charge in Argentina, a man clinging to concepts of the game as it used to be when Hungary were supreme. At a reception given for him by the Sports Writers' Association, Baroti said, with the air of a man embarking on a voyage which he fears: 'This

is the age of the artisan. The game has altered so radically in 25 years. When Puskas was at his peak he would run maybe two or three kilometres during a match. Now it is necessary to run seven kilometres, maybe more. We know the World Cup will be hard, but though we have a young team I think we can be as hard as anybody. It is very difficult for us having to play Argentina in our first match, yet because it is *their* first they will be nervous, and this may give us our chance. It is vital that the referees do their job: if not it will be the death of football. It is important that the referees should be selected from those countries where there is a high standard of football. I am optimistic that we have a young player, our centre-forward Torocsik, who may prove to be the most outstanding since Puskas. It is not our aim to be expedient; we would rather die beautifully.'

They were prophetic comments. Although there were some enthralling, classic matches, there were many which were all too artisan. Argentina were nervous; and the referees were weak, as Hungary tragically discovered to their cost when, following extensive provocation, they had Nyilasi and Torocsik sent off in the closing stages against Argentina, thereby terminating their chances. And Torocsik, in those 80-odd minutes, revealed that with self-discipline, and protection from referees, he could indeed become a super-player.

The referees were at times, without question, lamentable: Garrido of Portugal

Another ticker-tape welcome cascades down from the terraces of the River Plate stadium at the start of the World Cup Final.

and Dubach of Switzerland grossly favouring Argentina in their opening matches against Hungary and France, likewise Rainea of Romania and Barreto of Uruguay leaning towards Italy in their encounters with the luckless French and Hungarians. In many matches players were not cautioned for the most deliberate and cynical fouls, mostly committed to gain tactical advantage rather than done with malicious intent. And where players were deliberately dangerous, and should have been sent off, they were sometimes not even cautioned. In the frenetic encounter between Argentina and Brazil, in their second match in the Second Round, there were 14 fouls in the first 16 minutes, yet Karoly Palotai of Hungary, widely regarded as one of the world's best referees, did not issue one caution in that time.

And the Final? The process by which the referee, Sergio Gonella of Italy, was nominated was unsatisfactory to say the least. The appointment of referees is handled by the FIFA special standing committee of nine men, with Dr Artemio Franchi of Italy the chairman. Dr Roger Barde (France), José Codesal (Uruguay), Nikolai Latyschev (USSR), John Mowat (Scotland), Friedrich Seipelt (Austria), and Koe Ewe Teik (Malaysia) all have extensive experience as first-class referees, Javier Arriaga (Mexico) and Dr Ahmed Zouiten (Tunisia) comparatively little. When it came to deciding the Final, the Europeans—Barde, Latyschev, Mowat and Seipelt— all voted for Gonella, the other four for Barreto of Uruguay, leaving Franchi the casting vote. A South American had never refereed the World Cup Final, and there is little doubt that Barreto would have got the job had Uruguay's neighbours not been involved in the Final—even though Barreto was the man who had cravenly sent off Trevor Cherry, the victim, as well as Daniel Bertoni, the aggressor, in England's friendly with Argentina the year before. Barreto was also the man who had sent off Nanninga of Holland for laughing.

I personally can accept that Franchi gave his countryman the casting vote strictly on objective terms. Yet Franchi was confronted with two rather modest alternatives. Where the referee's committee slipped up, in my opinion, was in giving the Argentina–Italy First Round match to Abraham Klein of Israel, to whose extensive reputa-

Italian referee Sergio Gonella in training. His handling of the World Cup Final was heavily criticized.

tion for efficiency was added the advantage of coming from a neutral continent. But once Argentina had lost to Italy, with wails of protest about Klein's impartial and strict control of the Argentinians, he had been compromised for the Final. Argentina duly let it be known to FIFA that they would protest at the appointment of Klein for the Final on the grounds, not of his handling of their earlier game, but of Holland's political alignment with Israel! There was a mood within the referee's committee to appoint Klein and damn the consequences, but it lacked conviction; and the outcome was a final in which Gonella's feebleness, even over Argentina's gamesmanship before the kick-off, spoiled a potentially momentous event.

The fact which the Dutch must face is that, though dominating so much of the first 90 minutes, they failed to win their second successive Final because of poor finishing close to goal. As simple as that! But their frustration, and that of millions of neutrals, was intensified by the licence given by Gonella to Argentina to disrupt Holland's rhythm: the repeated handling of through passes by centre-back Luis Galvan, his outrageous foul on Johan Neeskens. On the other hand, Holland forfeited much sympathy by their barefaced attempt to reduce Argentina's impetus from the start with brutal tackling. The Dutch, of course, would argue that their physical attitude was the result of *knowing* which way the referee would lean. Enzo Bearzot, Italy's hugely experienced and fair-minded manager, had told Jeff Powell of the *Daily Mail*, while watching Argentina against Poland during the Second Round: 'Look at Argentina, not just how well Mario Kempes is playing; look at that Polish player brought down without a free-kick. It is nothing outrageous, but it is enough—enough to disrupt any team trying to beat Argentina. Men like Passarella are difficult enough opponents without additional licence. Our achievement in beating Argentina was such that they should have given us a little World Cup for winning that group! We may be the only nation to beat them here, but that is not because they are the best team.'

Before the tournament began, I had forecast in the *Daily Express* that the first three in the finals would be Argentina, Brazil and Holland; I had Brazil and Holland the wrong way round. I have to admit that my deep-seated conviction concerning the hosts was based to a degree on cynicism concerning the referees: that they would not withstand the colossal pressure imposed on them by the home crowds. Sir Walter Winterbottom, former England manager and now Chairman of the FIFA Technical Committee, said after Argentina's controversial 2–1 win over France: 'I'm expected not to criticize referees, which is a matter for the Referees' Committee, but I have to say that some of the refereeing has been slack and in the River Plate stadium the referees have been affected by the crowd.'

After Argentina's victory in the Final, the European press raged at Gonella's handling of the game. Patrick Mahé of *Le Figaro* of Paris said: 'What Gonella did was worse than awarding a penalty which was unjust. Little by little he allowed Argentina to prevent Holland from playing.' *De Volkskrant* of Amsterdam claimed: 'Gonella's performance was not a major factor in the result, but Argentina were always given the benefit of the doubt.'

Sour grapes? To some extent, possibly. Yet it has always been, will always be, a colossal advantage to the host nation to play in front of its own crowds. From 1930, when Uruguay won the inaugural competition, beating Argentina across the

The gesture that says it all. Mario Kempes, Argentina's storming match-winner, has just scored the opening goal of the World Cup Final. Goalkeeper Jongbloed and defender Brandts contemplate the damage.

River Plate in Montevideo, the pattern has been continuous. Italy won at home in 1934, then in neighbouring France in 1938. Uruguay beat Brazil, the hosts, in Rio in 1950, West Germany triumphed across the border in Switzerland in 1954, Sweden reached the Final against Brazil four years later, modest Chile the semi-final in 1962. England won at Wembley, and not without protest that all their matches were at the same stadium and that the referee and linesman awarded them a goal that wasn't in the Final. Mexico, with more hysterical support than Argentina, reached the quarter-final; West Germany won again in Munich, in 1974. There can be little doubt that Spain will profit from the advantage in four years' time. So I am certainly one of those who, while readily agreeing that the control of matches in 1978 was inadequate, does not begrudge the Argentinians their triumph. Menotti's team brought colour and excitement to the game, playing with a precarious insistence on attack which made every match a tightrope walk. They were the perfect antidote to the computer-football of Poland, whose manager Jacek Gmoch claimed after the goal-less opening against Germany: 'The fact that Poland succeeded in neutralizing Germany should in my opinion be regarded as positive.'

Ron Greenwood, the England manager whose succession to Don Revie, and introduction of adventurous policies comparable to Menotti's, had come too late to rescue England's World Cup qualifying campaign against Italy, Finland and Luxembourg, was adamant that Argentina had been good for football. He said: 'The finals have proved that the more adventurous you are, the more successful you will be. It is important to be unconventional, not to conform to modern patterns of defensiveness. The finals have re-emphasized the value of running with the ball at the right time, demonstrated by other teams as well as Argentina.'

It is usually said that a team needs at least five world-class players to win the World Cup, and Argentina possessed those five: Fillol, a remarkable goalkeeper whose catching technique is considered all 'wrong' in Europe, but whose succession of magnificent saves in almost every match was indispensable; Passarella, the dynamic *libero* (the free man or 'sweeper' as he is known in Britain), a defender with an attacking flair which recalled the illustrious Austrian, Ocwirc; Ardiles, suave schemer with a tactical intelligence to match his creative skills, subsequently bought by Tottenham Hotspur a fortnight after the finals, together with reserve midfielder Villa, in a breath-taking £700,000 coup; Luque, a volatile centre-forward with skill at speed and a tremendous shot; and Kempes, the talisman recalled from Valencia in Spain to inspire the team, match-winner, top scorer in the competition, another irresistible player at speed. Add to these five the two above-average wingers, Bertoni and Ortiz, and an attacking left-back Tarantini, and there was every justification for Argentina becoming only the sixth holders of the title in 48 years. It is a distinction they have long deserved, having produced a richer flow of world-class players than any nation except perhaps Yugoslavia, so many of whom have gone abroad, bleeding the game at home.

Menotti might well have had a stronger defence had he had the services of full-back Enrique Wolff of Real Madrid, and Oswaldo Piazza of St. Étienne, an even stronger attack had Renee Houseman reproduced his 1974 form; but he could not get Wolff's release in time, and Piazza was forced to return to France when his family was involved in a car crash. No matter, Argentina surged to victory on an emotional tidal wave which engulfed the whole country every time they played.

A nation celebrates. The crowds mass for a seventh time around the Obelisk on Aveneida 9 July, on the night of Argentina's 3–1 triumph over Holland.

It was spontaneous, infectious and harmless, though whether success in the World Cup really offered some symbolic route to political salvation for a nation emerging from years of internal strife and oppression must be doubtful. But while the wine of euphoria was flowing, the people were happy to drink it until it flooded their senses, and in their intense celebrations they were rarely objectionable.

On every match night in Buenos Aires, close on eight million people took to the streets of the capital's 700 square miles, yet there was never a vandal, a pickpocket or a drunk in sight. The only damage was to the suspension of groaning cars laden, inside and out, with wild-eyed delirious Latin Americans blowing whistles and beating a samba on a saucepan lid. On the night of the Final they perched in the trees of San Martin Square outside the Plaza Hotel, where the victory banquet was boy-cotted by the angry Dutch, for five hours or more just for a glimpse of Cesar and his heroes. They roamed the streets until dawn, thousands of impromptu percussion bands, little groups of up to 40, rhythmically beating out the message of hope and optimism for a people who have known so much strife and anxiety ... and fear. My hotel was the nearest building to the ceremonial centre of the city—the obelisk monument on Aveneida 9 July, one of the widest streets in the world outside Bra-zilia. It is almost 200 yards across, and for three hours before and after midnight on match evenings it was paved wall-to-wall with people, like some gigantic, open-air tube train in the rush hour. At some stages you could not leave the hotel because of the static, physical pressure against the doors of the crowds outside.

It may sound pretentious, to anyone who was not there to witness this spon-taneous emotional intoxication, yet a simple game of football provoked perhaps the largest peaceful demonstrations ever known to mankind. One moment the streets would be deserted, as a nation crouched round the cathode-ray images of men belting a ball into a net; 30 minutes later you could not hear your own voice above the cacophony of horns and hooters, whistles and saucepans.

At the press centre in Buenos Aires, where we would watch the transmission of those matches we could not attend, there was a waiter whose resemblance to the incompetent Manuel of 'Fawlty Towers' had been a matter of international anguish for more than a month. The night Argentina put six past Peru, he was galvanized by the sight of Kempes and Luque on TV into such a frenzy of action that coffee and fried eggs arrived ready-mixed on the tray. He was not the only one whose nerves at times were frayed. There was the girl at the accreditation desk who, vainly attempting to grapple simultaneously in Spanish, English, Italian and German with the frenzied demands of 4000 journalists for press tickets, which at that moment she simply did not possess, complained: 'My God, I am driving me crazy.'

For five weeks, across five major cities, with all the pressures imposed by the artificial, often impossible demands of this gigantic sports festival, I did not encounter a single rude or unco-operative Argentinian. The charm of the people was sincere. They were transparently neither unhappy nor, any longer, oppressed. When I arrived on one occasion in Mendoza, short of money, at a hotel which did not accept credit cards, the manager merely smiled and said: 'Are you coming back next week? OK, pay us when you return.' Can you imagine that in London, New York, Paris or Frankfurt? There are things which happen in Argentina on the darker side which need eliminating, but never have I met a people so clearly intent on putting their house in order. I do not believe this was an illusion.

Should Holland have won? Enzo Bearzot said early in the tournament: 'Ever since 1974 everybody took their inspiration from Holland. However, although everybody tried to imitate them, nobody was able to equal them. I believe that Holland play the best football in the world. It was possible to argue in 1974 that they were almost unbeatable, but today that is no longer so.' Perhaps the Dutch were undermined by their own slightly ambivalent attitude: undecided just how total to make their Total Football, how much to attack, how much to defend. Before the final Willy van der Kerkhof told Rob Hughes of *The Sunday Times*: 'People say that we do not have the passion to win a World Cup, that it does not mean enough to us. But to me it means everything, the absolute climax of a footballer's career. Club football gives us good rewards. I earn more than £1500 a week with PSV Eindhoven, but the final is above money. This is the end. On Sunday I will give everything. All of us will, and I honestly believe it will be enough. I think we are stronger than in 1974 with Cruyff, more collective. Cruyff is a wonderful player, but he dominated others; the team revolved around him. Now he is gone, men such as Rep and Rensenbrink and Krol come out and show their true worth. The strength of Dutch football is team strength. From the age of eight or nine we are taught the importance of running without the ball. Always we have movement. When I have the ball there are three or four others running, open for the pass. With that, we have the capacity to counter-attack against Argentina. They come at the goal with great speed, with many players pressing forward, but they leave spaces behind and we can use them. Kempes is a marvellous forward, a player of the top class, and Luque is powerful and always dangerous, but if we can neutralize those two they have not too much left. Of course, there will be a great noise at River Plate, much nervous pressure at the start, but we are not afraid.'

But Rep and Rensenbrink on the day failed to bury Argentina when they had the chance. It was Rep who, presented with an open goal by Cruyff in the second half of the 1974 Final, had struck the ball against Germany's goalkeeper Maier—though Rep has always claimed that Cruyff 'chickened' out of responsibility by passing the ball instead of going it alone. Now Rensenbrink was the major culprit: a player of such sublime skills in European club football now twice missed from a few yards, so that Neeskens, who for eight years has put fear in the heart of every opponent as he drives through a match like some relentless Roman charioteer, is forced to admit: 'Twice we have shown the world how we can play, twice we have nothing. When Rensenbrink shot at the end of normal time it seemed it must be a goal, and that would have been a fair result because we had dominated the second half. But the ball bounced off the post. In extra-time we attacked, but Argentina scored in their first counter-attack. Kempes, who is a great player, even then had luck; the ball bounces for him and not for our defenders. That has been our luck in the World Cup.'

Brazil's shoddy descent even further into physical intimidation than was evident in 1974 lost them many of the admirers they had won in 12 glorious years from 1958 to 1970, winning three titles. Yet I believe that, had their reversion to their traditional style come sooner than the last four matches, they might well have

14

Welsh referee Clive Thomas disallows Brazil's winning goal in the last minute against Sweden—one of many controversial decisions in the finals. Zico (*left*) scorer, Oscar (3) and Edinho look stunned; Sjoberg celebrates the 1–1 draw.

regained the title; and we would be praising rather than condemning them. An undercurrent of resentfulness remained even when they were outplaying Italy to take third place; but I am convinced that if they would learn from the example of Argentina and have faith in their own marvellously instinctive skills, they can go in four years' time to Spain, where once again the sun will be on their backs, in full bloom. Those who roundly dismiss Brazil for kicking, for attempting under Claudio Coutinho to become more European than the Europeans, should pause to reflect where Brazil first found themselves compromised: in England in 1966, when they were kicked to bits under the permissive eye of English referees.

It was a major loss to the tournament when France, suffering a ludicrous penalty awarded to Argentina and denied a justifiable one themselves, were eliminated—just as they began to reveal what they might have achieved with such magnificent players as Tresor, their *libero* from Guadeloupe, Platini and Bathenay in midfield, Rocheteau and Six in attack. The draw which placed Argentina, Italy, France and Hungary in the same group was one instance of gross mismanagement by FIFA, if its function is to stage the best possible football tournament and not some United Nations political festival.

On Italy we must reserve judgement. When it seemed that Bearzot had succeeded in an astonishing metamorphosis of the Italian mentality, from defence to attack, just when they were looking the most compact of all teams, their mental discipline crumbled; and we reflected ruefully on Baroti's opinion: 'If England, not Italy, had qualified I'm sure they would have reached the last four. They have that mental and physical discipline which is so essential in a tournament such as this, when you must play six or seven matches in under four weeks.' It is ironic that the same over-

crowded intensity of fixtures, which limits the development of English skills, perhaps also gives them that mental discipline which Bearzot and others such as Miljan
Miljanic so admire. As Miljanic says: 'The game in England is damaged by "industrial football", but the fact remains that England still has one of the richest supplies
of natural talent, and the best temperament for the game at the highest level anywhere in the world.'

And Scotland? The danger to Scottish football for the last few years has been,
and will continue to be, its inextricable identification with Scottish nationalism:
eleven men in blue jerseys shouldering the burden of that historic inferiority com-
plex of a nation of five million, many of whom place hating the English almost
on the level of a national industry. Why else should tens of thousands of Scots fans
march to Hampden Park for a match against Czechoslovakia in the World Cup
qualifying competition chanting: 'If you hate the f—— English, clap your hands.'

The thousands who believed the hollow, trite assurances of manager Ally
MacLeod that Scotland were heading for the World Cup with the scent of victory
already strong in their nostrils, believed him because they wanted to believe him,
because he talked like one of them. Alan Sharp, the Scottish novelist, who had been
to Germany four years before to watch Scotland in the World Cup, had written:
'Against Brazil it was possible to believe that we had taken that step forward, beyond
our intense infantilism, our terror of being found out. "Found out!" There's an
epitaph for you. I have lived all my life waiting for that dread moment when they'll
see what I'm really like, not what I claim I'm like. We're all Calvinists, throttled
by the horror of pre-election, doomed for ever to pretend elitism while endlessly
dreading discovery of the pretence.'

Duel for Third Place. Brazil's libero
Amaral makes another perfectly timed
tackle: this one on Italian winger Roberto
Bettega. Brazil won 2–1.

Hence the long-standing, illusory conviction of the Scots that they can lose to every team in the world and beat England and claim they are world champions! Instead of attempting to control or rationalize this emotional self-betrayal, MacLeod from the very start thrived upon it, actually fuelled it like someone rushing round opening all the doors of a blazing house, so that ultimately he was scorched by his own boasts, his own extravagant assertions and false optimism. It began with telling his squad, soon after his appointment halfway through the qualifying competition: 'I'm a born winner.' And from then on it continued upwards in ever-increasing hyperbole: 'I don't dislike the English, I hate their guts'; 'at the very least Scotland deserve third place in Argentina'; after defeat by England a fortnight before the finals, the assertion that the winning goal was scored 'by the worst player on the field, from a pass from the second-worst player'; all the way through the catastrophe of the first two matches to the statement after they had defeated Holland: 'We've all read what the media have been saying and this morning we got together and said: "We'll stuff the lot of them".' Was it really the press who swallowed the pills and missed the penalties, who didn't go to watch the opposition beforehand and then failed to mark them on the pitch? The nation back home had been seduced by the cries of an extrovert manager who was never equipped for the job for which he had been appointed.

Italian winger Roberto Bettega inflicts Argentina's only defeat with the only goal in the 67th minute of their first round encounter, as Tarantini's tackle fails. Olguin, Ardiles, Benetti, Galvan and Passarella look on.

For that, the men of the Scottish Football Association who selected MacLeod must take some of the blame. The tragedy for the Scots was that, for the second World Cup in succession, one of the most experienced and able managers in Europe, Jock Stein of Celtic, was merely a spectator. Yet had not Stein repeatedly rejected offers to lead his country to glory? The harsh truth is that for two decades the most prominent Scots managers have, reasonably, preferred the rewards and security of working with a top club. If patriotism is their uniting virtue, then Stein has dis-

appointed his countrymen as much as MacLeod ... for he had so much more to offer.

MacLeod, former Blackburn, St Mirren and Hibernian winger, had known nothing outside the confines of Scottish league football, yet he ensnared the Scottish press into joining him in the conspiracy of false optimism with his demagogue's empty oratory. 'We Scots are best with our backs to the wall.' Rubbish. 'The bad season Masson and Rioch have had at Derby is a blessing in disguise; when they join us they will be happy to get away and we will reap the benefit.' Rubbish. 'Our failure to win a match in the British Championship will make us all the better when we get to Argentina.' Rubbish.

The Scottish press, having jumped on the bandwagon with the rest of Ally's Army, found themselves trapped on a vehicle out of control, but open to charges of treason if they deserted. Meanwhile, MacLeod was stoking his own ultimate bonfire with rampant excursions into commercial exploitation of his new-found fame. Yet when he came to negotiate the players' bonus for reaching the Second Round, he got the figures wrong, informing them that they would share £15,000, when in fact it would be £30,000, increasing to £50,000 for reaching the last four and £100,000 if they were in the Final. Whatever the bargaining between MacLeod and the SFA, his handling of the finances only further reduced the players' confidence in him. The fact that the hotel at Alta Gracia, twenty-five miles outside

Left Teófilo Cubillas, whose two goals for Peru helped to sink Scotland in their opening match, exchanges shirts with Kenny Dalglish.

Right A man alone. Scots' winger Willie Johnston returns to the hotel as the drug row breaks over him.

18

Cordoba, was less than luxurious, that the training pitch was terrible, would all have been taken in their stride had the players believed the squad was under control.

When MacLeod selected out-of-form players for the opening match against Peru, then ignored the plea from his own substitutes' bench to make changes before it was too late, and finally the next morning blamed the players, that was the last straw. Professional sportsmen are selfish, almost by definition. When all is going well in a squad, antagonisms are buried because the interests of the squad are synonymous with the interest of the individual. But when things start to come apart at the hinges, then players immediately look for ways in which they can make the most capital for themselves. A squad solidly together would have survived the revelation of Willie Johnston's positive drug test in the same way that England rode the Bobby Moore affair* in Bogota eight years previously. But in the mood at the Scots camp at the time, it only served to deepen the rifts in which several players were not speaking to the manager, or to each other.

Lou Macari was subsequently disciplined for selling his comments on the Scots' circus to *The Sun*, but he had told Hugh McIlvanney during the First Round: 'If clever people had been in charge, they would have taken the pressure off by telling us we were coming to play the best players in the world. Instead, we were bombarded with crap about beating the rest of the world into the ground. How could anyone be so optimistic about our chances? When did you last see Scotland play really good football, play with positive rhythm and a consistent pattern? In the home internationals, and the qualifying games before them, it was a fight, a battering-ram job. It was a fight when we beat the Czechs and a fight when we beat the Welsh at Anfield. Meanwhile the likes of Tunisia and Iran would be slogging away in their training camps for the last two months with the World Cup as the only target. Tunisia and Iran are better prepared than we are. In our last match before coming here the lads exhausted themselves trying to beat England. It couldn't be any other way with 80,000 mad Scotsmen yelling "*Gie us an English heid*".'

At home, the Chrysler car company hurriedly withdrew its advertising campaign, depicting the Scots team round an Avenger model with the legend: 'They both run rings round the opposition.' It is not the slightest satisfaction for me to say that I was in no way surprised at any of the problems. Two weeks before the departure for Argentina, the *Daily Express* had headlined my story *Has Ally Blown It?*, after the drab draw with Ireland. I was invited to appear on Scottish television, rather as some insulting English freak, and patronizingly wished a 'safe' journey to Hampden for the match between England and Scotland two days later. As someone else has said, the Scots spend a lifetime lying in wait for the English insult.

As at least part of my information on the state of affairs within the squad came from the players themselves, I advocated after the Peru game that the players should take over the tactical direction and if possible the selection of the team—which is what happened, but only after the eclipse against Iran. The surging, spirited victory over Holland only served to show just what might have developed if Scotland had been properly directed from the start. Which is sadly an echo of what we were all saying four years ago after the finals in West Germany. The Johnston scandal

---

* Moore was falsely charged and detained in Columbia for the alleged theft of a jeweller's bracelet.

was in my opinion inflated out of proportion—conceived in naïvety, delivered out of stupidity. Johnston was foolish to have been taking pills, a stimulant containing the prohibited drug fencamfamin, and MacLeod should have been sufficiently in touch to know that he possessed them. The worst aspect of the case was the exposure of the use of the drug by Johnston's club, West Bromwich Albion, and by implication other English clubs. Scotland had no option but to take the most severe action, an instant life-ban on Johnston, to protect what was left of their reputation.

The furore surrounding the demise of the champions, Germany, was only slightly less heated than at Alta Gracia. The two draws, by Tunisia and Iran against Germany and Scotland, were the results which will give most impetus to Afro-Asia's demand for a larger proportion of places in the finals. Although Germany progressed to the Second Round, they were governed by fear, and disproved the tribute from Andy Roxburgh, Scotland's director of coaching, who had said: 'The difference between Scotland and Germany is that when things are going badly, Germany can fall back on their method.' They did, and nothing happened—confirming the forecast given to me a whole year before by Miljan Miljanic, the famous Yugoslav manager, when he said: 'Germany's domination is drawing to a close, because they have no new young players of real quality coming through.' We await with interest their European Championship qualifying group with Wales, Turkey and Malta.

Afro-Asia once again were airing their claims during the FIFA Congress immediately before the finals. It is they who are pressing the President, Joao Havelange of Brazil, to extend the 1982 finals in Spain to 24 nations; and their argument will have been swollen by the 'success' of Tunisia and Iran. I believe it is only a matter of time before the emerging Third World *does* draw level with the traditional areas of soccer power, Europe and South America; though it will take at least another 20 years *if*, and only if, Europe and South America concentrate on being positive instead of being afraid, on following the lead of Argentina and France. It was obvious to me, watching Sudan in the 1972 Olympics, that Africa is sitting on a mine of talent only waiting to be developed. But for the moment there is no case for Afro-Asia to be granted a larger share of the finals to the exclusion of more prominent European nations such as England, USSR and Yugoslavia, in 1978. Professor Sir Harold Thompson, chairman of the FA, firmly shot down the Afro-Asian plea for 1982 in a severe speech at the Congress, pointing out that European nations provide more than 80 per cent of FIFA's revenue.

FIFA will be crazy if they expand from 16 to 24 nations for 1982, for three reasons: (1) they will have to revert to 16 in 1986 because Colombia cannot accommodate 24; (2) it will increase the expense of the finals by 50 per cent with *no* increase in the fee which worldwide TV will be prepared to pay; and (3) it will double the number of bad matches without adding to the number of spectacular matches. At its Congress in Istanbul in April 1978, UEFA (the European federation) passed a resolution to agree to an increase to 24 only if their percentage share of places is maintained, i.e. 13 instead of nine, plus Spain the hosts making 14. The Third World will never sanction that; and as UEFA have stated, *they* will pull out of the World Cup if their conditions are not met, taking Spain with them. It seems unlikely that Havelange will be able to keep his promise of expansion.

20

CHAPTER TWO

History of the World Cup

The idea of a world football championship was first put forward in 1904, year of the formation of FIFA, the governing body. Britain, home of the game, can take little credit for the launching of what was to become the world's major sporting spectacle, greater even than the Olympics... because Britain, or rather the separate associations of England, Scotland, Northern Ireland and Wales, adopted a consistently isolationist attitude to the rest of the world, withdrew from FIFA long before the inaugural competition of 1930, and did not rejoin until after the Second World War. It was not until the fourth World Cup of 1950, in Brazil, that England at last took part in the finals.

The popularity of the Olympic football tournaments of the twenties, in Antwerp, Paris and Amsterdam, was the prime force in bringing about the World Cup. In 1926, Austria, Hungary, Czechoslovakia and Italy proposed the formation of a European Championship—for full professionals as opposed to the 'restricted' Olympic amateurs—but this was shelved because of the impending global competition and did not reappear until its present form in 1958–60. After the 1928 Amsterdam Olympics, the World Cup finally took root, and was formally agreed at the 1929 FIFA Congress—the same year as England's first defeat by a foreign side, Spain, who won 4–3 in Madrid.

There were six applicants to stage the first tournament: Italy, the Netherlands, Hungary, Sweden, Spain and Uruguay. But the condition that the hosts must pay the travelling and accommodation expenses of all the teams led to some hasty withdrawals, the honour finally going to Uruguay, Olympic Champions of 1924 and 1928, for whom 1930 would be the centenary of their independence.

1930

An Atlantic crossing by boat in the years of the great depression was not what it is today. With the expense, even in those modest days, of paying their players for the two-month trip, many European countries backed out, only Belgium, France, Yugoslavia and Romania—under the patronage of King Carol—making the journey. The form of the first competition consisted of four pools, played as mini-leagues, the winners going into the semi-finals. In fact, because of withdrawals, three pools had only three teams, thus:

Argentina, Chile, France, Mexico
Brazil, Yugoslavia, Bolivia
Uruguay, Romania, Peru
Belgium, Paraguay, USA

1930 The captains, Jose Nasazzi (Uruguay) and Nolo Ferreyra (Argentina), shake hands before the kick-off in the first World Cup Final in Montevideo, watched by referee John Langenus of Belgium. Uruguay won 4–2.

Predictably, Uruguay met Argentina in the final, establishing the pattern of ascendancy of the stronger teams from the home continent which remained for half a century. This was a repeat of the 1928 Olympic Final, which had gone to a replay. Uruguay, 2–1 down at half-time, won 4–2. The tournament made a healthy profit and the South Americans had established a reputation which would arouse excitement for the next ten World Cups.

1934

With 32 entries for the second World Cup, so successful was the first, a qualifying competition had to be introduced. Politics intruded for the first time, Mussolini's fascist regime anxious to stage the finals in 'unison' with the 1936 Berlin Olympics. Italy eventually were nominated because they had sufficient stadia in which to play the expanding number of matches. Uruguay, still smarting from the lack of European support in 1930, refused to defend their title.

Austria, the outstanding European team of the era, were favourites, but had a rough passage. After beating France 3–2 in extra-time, they played Hungary in the quarter-finals. The clash of these historic neighbours became a brawl when Hungary were awarded a penalty with Austria leading 2–0. Sarosi scored, fighting broke out, and Markos, Hungary's right-winger, was sent off. Austria held out, but in the semi-final were beaten by the only goal from Guaita of Italy . . . one of three Argentinians in the Italian side.

The others were Orsi and Monti, centre-half in the 1930 final. Vittorio Pozzo, Italy's manager, justified their inclusion on the grounds that because of their paren-

1934 Italy, one of the first of the 'tough' teams, and 2–1 final winners over Czechoslovakia. *From left, standing:* Combi, Monti, Ferraris, Allemandi, Guaita, Ferrari. *Kneeling:* Schiavio, Meazza, Monzeglio, Bertolini, Orsi.

tage they could have fought for Italy in the First World War, therefore they could play football. In the final in Rome, Italy met Czechoslovakia in a hard, physical match, winning 2–1 after being behind.

The receipts were huge, both finalists receiving handsome bonuses; the pattern of commercialization and nationalism which was to mar later finals was emerging. Fanatical support of the home team had again proved invaluable, and would regularly do so again. England were still absent, though it was the opinion of the Austrian manager, Hugo Mcisl, that had they competed they would not even have reached the final.

1938

In recognition of the work of Jules Rimet, after whom the trophy was now known, the third World Cup was given to France, already nervously glancing once again at her German neighbour. There were 36 entries, but Austria, overrun by Germany in the spring, withdrew without even sympathetic protest from the rest. Spain entered, but could not mobilize a team because of the Civil War. Uruguay again stayed away; Argentina entered, then withdrew. Among the entries were Estonia, Latvia and Lithuania, shortly due for Soviet 'amalgamation'. For the first time the hosts and holders (Italy) were exempted from qualifying for motives of sportsmanship(?) and financial expediency.

The shock of the first round—moral retribution!—was the defeat of a German side including four Austrians by Switzerland, 4–2 in a replay. Brazil, with a Hungarian coach, were emerging for the first time, beat Poland 6–5, then met Czechoslovakia in a punch-up in which two Brazilians and a Czech were sent off; two

23

Czech players ended up in hospital with broken limbs. After a 1–1 draw, Brazil made nine changes, won the replay 2–1, then lost by the same score to Italy in the semi-final. In the other semi-final, Hungary beat Sweden 5–1.

Before the final, Vittorio Pozzo and the manager of Hungary, Dr Dietz, were warned about the conduct of their players. In the event it was a classic match between supremely gifted sides. The decisive factor proved to be the brilliance of Piola, Italy's centre-forward, a fluent scorer with either foot or with his head. He and outside-left Colaussi scored two each in a 4–2 victory, though Hungary pressed hard when pulling back from 1–3 to 2–3 in the second half. Pozzo was now a national hero; in five years Italy had twice won the World Cup, and the Olympics (1936). Then Pozzo was a strident leader; when I used to meet him 30 years later in the press boxes of Europe's most famous clubs he was a frail, white-haired sage who still knew instinctively and instantly which players could play and which were make-weight.

England, invited to take the place of Austria in 1938, rejected the offer, thereby sustaining the illusion for another 12 years or more that they were still the masters, when the truth was that Italy, Brazil and Hungary were already strides ahead.

1938 Piola, brilliant two-footed Italian centre-forward and reputedly one of the greatest of all players, evades two Brazilians in the semi-final. In the final Italy beat Hungary 4–2.

1950

The fourth World Cup was scheduled for Brazil in 1942, but once the war was over it required another five years to prepare. Brazil, worried about the financial success of the finals, insisted that the 16 finalists should be divided into four mini-leagues, with the winners going into a further league. It was therefore only by chance that the final match between Uruguay and Brazil was the decisive game, Uruguay winning 2–1. It was also agreed that no match should be played under floodlights, and that boots *must* be worn.

Because of the ideological turmoil in central Europe, the USSR, Hungary and Czechoslovakia were not represented, Austria did not enter, and Germany East and West were excluded by FIFA. The withdrawal of Argentina, Scotland and France left the finals with only 13 teams, Scotland being eliminated by a rule of their own making. The British Championship was used as a qualifying group with the first *two* teams to qualify, but the Scots decided they would not go to Brazil unless they finished top. A large contingent from Brazil, including their manager, Flavio Costa, flew to Glasgow—no short hop in those days—as a hospitable gesture, for the match against England. Scotland lost by the only goal, refused to play in the finals, and at the next FIFA Congress the Scottish vice-president was not re-elected!

Back in Rio, the Brazilians battled against time to complete their gigantic new Maracana Stadium, a stunning two-tier sweep of 435,000 tons of concrete, holding 200,000 spectators. The shock of the opening round was the 3–2 defeat of Italy, the holders, by Sweden, the 1948 Olympic champions in London. Coached by George Raynor from England, a shrewd tactician unrecognized in his own country, Sweden took revenge for the plunder of her players by Italian professional clubs. But this surprise was nothing compared with what was to come.

Although England had lost Neil Franklin, one of their greatest ever centre-halves, suspended by FIFA for playing in Bogota when Colombia were unaffiliated, they possessed some of their most famous names of all time: Matthews, Finney, Mannion and Mortensen, not to mention a full-back named Ramsey. In their opening match they beat Chile 2–0, with the following team: Williams; Ramsey, Aston; Wright, Hughes, Dickinson; Finney, Mortensen, Bentley, Mannion, Mullen.

It was a less than confident performance, but the same team—without Matthews—played the USA in Belo Horizonte. After 37 minutes Gaetjens deflected a cross by Bahr past Williams for the only goal in a result which the soccer world could hardly believe. When the scoreline was flashed to agencies in London it was queried. Surely it should be 10–1, not 0–1? England had pounded the Americans to no avail. Mannion admitted: 'I must have missed about 40 chances.'

Bentley recalls: 'Once Finney went through their entire defence, and passed across an open goal to me. Someone shouted "leave it", and I did. It went to Morty, and he shot wide. The game was full of disasters like that.' In the second half Williams in goal never touched the ball, but England had suffered their worst ever humiliation.

Only afterwards did Walter Winterbottom, the manager, admit the need for *building* a team as opposed to merely selecting one. The side in 1950 had met for one week's get-together, leaving for Rio only six days before their opening match. Some of the players had to change their rooms in the hotel in Rio because of smells from the drains; the food was strange, and when they arrived in Belo Horizonte, they found a pitch which was like a public park. That was some small excuse. For the final match against Spain, Matthews, Baily and Milburn were brought into attack, but all the brilliance of Matthews and Finney was wasted, Spain obstructing their way to a 1–0 victory and Sir Stanley Rous commenting: 'We were the better gentlemen; they were the better players.'

The final pool consisted of Brazil, Uruguay, Spain and Sweden. With a glittering inside-forward trio—in the old 2–3–5 formation—of Zizinho, Ademir and Jair, Brazil whipped Sweden 7–1 and Spain 6–1. They needed only to draw with Uruguay, who had drawn 2–2 with Spain, to take the Cup.

The whole of Brazil was convinced the trophy was already won, but the wily Uruguayans, habitually masters at chiselling a result beyond their means, won 2–1. Their key players were right-winger Ghiggia and inside-left Schiaffino, who between them contrived the equalizing goal after an hour. In those days wingers were still marked by wing-halves, and Bigode, Brazil's left-half, allowed Ghiggia too much room throughout. Five minutes from time, Ghiggia swept through to beat goalkeeper Barbosa inside the near post, a sad error in narrowing the angle. The vast Maracana crowd, thousands in tears, stood to applaud the winners in a gesture of sportsmanship by a home crowd unlikely ever to be repeated. England had not waited to see the final pool of matches; at home, belief in their ability persisted for another three years.

1954

England went to the fifth World Cup in Switzerland with their false reputation as world masters at last exposed, two crushing defeats at the hands of the Hungarian Olympic champions confirming what many had long believed. The incomparable team raised by Gustav Sebes and Guyla Mandi had won 6–3 at Wembley in 1953—the first home defeat by a foreign team—then 7–1 in Budapest the following spring. Again England had qualified by winning the British Championship, this time Scotland accepting their place in the finals.

The form of the competition was changed, with four first round groups of four, the first two from each mini-league going into knock-out quarter-finals. The anomaly was that the new 'West' Germany, competing for the first time, beat hot favourites Hungary in the final after losing to them 8–3 in the first round. Hungary's legendary captain Ferenc Puskas was injured in the first encounter, a decisive factor in the final.

This was, according to many of the most experienced observers such as Geoffrey Green of *The Times*, the finest gathering of teams in the competition's history. Brazil, flawed only by temperament; Yugoslavia, with such noble players as Beara, Bobek, Boskov and Milutinovic; Austria, with their famous attacking centre-half Ocwirk, and Uruguay; Hungary and Germany; England, failing to respond to the inspiration of Matthews; and Italy. Yet, losing 2–1 and again 4–1 in a play-off with Switzerland, Italy began an unhappy run which was to stay with them for over a decade.

England's form against Belgium in their opening game was less than auspicious: from 3–1 in front they were held 4–4, after leading 4–3 in extra-time. Matthews was bewildering, but found little support. The team was: Merrick; Staniforth, Byrne; Wright, Owen, Dickinson; Matthews, Broadis, Lofthouse, Taylor, Finney.

1954 Finney and
Lofthouse lunge
and miss;
Uruguayan keeper
Maspoli gathers
the ball watched
by Santamaria
(subsequently star
of Real Madrid).
Uruguay won this
quarter-final 4–2.

Broadis and Lofthouse scored twice each. Beating Switzerland 2–0, England were
confronted in the quarter-final by Uruguay. In a 4–2 defeat Merrick was blamed
for two of the goals, but there was no matching Schiaffino in midfield. England
had included McGarry and Wilshaw in place of Owen and Taylor, but the blame
placed on Merrick camouflaged deficiencies in teamwork as much as technique.

In an astonishing 12-goal quarter-final Switzerland went down 7–5 to Austria,
after leading 3–0. Germany beat Yugoslavia 2–0, but in the fourth quarter-final
Brazil and Hungary engaged in the infamous Battle of Berne, played in heavy rain.
Brazil conceded two early goals to Hidegkuti and Kocsis; the game became vicious.
Djalmar Santos, Brazil's right-back, scored from a penalty; both sides were booed
by the Swiss crowd. Hungary, already without Puskas, started the second half with
10 men—no substitutes then—but they were awarded a penalty by English referee
Arthur Ellis when both teams expected a free-kick to Brazil; Lantos scored to make
it 3–1. Soon Humberto, Brazil's inside-left, and Czibor, the famed little Hungarian
left-winger, should have been sent off but were not. Julinho made it 3–2, Bozsik
and Nilton Santos were ordered off for fighting; Humberto and Didi hit the post
for Brazil, Kocsis headed Hungary's fourth; finally Humberto was also sent off.
Part brilliant, part brawl, the game had run totally out of control. The fighting
continued in the corridor to the dressing-room.

Hungary's semi-final with Uruguay touched a plane of perfection, without the
violence. Czibor and Hidegkuti put Hungary two up, Schiaffino and Hohberg—
later manager in 1970—twice combined to level the score in the last quarter of an

hour. In the first half of extra-time Hohberg hit a post, but two headers by Kocsis, possibly the fiercest header of the ball ever, gave Hungary victory in a game which ranks with any played. In the final against Germany, 6–1 winners over Austria, Puskas returned for Hungary, semi-fit; the decision seemed justified when he scored after only six minutes.

Czibor made it 2–0, but Morlock and Rahn levelled the game, all within 18 minutes. Before half-time Hidegkuti hit a post; the football was mesmeric; both sides attacked relentlessly. Six minutes from the end Bozsik lost the ball to Schaefer, who sent Rahn through for the winner. Puskas equalized but was given off-side; Czibor had a tremendous drive saved by Turek, the German keeper who gave an unprecedented performance. Hungary, the greatest team of theirs and possibly any generation, had been beaten for the first time in four seasons and over 30 matches. They might have lost the prize, but they would never be forgotten as long as football was talked about. Their team of all talents, in 4–2–4 formation, was: Grosics; Buzansky, Lorant, Zakarias, Lantos; Bozsik, Hidegkuti; Toth (or Budai), Kocsis, Puskas, Czibor.

1958

The sixth World Cup is remembered above all for the arrival of the 17-year-old Pele, the dark, bubbling genius of a boy who was to be the focus of the world game for the next 12 years. Yet the tournament was influenced by two external tragedies. Hungary were without Puskas, Czibor and Kocsis who, away on tour with Honved, had not returned home after the Hungarian Uprising of 1956. England, with a team climbing back towards international respectability, were without Roger Byrne, Tommy Taylor and the *nonpareil* Duncan Edwards, killed with five other Manchester United players in the Munich air crash. But for these events, either might have won in Stockholm.

Following complaints that Britain was favoured by an exclusive qualifying group producing two teams for the finals, the four home associations were split into different groups in 1958 . . . and all qualified. Wales, eliminated by Czechoslovakia, were drawn to play-off with Israel, and won, Israel's Afro-Asian opponents having staged a political walk-out. The match in Cardiff probably saved the lives of Jimmy Murphy, manager of Wales and assistant to Matt Busby at Old Trafford, and Geoffrey Green of *The Times*, who would otherwise have been on the plane from Belgrade.

England qualified without incident against Eire and Denmark; Scotland under Busby eliminated Spain, but he was still too injured to take charge in Sweden. Ireland eliminated Italy, who had 'transferred' the formidable Schiaffino from Uruguay on an Italian father's passport. The tie in Belfast had to be replayed when the match was first played as a 'friendly' because fog prevented the Hungarian referee arriving. Never was a friendly more brutal.

The British were kept apart in the first round of the finals. Ireland, up against West Germany, Czechoslovakia and Argentina, beat the Czechs with the only goal by Cush, held the Germans 2–2 with both goals from McParland (after losing to Argentina) and had to play-off with the Czechs, who had crushed Argentina 6–1.

1958 *Left*
England's hopes
were dimmed by
the death at
Munich of Roger
Byrne, Duncan
Edwards, and
Tommy Taylor—
seen here framed
by Eire defenders
during the 5–1
qualifying win at
Wembley. *Right*
Harry Gregg,
Munich survivor,
and hero of
Northern Ireland's
crusade to the
quarter-finals, flies
through the air
against West
Germany.

Inspired by the management of Peter Doherty and the midfield leadership of Danny Blanchflower and Jimmy McIlroy, they won 2–1—again McParland scoring both goals.

Wales, with their greatest ever team, began by holding Hungary, John Charles heading the equalizer after Bozsik had scored for Hungary. Drawing with Mexico, when they should have won, and with Sweden, when they might have lost, Wales won 2–1 in a foul-ridden play-off with Hungary, with goals from Ivor Allchurch and Medwin. Kelsey was a hero in goal.

Scotland, with a fair start in which they held Yugoslavia—recent 5–0 winners over England in Belgrade—then slumped 3–2 and 2–1 to Paraguay and France, Spurs keeper Bill Brown averting a worse defeat by the French. Meanwhile England pulled back from two down against the USSR with goals by Kevan and Finney (penalty), then drew 0–0 with Brazil, the only match in which Brazil failed to score. McDonald of Burnley was brilliant in goal. Twice behind against Austria, England twice drew level through Haynes and Kevan, then lost the play-off with the USSR. Still excluding the dazzling power of the young Charlton—a Munich survivor— Walter Winterbottom played Brabrook and Broadbent on the right-wing. Finney had not played since a brutal tackle in the first encounter with the USSR, who now won with the only goal by Ilyin after 67 minutes.

Like Wales and Ireland, the USSR had little chance of recovering in time for their quarter-final 48 hours later. Ireland, with no alternative hotels booked, travelled for almost a whole day and night to reach Norkopping for the game with France— whose forward line of Wiesnieski, Fontaine, Kopa, Piantoni and Vincent rivalled any in those or most other finals. Ireland had both keepers injured, Gregg playing on one good leg rather than Uprichard with one good hand. France won 4–0, Fontaine scoring two of the 13 goals, which still stands as a record for the finals of one competition. Wales lost by the only goal to Brazil, a mis-hit shot by Pele, who had not played in the first two preliminary games. Germany beat Yugoslavia; Sweden beat the USSR. Roused by fanatical cheer-leaders, who were banned for the final, Sweden beat Germany in the semi-final; Germany scored first, had full-back Juskowiak sent off for retaliating, and lost 3–1. France, losing centre-half Jonquet after 25 minutes with the score 1–1, were beaten 5–2 by Brazil, Pele claiming three. The final surpassed even 1954. Sweden scored first, Garrincha marvellously made the equalizer for Vava, and Sweden's hopes faded as it became clear that their wingers, Hamrin and Skoglund, were matched by Brazil's full-backs, Djalmar Santos and Nilton Santos. Garrincha made a second for Vava, Pele scored twice in the second half, once with a piece of astonishing jugglery that had the soccer public agog. Their tempers of 1950 and 1954 now disciplined by manager Vicente Feola, Brazil would dominate the game for the next six years. Their team was: Gylmar; Djalmar Santos, Bellini, Orlando, Nilton Santos; Zito, Didi; Garrincha, Vava, Pele, Zagalo.

1962

The seventh World Cup in Chile saw the end of football as essentially an exercise in skill, and the beginning of an era in which tactics, based on negative, defensive expediency, removed much of the fun. It had become a manager's rather than a players' or spectators' game. There was no outstanding team, only an outstanding amount of rough play. If the idea of the World Cup was to elevate the game, more than merely to make money for the organizers and contestants—which at times seemed doubtful—then the World Cup of 1962 marked the start of a decline. It was saved in the end by a tidy but rather unemotional final in which Brazil retained their title after various scares, including the loss of Pele through injury in the early stages.

England were this time the only British finalists. Wales lost 2–1 at home to Spain, an ageing Di Stefano scoring a stunning goal from a seemingly impossible angle. Without Woosnam, injured the day before in training, Wales drew in Madrid. Scotland were desperately unlucky to go out to Czechoslovakia in a play-off in Brussels, in extra-time, robbed of wingers Scott and Wilson by injury. Ireland fell to West Germany. England, with an edgy draw in Lisbon thanks to Flowers' pulverizing shot in the fierce heat, gained a place by beating Portugal 2–0 at Wembley (Connelly and Pointer); they needed only a draw, Portugal absurdly losing 4–2 to Luxembourg the previous week.

It was hoped that, in Chile, England's goal-scoring problems would be resolved once Greaves and Hitchens were integrated into the side upon release from Italy. The optimism turned sour. Neither was a success, nor was Peacock, and after three tepid performances against Hungary (1–2), Argentina (3–1) and Bulgaria (0–0), England went out 3–1 to Brazil in the quarter-final.

The team was sadly feeble in spirit, in spite of the class of players such as Douglas, Haynes, Greaves, Charlton, Armfield and young Moore. Haynes was a poor cap-

tain; many of the players, though professionals at the summit of their career, were disenchanted with their training camp in the mountains and wanted to get home to the beer and skittles. The first goal by Hungary compounded all the faults in the team—no tackling back, weak central defence, uncertain goalkeeping.

There was little to cheer elsewhere. The USSR and Yugoslavia, Chile and Italy produced two matches of grim, degrading violence. Two Italians were sent off, while Leonel Sanchez, Chile's outside-left, broke the nose of Maschio, Italy's centre-forward, unseen by referee Ken Aston of England or his linesmen. Szymaniak of Germany broke the leg of Eschmann of Switzerland in the tackle. Only in beautiful Vina del Mar did the game sparkle, Brazil surviving by a hair's-breadth against Spain. Dropping the legendary Suarez and Del Sol for this final group match, Spain led 1–0 till a quarter of an hour from the end. Only a performance in a thousand by Gylmar in goal prevented a rout, two late goals by Amarildo, deputy for Pele, distorting the result. Di Stefano, injured before the finals began, thus never played in the finals for either Argentina or his adopted Spain.

The quarter-finals continued without quality. Chile beat the USSR, the veteran Yashin at fault with both goals. Hungary dominated the whole game against Czechoslovakia, but could not get past Schroiff to nullify Scherer's early goal. Yugoslavia, emerging as one of few teams with genuine claims to dispute a world championship, beat Germany with Radakovic's goal four minutes from the end. England, baffled by Garrincha, lost to Brazil. Garrincha scored, Hitchens equalized after Greaves had hit the bar, but misjudgements by Springett in goal aided further goals by Vava and Garrincha.

Garrincha, with two inside half an hour, ended Chile's slightly hysterical hopes in a 4–2 semi-final. Landa, Chile's centre-half, and Garrincha were sent off. The

31

Czechs, the better tacticians, beat the Slavs, the better players, against all expectation, Masopust and Kvasniak superb for the winners. For the final, Pele was still injured, Garrincha was illogically permitted to play. Masopust put the Czechs in front, but errors by Schroiff aided two of Brazil's three goals. England continued their errors at home; Winterbottom was passed over for the post of FA secretary in some nasty political in-fighting aimed at Sir Stanley Rous, now elevated to President of FIFA. The loss of Winterbottom's wisdom and worldwide esteem would take its toll over the years. Meanwhile, a new manager was required, not to say a new formula.

1966

The man and the formula arrived in the person of Alf Ramsey, after Jimmy Adamson of Burnley had turned down the offer of FA chairman, Graham Doggart. Ramsey, dapper full-back for Southampton, Spurs and England, had just taken Ipswich from the Third to the First Division, winning the League Championship at the first attempt—an achievement of unusual shrewdness accomplished with players many of whom were the rejects of more prosperous clubs. Ramsey, virtually unknown when he took charge against France in the European Championship in February 1963, was a singular, stubborn and immensely professional man. He promised to win the World Cup for England . . . and did. Though England were not the most skilful of the 1966 finalists—a position which belonged to Hungary—they were the best organized, exploiting what talent they had to the full. They were the best team measured in terms of contemporary tactics.

Wales were eliminated in the qualifying competition by the USSR. Northern Ireland, needing to win their final qualifying game in Albania to force a play-off with Switzerland, drew. Scotland, squandering two points at home to Poland, left themselves needing to win in Naples to force a play-off, and lost 3–0. Jock Stein, hired as 'flying doctor' halfway through the qualifying stages, was unable to save a patient needing prolonged treatment of the kind supplied by Ramsey—who, it should be admitted, did not have to qualify.

The opening game of the finals was a disaster, a goal-less draw against Uruguay hailed by the world's press as evidence of England's lack of class. The front line of Greaves, Hunt and Connelly was totally frustrated by Uruguay's blanket defence. It was little better when Bobby Charlton ran 40 yards to score a glorious solo goal to put modest Mexico in their place. Hunt scored another, then two against France, the second coming while Simon was lying injured from a late tackle by the notorious Stiles. It looked malevolent, at least from the stands, and increased England's burden of criticism. Ramsey allegedly refused an FA request to drop Stiles.

Pele, meanwhile, had scored the first goal of the finals, a free-kick of momentous power against Bulgaria. But the Brazilian magic had gone, they could not paper the cracks, and without Pele were destroyed by brilliant Hungary in their next game, Farkas hitting the most dazzling goal of the whole finals in a 3–1 win. But Hungary's fate had been turned by the previous 3–1 defeat by Portugal, hinging on two errors by their keeper Szentmihalyi. Had Hungary won or even drawn this match they, and not Portugal, would have played North Korea in the quarter-final, and the outcome of 1966 might have been very different.

1966 Geoff Hurst's header, from a cross by Martin Peters (*background*), beats Roma for the only goal in England's heated quarter-final against Argentina.

Brazil were beaten again by Portugal, Pele brutally chopped down by Morais and Baptista under the permissive eye of English referee McCabe. Pele's limping departure from the arena at Goodison epitomized the failure of authority to prevent the sacrifice of great talent to mean, often illegal functionalism. The Koreans, with an historic goal from Pak Doo Ik, gave Italy a humiliating, early return home.

From the Midlands there had been rumblings of Argentinian strong-arm stuff ...which suddenly mushroomed at Wembley. For the quarter-final, Ramsey recalled Ball and introduced Hurst, in place of Callaghan and the injured Greaves. The Argentinians, under the Machiavellian guidance of the infamous Juan Carlos Lorenzo, had decided that the only way to combat the England machine—its superior strength, its huge, vociferous crowd—was a policy of systematic fouling. Four names had already gone into the book of West German referee Rudolf Kreitlein, one of them Antonio Rattin's, when he decided that the Argentinian captain's persistent arguing and attempted intimidation was too much; and sent him off. Rattin refused to go; the whole team nearly went with him, and it took eight minutes of persuasion by police and FIFA officials to restart the game. Argentina had been doubly stupid, because with only 10 men it was soon apparent they were the superior team, stretching England with their spontaneous skills. Only Hurst's glancing near-post cross from Peters' centre with 12 minutes to go—a West Ham special—squeezed England into the semi-finals. Argentina were threatened with expulsion from the next World Cup—they continued fighting in the tunnel to the dressing-rooms—but appeased their conscience with the belief that the whole thing was a plot between Sir Stanley Rous and the referees!

The suspicion of European prejudice—false, but fanned by the unfortunate

33

selection of referees—was strengthened when Finney of England sent off two Uruguayans in the quarter-final against Germany. Korea, three up against Portugal, were toppled by four from Eusebio, including two penalties. More goalkeeping errors, this time by Gelei, led to Hungary's downfall against the USSR, who lost a semi-final against Germany which is best forgotten. Germany won with goals from Haller and the youthful Beckenbauer. Chislenko of the USSR was sent off, Germany played safe against nine fit men. In the other semi-final England beat Portugal. Eusebio was mastered by Stiles, as he was again in the 1968 European Cup final, not without intimidation. But at last Hurst, Hunt, Ball and Bobby Charlton began to shine, Charlton scoring both goals, and Eusebio one from a penalty when Jack Charlton handled. Banks made a vital save from the ageing Coluna.

The final against Germany was won in extra-time by the goal that wasn't. Hurst's shot, which bounced off the bar behind keeper Tilkowski, landed on or just in front of the goal-line. That is not a matter of opinion but scientific fact, established by photographs of the position of the *shadow* of the ball in bright sunlight. Since the photo shows the shadow almost on the line *behind* it, with the ball off the ground and the sun coming from the other end of the stadium, therefore when ball and shadow coincided on impact, it must have been in *front*. But the Russian linesman Bakhramov insisted from his position 35 yards away, to Swiss referee Dienst, that it was a goal.

That is just one instance of the swings and roundabouts of fortune, because the German free-kick from which Emmerich equalized just before full-time (2–2)

1966 Hurst's shot rebounds off the cross-bar in the final, bouncing behind goalkeeper Tilkowski. Position of the ball's shadow (*arrowed*), and angle of sun, mean that the ball *must* have bounced in front of the line, not behind for a goal as ruled by linesman (half seen beyond Tilkowski's body).

should not only have been awarded the other way for a foul *against* Jack Charlton, but the ball was handled by the German defender Weber before it went in.

The final had begun with Haller giving Germany the lead from England's first unforced error of the tournament, by the redoubtable Wilson at left-back. Soon Hurst, from Moore's quick free-kick, headed the equalizer. Gambling on using Beckenbauer to stifle Bobby Charlton, Germany had sacrificed their own most intuitive influence in midfield. With 12 minutes to go Peters shot England ahead, then Emmerich forced extra-time. Thankfully, after Hurst's controversial second he hit a third for a unique hat-trick in the final, to silence some of the criticism. Yet it had been a performance of sterling character and resolution by Ramsey's team, not least by Ball, with Hurst and Peters adding a dimension of tactical subtlety. England were known as the 'wingless wonders', yet Ramsey had tried to use wingers and found them lacking. His success would have, ironically, an adverse influence on English soccer for the next 11 years, through ignorant imitation among thousands of lesser managers and coaches. The teams in the 1966 final were:

England: Banks; Cohen, J. Charlton, Moore, Wilson; Stiles, R. Charlton, Peters; Ball, Hurst, Hunt.
West Germany: Tilkowski; Hoettges, Schulz, Weber, Schnellinger; Haller, Beckenbauer, Overath; Seeler, Held, Emmerich.

1970

The ninth World Cup was said to have been high-scoring, entertaining, clean and well controlled. To an extent, each of these factors was an illusion, brought about in no small measure by the altitude, ranging from 7500 feet in Toluca to 5000 feet in Guadalajara.

Although 95 goals were scored, six more than in 1966, no fewer than 43 came in the last half-hour or extra-time, when teams were often overcome with heat and fatigue and defences wilted. In 15 of the 32 matches, conspicuously those between the strongest teams, there were three goals or fewer, while in four key matches, 13 out of 21 goals were scored after the 70th minute. Over half the goals (48) were scored in under a third (10) of the matches. The goal-scoring rate was therefore partially a product of the physical circumstances, as was the entertainment factor. The only teams committed to attack were Brazil, Peru (incapable of defending) and Belgium, who misfired. West Germany *had* to attack because they were behind in four of their first five matches: against England they were two down with 20 minutes to go without having had a shot. The major teams played, as in the last three tournaments, to win, not to entertain. If there was entertainment, it was not a motivating force from within the teams—again often arising from the breakdown of defence discipline with fatigue. Italy beat Germany 4–3 in the semi-final with five goals in extra-time, and as Helmut Schoen, Germany's manager, admitted: 'Perhaps we should always play extra-time, and only admit the public after the first 90 minutes!'

The impression of a clean competition well refereed was also influenced by the altitude. Teams conserved their energy, tackled and challenged less, disputed possession primarily around the penalty areas—so there were fewer fouls. Yet there were examples of deplorable refereeing which influenced the outcome of the competition. No player was sent off, though several should have been; there were monstrous decisions in favour of the hosts, Mexico.

England, as holders, were exempt from qualifying. Scotland, grouped with West Germany, Austria and Cyprus, reached their final two matches, away to Germany and Austria, needing to draw and win respectively to force a play-off with Germany. Bobby Brown, the manager, strangely decided the easier game to win was in Hamburg, where he had nine changes from the team which had drawn with Germany at Hampden. Johnstone put the Scots ahead, Fichtel and Muller gave Germany the lead, Gilzean equalized; instead of settling for a draw, Scotland went surging forward, and were sunk by Libuda's break-away goal six minutes from time. The Austria match now mattered not. Germany had still to lose their first qualifying tie . . . *and still have*. Wales, losing at home to both Italy and East Germany, finished bottom, Italy top. Northern Ireland's chances depended on two meetings with Russia; after 0–0 at home they lost in Moscow 2–0, denied George Best by, of all things, a League Cup replay between Manchester United and Burnley 48 hours previously!

The finals opened in the Aztec Stadium in Mexico City (7000 feet) with, once more, a goal-less draw between the hosts and Russia immediately exposing the limitations of the Mexicans. Yet Mexico gained a place in the last eight thanks to two remarkable decisions by referees. Against their tiny neighbours El Salvador, who stayed in a fourth-rate motel beside an eight-lane motorway, Mexico had failed to score for 43 minutes. Then Aly Hussein Kandil, 49, from the United Arab Republic, gave a free-kick to El Salvador on the halfway line; Mexico took the kick, Valdivia scored. Uproar. El Salvador protested, jostled Kandil, lay on the ground in tears, refused to restart. So Kandil blew for half-time!

Hardly surprisingly El Salvador, who had precipitated a three-day war when eliminating Honduras, had no stomach for the second half. An equally atrocious decision followed against Belgium, when Coerezza of Argentina awarded a penalty as Valdivia fell over a defender's leg seconds after the ball had been cleared upfield. These two victories were greeted by hysteria in the streets: trees were uprooted, cars overturned, foreigners assaulted. Mercifully Italy put a stop to the emotional blackmail with a 4–1 quarter-final victory at Toluca, the highest ground, in which Rivera, golden boy of Milan, mesmerized the Mexicans—yet failed to keep his place for the semi-final.

Italy had reached the quarter-final with one meagre goal in three matches—their first against Sweden—through a bad error by keeper Hellstrom. They then drew without score against Uruguay and Israel in a group producing only seven goals in the six matches.

England were grouped in Guadalajara with Brazil, Romania and Czechoslovakia. They brought their own bus and their own water from home, offending the Mexicans whose public hostility was further roused by Sir Alf Ramsey's insensitive press comments. Romania, ruthless and uncensored in the tackle, were beaten 1–0; a match of breathtaking excellence against Brazil was lost to the only goal by Jairzinho, Banks making his historic, 'impossible' save from Pele. With a 1–0 win over the Czechs, the holders were through to the quarter-final against West Germany, who

36

1970 Jairzinho, Brazil's right-winger, about to shoot past Gordon Banks for the only goal in Guadalajara as Martin Peters (11), Brian Labone (5) and Alan Mullery (4) close in too late.

had been far from impressive in coming from behind against Morocco, Bulgaria and Peru.

Having seen both teams, I was in no doubt that, playing to form, there was no way in which Germany could win. With 20 minutes to go under the intense midday sun in Leon, England were two up through Mullery and Peters...yet lost.

The hand of fate was at work, as if to atone for that goal at Wembley. Banks was taken ill the night before the match, his deputy Bonetti was, unknown to most, in a state of some anxiety over personal problems. In a devastating collapse, poor Bonetti was at fault with two if not three of the goals which swept Germany to victory.

They had morally conceded the game before Beckenbauer scored the first with a modest shot from a wide angle, Bonetti's dive going over the top of the ball as it went into the middle of the goal. At this point Ramsey already had Bell warming up to replace, and rest, Bobby Charlton, and now sent him on. Within minutes Bell made a chance for Hurst, whose header beat Maier but bounced inches wide of an empty goal. That should have been 3–1. With 10 minutes to go, Ramsey made his second controversial substitution, Hunter for Peters, reasoning that Hunter would check a German attack beginning to take wings and England would still win in normal time. But Germany equalized with a freak goal, off the back of Seeler's head, which caught Bonetti in no man's land coming for a cross he could not reach. In extra-time England were the more consistent attackers, but Germany

37

b

c

won with a goal by Muller, volleying from only three yards a dropping cross which Bonetti might well have reached. Ramsey was blamed for taking off Charlton, thereby freeing Beckenbauer to attack: but the goal which turned the game came *beforehand*. Ramsey commented bleakly: 'In all my time as manager I cannot remember England giving away three such bad goals.'

In the semi-finals Italy won the extra-time extravaganza with Germany, Brazil beat negative, dirty Uruguay. The final, happily, was a celebration of the game's skills, with Brazil opening up the Italian defence with delayed but ultimate ease. With players of the sublime artistry of Pele, Tostao, Jairzinho and Rivelino, and a goalkeeper as bad as Felix, it was difficult for Brazil not to entertain. Pele opened the scoring with a memorable header, Boninsegna equalized, Gerson regained the lead with a cross shot struck with the eye of a cobra. Italy chopped and hacked in vain

1970 Pele, greatest of all time (?), beats Burgnich to head Brazil's first in the 4–1 final victory over Italy.

at Brazil's heels, Jairzinho and Carlos Alberto added further goals. Brazil were again the undisputed masters, with a velvet performance against cynical spoilers. With three victories, the Jules Rimet trophy was theirs for keeps; a new cup would have to be found. Yet had England not thrown away victory in Leon, there were many who tipped them to have won a likely final with Brazil. Ramsey had produced if anything a better team than in 1966, certainly the tactical system was more refined and, ironically, fail-safe. The respected German coach Dettmar Cramer said: 'In any match between the present Brazil and England teams, I would expect England to have an equal chance of victory.' The game in Guadalajara had proved that.

1974

What might England have achieved had they qualified? On the evidence in Germany of the tenth World Cup, they might well have reached the last four. Yet had they survived their qualifying group with Wales and Poland, Sir Alf Ramsey would still have been the manager in the finals, and had he hung on to the same players who in fact fell to Poland, they might have suffered the same fate as Italy. The failure was not so much against Poland at Wembley, but in Katowice previously, and against Wales at Wembley. In these two matches three points were lost, but for which the draw against Poland at Wembley, 1–1, would have been adequate. England went into steady decline after 1970, Ramsey reluctant to introduce new, younger players. The writing was on the wall when England struggled to master such minor teams as Malta and Greece in the European Championship, fell to Germany at home, then played an appallingly negative return match in Berlin. The same policy of midfield caution was retained in the World Cup qualifying competition. England failed to win an ugly match against the excessively physical Welsh at Wembley, and followed this with an incredible blunder in Katowice.

With Channon emerging as a striker of real force, Ramsey left him out and played four in midfield, including the technically limited Storey. England dominated the centre-circle but lost the match, with Moore badly exposed. Now they *had* to win at Wembley, Poland had only to draw. Ramsey persisted with the out-of-form Chivers, watched his team squander a multitude of chances in the face of the magical luck of Tomaszewski in goal; and only sent out a substitute, Hector, with 90 seconds to go. Moore, relegated to the bench, had pleaded for change, but Ramsey had mentally 'frozen'. Failure to adapt had cost England a place ... and cost Ramsey his job.

The irony was that Scotland, with a manager, Willie Ormond, far less experienced and knowledgeable than Ramsey, reached the finals, eliminating Denmark and Czechoslovakia, thanks to the Danes holding the Czechs at home. They gave to the finals a burning sense of adventure which communicated itself to all nations and supporters. There was no other team in Germany which ran at their opponents as Scotland did, except possibly Poland. Their spirit was epitomized by David Hay, who said: 'If patriotism is silly, O.K., we're silly. When we go on the field for Scotland, we are ready to give blood. Of course we'd like a lot of money, but even without it we'll play till we drop.'

Scotland were the only team not to lose in the finals, yet failed to reach the second round, eliminated by 'only' scoring two against Zaire in their first match, then drawing with Brazil and Yugoslavia. Their unquenchable character, marshalled by Bremner, was not supported by sound tactical planning and selection. The errors included: failing to grasp the mathematical significance against Zaire; arriving in Germany disrupted by internal friction; delayed substitutions at critical stages; lack of knowledge of the opposition. Lack of a real goal-scorer they could not help. But indifference to the quality of the opposition can be a two-edged virtue. It was in their own hands to have achieved more. Scotland's unfulfilled promise apart, the disappointment of 1974 was Holland's failure to establish for all time their incomparable quality by winning the Cup. There was no questioning their superiority, a tactical and technical fluency which rivalled the peaks of Brazil and Hungary in the past. Their collective understanding was on a plane not reached since the days of Bozsik and Puskas, and in Cruyff they possessed a unique talent. As Cramer said: 'He has shown us how far ahead of his time Di Stefano was 20 years ago; in many ways they are identical. They operate over the whole length of the pitch, directing the start of attacks, yet being there to help conclude them. Cruyff has the same even temperament as Di Stefano, yet can be hard, and brave, when necessary. A super-player.'

Holland alternately coasted and galloped through their six matches in the first and second rounds, ripping apart Bulgaria, Argentina and Brazil. The scene was set for a consummation in the final. Their only flaw was mental; they believed they would win easily, and intended to humiliate the Germans in front of their own crowd to avenge some old wounds from other spheres. When they scored after 90 seconds, it was too good to be true; they fatally relaxed against the world's best competitors.

40

1974 *Above* Johan Neeskens fires Holland in front from the penalty spot after only 90 seconds of the final. *Below* Paul Breitner makes it 1–1 for West Germany. Muller (13) scored the winner.

Germany had reached the final without flair. Narrowly beating Chile, losing to East Germany, behind against Sweden, they were by no means a settled unit. It was said that Beckenbauer, not Helmut Schoen, was running the team, but Schoen told me later: 'I was angry after the defeat by GDR, and had made up my mind to bring in Bonhof and Holzenbein. The night before we played Yugoslavia in the second round, I went to tell Beckenbauer and Muller, who shared a room, what I had in mind. They persuaded me not to drop Breitner. The next day, before I had told the team the line-up, Beckenbauer gave a press conference, indicating the changes. This gave rise to the talk that his influence was important. It was improper.'

The introduction of the second round system, replacing quarter- and semi-finals, meant it was only by chance that the last matches in each group, Holland *v* Brazil and Germany *v* Poland, determined the finalists. The Munich crowd was stunned when, in the final, referee Jack Taylor of England gave the penalty as Hoeness brought down Cruyff at the end of a 15-pass move. Neeskens rammed in the kick, Germany were seemingly skewered. But no. Before half-time Breitner and Muller put Germany ahead as Holland let their rhythm drop, Rep squandering the most glaring chance of the match following Cruyff's rippling run just prior to Muller's goal. Holland were back on top in the second half but the goals would not come; Breitner and Bonhof cleared off the line, Neeskens volleyed against Maier in goal from close range. The prize had escaped one of the most accomplished of all teams.

CHAPTER THREE

England's Elimination

	W	D	L	F	A	Pts
Italy	5	0	1	18	4	10
England	5	0	1	15	4	10
Finland	2	0	4	11	16	4
Luxembourg	0	0	6	2	22	0

England's elimination from the World Cup Finals in Argentina, for the second time running, can be traced to several factors avoidable with hindsight, all interwoven with the decision by the FA first to sack Sir Alf Ramsey, and then to replace him with Don Revie. While Revie's appointment, during the climax of the 1974 Finals, was greeted with almost unanimous approval by press and public, there were sound reasons for apprehension. Not only his many practical virtues, but his limitations, had been clearly apparent during the years of prominence with Leeds. Had they not lost more trophies, in the moment of truth, than they had won? Had they not been responsible for some of the most cynical and retrograde trends of so-called professionalism over the past decade? Again and again his own anxiety had communicated itself in moments of peak stress to his team, betraying all those hours, weeks and years of painstaking training. The perfection of the football—and there was near-perfection in the early seventies—was nevertheless flawed. But such matters were largely foreign territory to the FA committee making the appointment, their knowledge restricted mostly to the view from the directors' box. My own preference, stated at the time in the *Daily Express*, had been for a dual appointment of Ron Greenwood together with another, younger track-suited coach. This was precisely the course adopted by the FA after Revie's infamous defection three years, and another elimination, later.

But this is running ahead of the story. Following the traumatic failure against Poland at Wembley in the autumn of 1973, Ramsey made two changes a month later against Italy, bringing back Bobby Moore in place of Hunter, dropping Chivers and recalling Osgood. Again England received a bloodied nose, losing 1–0. Ramsey's stock was zero, and belatedly he made changes for the summer tour of East Germany, Bulgaria and Yugoslavia . . . but was never allowed to put them to the test.

Unknown to Ramsey, the decision to terminate his 11-year reign had been taken at the FA offices in Lancaster Gate the same morning as England left for a spring friendly against Portugal in Lisbon, with a depleted squad. What was doubly ironic was that on this trip, and in subsequent weeks, Ramsey suddenly became more affable, more willing to define his view of England's problems, when the die was already cast. Shortly after the announcement of the squad for the tour, the bombshell dropped—the FA were giving notice to their Knight. Joe Mercer, now general

Don Revie training with Alan Ball for his first match as England manager against Czechoslovakia. Already the team is parading the controversial Admiral kit, including the 'liquorice all-sorts' shirts, sharply departing from tradition. Ball was one of five captains under Revie, though Emlyn Hughes was the first.

manager at Coventry, would temporarily take charge for the home championship and the tour. 'Uncle Joe', renowned ex-Arsenal and England wing-half whose partnership with Malcolm Allison had taken Manchester City back to the top, had a carefree few weeks in which England beat Wales, Ireland and Bulgaria, lost to Scotland at Hampden and drew with Argentina (at Wembley), East Germany and Yugoslavia. The new players whom Ramsey had earlier spurned, such as Brooking, Todd, Watson and Keegan, gave England a lift which suggested that, had they been in the finals about to begin in West Germany, they would have been among the more entertaining teams. Mercer smiled his way through his brief appointment, consistently getting the names of players wrong, even in team talks—one was actually missing when addressed at some length!—but he succeeded in reminding everyone that football is, after all, a game.

After the usual mountain of speculation, Revie emerged as the new messiah, just in time to arrive in Munich for the World Cup Final between Germany and Holland: in many ways the replica of Ramsey, the professional pragmatist, exacting the last ounce of advantage from the laws, a man whose essential view of a football team was not as an instrument for display, aesthetic pleasure or athletic ideology, but for getting a result. For that reason he admired Germany more than the eloquent losers, Holland, and seemingly forgot what he had seen of Holland when he came to play them three years later.

Revie's first major action back home was to call a meeting of 81 potential international players for an address in Manchester. He meant well, but it is hard enough to communicate with 18 players never mind 80, especially when they come from 30 different clubs playing to 15 different patterns—one of the main impediments of the English game. Revie's address was full of optimism and progressive thinking. He said:

'Average players need three touches to set things up, good players need two, great players like Jimmy Greaves need one. I am looking for the one-touch players. At international level, the game is quite different from club football. There is less tackling and physical challenge, and the ability to do the unexpected cannot be over-emphasized. Of course, there has to be basic method, but I shall be searching for flexibility, for players who will run at the opposition, challenge them and frighten them the way Ian Moore did before his unfortunate injury. The club game, always playing for a result, discourages this. Possession football is all very well, but it allows opposing defences to regroup and ultimately makes the task more difficult.'

If he sensed the priorities then, he was to forget some of them before he quit, but for the moment all was euphoria, especially with his introduction of a new wage structure, with £100 for a draw, £200 for a win, in addition to the existing £100 appearance money. If that was consistent with his belief in financial motivation, he did a swift somersault in another direction, telling the players:

'The image of football has to be vastly improved, its behaviour as well as its attacking outlook. I was responsible for things which were not right at Leeds, but now I've got the job of improving the game at all levels. As players you don't realize how bad the dissent and the snarling looks in close-up on TV.'

1974–5

The revolution got under way with the squad to face Czechoslovakia in the European Championship at Wembley—including six of the most exciting Under-23 players from the previous season: Maddren, Beattie, Hudson, Thomas, Gerry Francis and Trevor Francis. In the event, with 85,000 there to attend England's medical check-up, only the tactical substitution of Brooking for Dobson and Thomas for Worthington, after an hour's stalemate, tipped the scales. Goals in the last 18 minutes from Channon and Bell (2) slightly concealed the fact that Revie's England was little different from Ramsey's. Revie's first team was: Clemence; Madeley, Watson, Hunter, Hughes; G. Francis, Dobson, Bell; Channon, Worthington, Keegan.

Expectation for the second European tie against Portugal was distorted by the Portuguese defeat a week before, 3–0 by Switzerland in Berne. Revie, accompanied by most of the national press, attended the match, in which Portugal looked third rate. Motivated by the urge to see England doing well again, encouraged by Revie, we all reported that the only doubt at Wembley could concern the margin of England's victory. Only four of the Portuguese team had more than four caps, but the sweet music of clicking turnstiles turned to a discordant hand-clap as the no-hopers held England to a goal-less draw. 'The 0–0 Massacre' blared one sarcastic headline. It was Revie's first reverse, the worse because the Wembley crowd felt cheated, for which I and other journalists had to take some of the blame for raising

44

false hopes. Malcolm Allison had in fact perceptively warned me the previous week-end: 'Even with international players, you cannot expect to tell them to play to a particular plan foreign to their normal game. They are not capable of such instant tactical flexibility. Don may intend to play without a central target striker'—Channon, Clarke and Thomas were the front three—'but in the end the team will revert to this type of game.' They did.

Four months later the gloom lifted when England became the first team to beat the world champions, West Germany, winning 2–0 at Wembley on a night remembered chiefly for a performance of sparkling inventiveness by Hudson. Bell and Macdonald scored the goals, and although Germany were weakened, with only five of the team which won the World Cup, Hudson, Ball and Bell had given the team a midfield dimension missing since the best days of Peters. Miljan Miljanic, the former Yugoslav national manager now with Real Madrid, said:

> 'England are once again the team everyone wants to beat. The difference between the teams was wider than the other way round when Germany won 3–1 at Wembley in the European Championship. But England still lack three qualities: width in attack, one "super" player, and enough left-sided players. And I am not sure about Gillard at left-back.'

That last observation was to prove particularly accurate when England played the return in Bratislava with the Czechs. Meanwhile Cyprus were disposed of at Wembley with five goals from Macdonald, the Supermac tag for once acquiring real currency in only his third complete international. He was only the second man this century to achieve such a feat, joining Willie Hall (*v* Ireland, 1938). All was less rosy in the return on the sandy, rutted pitch in Limassol, Keegan scoring the only goal against a nine-man barricade. The shortage of goals from key players was becoming a matter of concern—Channon had not scored in four matches, Thomas in three, Keegan only three in 12, Macdonald none in eight out of nine. It continued against Ireland (0–0), followed by a 2–2 draw with Wales, Johnson of Ipswich getting both. Then, with some inadvertent help from the Scotland keeper, Kennedy, there was a 5–1 rout of the Celtic foe at Wembley, significantly Gerry Francis coming into the side and scoring twice. Keegan, deserting the squad's headquarters when dropped against Wales, was forgiven and reinstated.

1975–6

But any confidence for the next encounter with the Czechs was dispelled by an unsatisfactory 2–1 win over the Swiss, in early autumn. In cold, misty Bratislava, with a few leaves still clinging to the trees along the banks of the Danube, Revie persisted with his policy of attack, using Keegan in midfield with Gerry Francis and Bell behind an attack of Channon, Macdonald, Clarke. His explanation was:

> 'To play a defensive formation, to go for a point the way we used to do at Leeds, requires the perfection of a system which can only be gained when the players are together for a long time. To come here and play cautiously, to risk

45

going one down to a lucky goal, would be to invite real problems. Win or lose, I shall not be diverted from the conviction that our future policy and success lies in attack.'

The game was fogged off after 20 minutes, with England well on top, and re-scheduled for 13.00 the next day, when it soon became obvious that the one factor Revie had seriously misjudged was the ability of Gillard at left-back to hold Masny, the quick-silver, right-flank Czech striker.

In front after 24 minutes through Channon, England were seemingly in control. But in the space of six minutes either side of half-time, unwisely relaxing, they were cut to bits as Masny pulled a razor on them. Watson took over from an injured McFarland at centre-back for the second half, but could not avert Revie's first defeat. The Czechs were scandalously physical once they had gone in front, but it was effectively the end of England's hopes in the European Championship. In the final match in Lisbon, needing to win to have a chance of qualifying on goal difference, England could only draw 1–1. Macdonald, badly missing twice from close in, was substituted without avail by Clarke. The squad returned home to the indignity of finding that they were not even seeded in the World Cup draw taking place in Argentina the following evening—and that Alan Hardaker, the Football League secretary, was busy having another stab at the 'unimportance' of international soccer just when England were at their lowest ebb for 112 years.

Three successive failures in the European, World and again the European tourna-ment could not be lightly explained—not when English club teams could hold their own in European competition, even though the domestic game demanded too much physical bravery, too little subtlety. The depression was deepened when the draw produced a formidable pairing with Italy, defensive experts of the kind best equipped to frustrate English 'runners'. Two countries with the most professional leagues in the world, both without recent success in the World Cup or Europe, now blocked each other's path to a return to glory. Remembering England's defeat by Italy in their two previous encounters under Ramsey, the omens were sombre. In six months Revie's squad had not progressed at all, and when he attempted to put on a bright front by claiming 'we are lucky to have got a group like this', there were not many who shared his optimism.

Some progress was made a week later when Ted Croker and Alan Hardaker, respective FA and League secretaries, agreed to a programme of collaboration over World Cup fixtures, with the postponement the previous Saturday of League matches involving clubs with international players. But Revie, pleased when he managed to persuade the Italians to agree to play England first in Rome, had con-ceded more ground than he at first thought with the proviso that Italy should have Luxembourg at home as their final qualifying tie. It did not require too great a strength of the imagination to think of the negotiations which might take place should Italy need to win by a certain margin to qualify on goal difference.

In March, Peter Taylor of Crystal Palace became the first Third Division player for 15 years to play for England, and did so with verve, scoring the second goal in a 2–1 win in the Wales Centenary match at Wrexham. He gave the team width and pace with some exciting runs, but the match was otherwise unmemorable, as was the scruffy 1–0 repeat at Cardiff at the start of the home championship, following which a Brazilian commentator remarked: 'Britain should be sending Wales, not England, to the US Bicentennial Tournament this summer.'

England had McFarland, Beattie and Brooking injured on the day, and had permanently lost the services of Colin Bell—a factor which was to prove critical to Revie in the long run. The team had eight players with a mere six caps between them—Clement, Brian Greenhoff, Thompson, Pearson, Towers and Taylor. That gives some indication of the hazards which perennially confront any England manager. The picture improved when Gerry Francis, Channon (2) and Pearson put four past Ireland at Wembley, then clouded with the 2–1 defeat at Hampden. Revie had made the first major compromise of his control of England, abandoning the attempt to play without a target striker—hence the introduction of Pearson from Manchester United and, as substitute against Ireland, Royle.

Before the Scots game, Revie was in an enigmatic mood, saying: 'This is the most impressive England squad since I took over.' Was this the psychology of the politician, hoping to convince a sceptical public? Scotland soon took the bones out of the theory, with their midfield trio of Rioch, Masson and Gemmill insisting: 'If we'd played really well, we'd have hammered England.' It was abundantly clear that on this form England's chances in the World Cup were no better than slim.

Enzo Bearzot, the Italian manager who was impressively frank throughout the qualifying competition, about not only his own but England's problems, observed: 'The fundamental requirement for England is a midfield player like Bobby Charlton or Johnny Giles. This would allow Francis and Keegan freedom to go forward. With so much imagination, Keegan should be allowed total freedom. By making him conform to the necessary geometry of the side in midfield, you limit his potential.'

Thus did Bearzot go straight to the heart of the matter, sensing England's dilemma long before Revie, offering even the advice which could turn the tables against Italy. Miljan Miljanic had this to say: 'It is no surprise that England are suffering from a list of injuries, because of the impossible strain you impose on them by playing too much football. There is a marked decline between October and April in the performance of your players, and you cannot underestimate the psychological effect of recent club defeats in Cup semi-finals and finals. Such blows to the nervous system take weeks to heal. You are plagued with "industrial football", yet the potential you have remains enormous.'

So England crossed the Atlantic in no great shape to meet Brazil in Los Angeles in the opening match of the US tournament. Yet they produced as fine a performance as any since Revie took charge, losing unluckily to a goal by Roberto in the last 90 seconds. It was the most unjust result since the Wembley draw with Poland, and Revie said: 'I've had some disappointments as a manager, but this was the worst in 14 years. We've really got something to build on now.' That team was: Clemence; Todd, Thompson, Doyle, Mills; G. Francis, Cherry, Brooking; Keegan, Pearson, Channon.

It was in fact the most complete performance abroad since the Mexico World Cup, and Brazil's manager Oswaldo Brandao admitted: 'Our luckiest result for 20 years!' With a changed, weakened team, though one including Wilkins, England

When England narrowly lost to Brazil in Los Angeles
in 1976, it seemed Revie was on the right road. Here
Trevor Brooking tussles with Zico, the latest 'new'
Pele.

Italy's general manager, Fulvio Bernardini, gives Revie a tip in New York, but England won 3–2, Bernardini was replaced by his coach Enzo Bearzot—who turned the tables in Rome.

proceeded to New York and a stirring 3–2 victory over World Cup opponents Italy, after being two down. Channon (2) and Thompson scored the goals; Wilkins had an outstanding game in midfield. Suddenly we all felt better about the prospects in Rome in November. In the final match in Philadelphia against 'Team America', a 3–1 win produced a cautionary note from the perceptive Pele: 'Without support from midfield, George Chinaglia and I gave England problems. They will have to raise their individual skills to produce. a major threat in the World Cup.'

The team returned home, rested, and reassembled in Helsinki 10 days later for the opening World Cup tie against Finland. All was well as Keegan (2), Channon and Pearson gave England a 4–1 margin against a massed, provocative defence. Finland attempted to turn the tie into a side-street mugging job, and failed conspicuously. It required two goals in four minutes on the hour for England to break free, with Finland briefly equalizing in between. Pearson's second on the far post was at a critical moment, but for which England might have nose-dived. It was slightly disturbing that in spite of the promise of Wilkins in America, Revie now reverted to Cherry as the 'hit-man' in midfield between Francis and Brooking, with Keegan the only player remotely resembling a winger.

1976–7

By the autumn and the start of a new league season, further blows had overtaken Revie. Francis had a prolonged injury and for the friendly with Eire at Wembley Revie reintroduced Brian Greenhoff. But what was he doing suddenly sending for the erratic Charlie George, then taking him off before the finish? It was definitive

49

straw snatching, and in an embarrassing encounter with an Irish midfield of Daly, Giles and Brady, England were held 1–1.

Revie's thoughts seem to have been particularly confused by this result, especially the 'failure' by Wilkins to follow Giles deep into the Irish half and restrict his direction of his side from behind. Revie insisted at his customary egg-and-bacon-sandwich breakfast with the press the next morning that he was not going to scrap the team because of one bad result. One was inclined to ask 'What team?' The changes in selection were too many for comfort, even allowing for harassing injuries—and there were more to come for the home cup-tie with Finland. Beattie, another player with recurring injuries, was suddenly included at left-back; Tueart, the unpredictable Manchester City winger, was recalled for the first time for 18 months, together with Royle; nine attackers, in a 4–2–4 formation, if one was to include Todd, the right-back. 'It's a team to do a job,' said Revie, with the now disconcerting belief that it was possible to change teams as easily as shirts, only a week or so after insisting that he would not be changing the team. The *Daily Express* headline on the morning of the match was: 'Charge in with Channon', a sentiment which probably reflected a little too accurately the attitude of not only the manager but English football as a whole.

The outcome was an alarmingly close 2–1 win against the amateur Finns, who came desperately close to drawing. Tueart put England ahead after only four minutes, but the avalanche from the nine-man attack just melted away, and there was the degrading sight of Clemence committing a deliberate foul on a Finnish forward, two yards outside the penalty area just before half-time, to prevent a cer-

Dennis Tueart (*arms raised*) gives England a fine start with his fourth-minute goal in the tie at Wembley, but modest Finland restricted the score to 2–1—not enough for England's needs in a group determined by goal difference.

50

tain goal. Revie's dour Yorkshire caution was beginning to take its toll, overburdening the team with dossiers of doubt, of too great an emphasis on the qualities of the opposition. The fear of failure was stalking England like a ghost, with the manager the most afraid. The next morning he was saying: 'The problems they caused our defence worried me.' Yet the gaps left by Todd and Beattie were partly as a result of insistence that they attack. Now Revie was confronted with the need to find—in his terms—a team to do a different, defensive job against Italy.

Once again the nation was in a lather. One League chairman even came up with the absurd accusation that Revie had somehow damaged the players in the week's special training, and it was a good thing he did not have them for two! The principle was not wrong, it was unarguable; the danger lay in Revie's fluctuation. Four days after the disappointment of failing to achieve a large score against Finland, Revie had his anxieties about Italy reinforced when he saw them beat Luxembourg 4–1 in the principality, with Juventus left-winger Roberto Bettega the most obvious threat to an uncertain English defence. Revie had probably decided on the spot to use his old Leeds utility player, Madeley, to stifle Bettega, but in the event was foiled by an injury to Madeley.

The anxiety soon showed itself, with the recall of Hughes, his discarded former skipper, to replace Madeley, Hughes not having played for over a year. The squad, when it was announced, had significantly not included Wilkins. While Italy's team almost picked itself, Revie's had half a dozen permutations at least. More than anything, that fact pinpointed the odds against England as they flew to Rome.

When Revie announced his team, I was full of misgiving. Once again, English soccer was relying on the cavalry to outwit the Indians, on the cannon to beat the arrow. It contained only three players, Clement, Cherry and Brian Greenhoff, not tried by Sir Alf Ramsey. It was an experienced team—without experience. A team of mostly outstanding players who had largely never played together. There were no fewer than six changes from the previous game against Finland, and 20 in the last four games. McFarland and Hughes, never previously tested together, were

No amount of exhortation by Revie and assistant Les Cocker, from the bench, can save Stan Bowles (*grounded*) and Mike Channon (*right*) from a 2–0 defeat by Italy. Also on the bench Fred Street (*trainer*), Bill Taylor (*coach*), Dennis Tueart and Peter Shilton.

the tenth centre-back partnership in Revie's 21 matches. It would be Bowles's first match for two and a half years!

There were, almost inevitably it seemed, two hard men in midfield, Cherry and Greenhoff, with Clement getting the job of stopping the formidable Bettega. Whatever the club reputations of the individuals, it was a hotch-potch of a team, compared with Italy's use of seven of the Juventus side which had successively eliminated Manchester City and United from European competition. The only hope for England, I was convinced, was that the character of the more experienced players would prove superior to the introverted Italians. As England left the pitch at the beautiful Olympic Stadium at the end of their final training session I asked Revie, on one side, if he was not worried about the collective inexperience of the team. Once again he replied, guardedly: 'I think it's the team for the job.' It was a fatal misjudgement of the international team manager's role.

Chosen to succeed where Ramsey had failed, Revie took a badly prepared England team into their most critical match for three years, and the 2–0 defeat was for him the beginning of the end—though the end would have a sharp twist. At the finish of the match, victim of his own caution as much as England's shortage of world-class players, he walked from the pitch shoulders down, hands thrust deep in pockets, alone. Only twice in the last seven World Cup competitions had England qualified against foreign opposition, and now their chance had been severely restricted again. In a group always likely to be decided by goal difference, it would have been a priceless advantage to take a point in Rome. But what hope with six changes!

The long years of English emphasis on speed and fitness instead of control and passing once more paid its penalty. A quarter of a century after the exposure of English methods by Hungary at Wembley, England were anxious prey for Italy's superior technique. Revie had attempted to reach the sanctuary of Wembley the following year with a team largely consisting of tacklers.

It was no more than predictable that the first goal which liberated Italy from their fear—theirs was every bit as deep as England's—came from one of the many

Italy's victory in Rome is assured by the second goal from left-winger Roberto Bettega, watched by Franco Causio, who began the move, Trevor Cherry and Roy McFarland.

free-kicks conceded around the penalty area by Roy McFarland and his defence. It was, in this instance, Cherry—attempting to halt the endlessly elusive Causio. From about 22 yards, Causio took a short kick to Antognoni, whose drive was inadvertently deflected by Keegan past a helpless Clemence as the wall started to break up.

Football is essentially a passing game, and now England's passing was often inaccurate. The front line of Channon, Bowles and Keegan never really functioned, except when Bowles showed, tantalizingly during a second half spell, what he might have achieved with better support. Twice in four minutes on the hour England had chances to draw level—which, if taken, would have sent Italy into shivers of panic. First Bowles drew three men on the right, slipped the ball to Channon, who went round Tardelli, was tripped but recovered his balance. Yet the Israeli referee Abraham Klein gave a free-kick with Channon dangerously positioned now 12 yards from goal with the ball at his feet. Then Greenhoff, meeting a cross by Channon on the half-volley, shot wide. The second goal again stemmed from Causio, who sent Benetti through on the left. Benetti's cross from the line was met by Bettega, bursting through the defence at speed to take the ball full-length in a waisthigh dive.

There are two ways to win World Cup matches—with outstanding individuals or outstanding teamwork. England had neither. They resorted, incredibly, to timewasting tactics from the start, their fear greater than that of their opponents. Yet the depressing aspect was that, on the plane home, hardly a player seemed to sense the gulf between the teams, other than young Talbot, the reserve from Ipswich. The general view was that they had been unlucky not to *steal* a result. Without realizing it, the mentality of the team had become self-confessed second class. The teams in Rome were:

Italy: Zoff; Cuccureddu, Gentile, Facchetti, Tardelli; Causio, Antognoni, Benetti; Capello, Graziani, Bettega.
England: Clemence; Clement (Beattie), McFarland, Hughes, Mills; Greenhoff, Cherry, Brooking; Channon, Bowles, Keegan.

Revie was left with 10 matches to find a formula before the return match with Italy at Wembley, and the hope that Finland might possibly take a point in their home tie with Italy in June. But in the next match Revie again got it wrong. The opponents were Holland, with Cruyff. In his first official engagement as England manager Revie had watched the final in Munich. He must have known that the whole concept of the Dutch tactics was to leave the central attacking area empty between two wingers, with midfield players breaking into that space. Yet Revie announced a team with not one but *two* stopper centre-halves, Watson and Doyle of Manchester City. Wholly predictably, they had no-one to mark, and spent an embarrassing night looking around for somebody to tackle, while Jan Peters of AZ 67 nipped in smartly to score Holland's two goals.

Furthermore, Revie made no special plan to combat Cruyff, in the way Germany had put Vogts on him in the final: and dropped Channon. There were changes in every department except goal, and a 92,000 crowd paid £260,000 to see England

play humble mouse to Holland's strolling, arrogant cat. The only thing 'total' about England's football was their incompetence. Cruyff enjoyed the freedom of the pitch, and Holland joined Hungary ('53), Sweden ('59), Austria ('65), West Germany ('72) and Italy ('73) as foreign victors at Wembley.

Revie, the dossier addict, had made his biggest blunder yet. Confronted with a known tactical problem, he had produced an inept solution. As Enzo Bearzot, his Italian opposite number said: 'In three vital matches, in New York, Rome and now London, England have played different teams with a different method.' Was this the moment for Revie to go? In two and a half years England had declined rather than advanced. In the *Daily Express* I voiced the opinion that only two men were equipped to do a better job—Jock Stein of Celtic and Ron Greenwood of West Ham, the man I had advocated when Ramsey was sacked. Within the FA there were again rumblings, as England's prospects for Argentina grew ever slimmer.

Luxembourg at Wembley . . . and more changes. Back came the 'touch' players, Kennedy and Hill, with a reversion also to a target striker, Royle, who sustained an injury and was replaced in the second half by Mariner. Keegan, Channon (2), Kennedy and Francis scored the goals, but when asked how many of the side would

A formula still eludes Revie, as Holland win the friendly at Wembley with two goals by Jan Peters (*arms aloft*). Mike Doyle, Kevin Keegan, Kevin Beattie (3) and Dave Watson wonder what to do next.

54

survive to play against Italy, Revie would only say 'No comment'. Brooking had not even been in the squad.

Against Northern Ireland in Belfast at the start of the home championship, England scraped a 2–1 win, then lost to both Wales and Scotland at Wembley. Things were going from bad to worse. The sharpest lesson, in a sense, came from the Welsh, so ably managed by Englishman Mike Smith. The same eleven who beat the Czechs in the World Cup qualifying tie, then drew with Scotland, now scored the only goal at Wembley, a penalty by James a minute before half-time, after he had been fouled by Shilton. A blatant penalty for England, when the Wales keeper Davies fouled Pearson, was ignored by Scots World Cup referee Gordon. McQueen and Dalglish scored the goals which sent the highland barbarians wild with glee on the Wembley terraces, but it was not a memorable Scots win, McGrain's excellence at left-back apart. England finished a sad third in the table.

Revie's credibility was now rock-bottom. The first ever successive defeats at Wembley to 'local' opposition, following those against Italy and Holland, left England looking morally bankrupt—with, additionally, £1 million slipping away if they failed to qualify (the value of reaching Argentina). Revie's actions, under enormous pressure and with continuing injury problems, had only magnified the crisis:

If, as he claimed, the team against Wales, with Brooking in central midfield, was one he had wanted to see 'for a long time', why had he not picked it before? To claim publicly, as he now did, that his squad lacked the intelligence to absorb his infamous dossiers was a self-defensive blunder damaging to morale. To deny publicly, in the middle of a six-match spell—a South American tour to follow—that he was a failure or that he would resign was merely to acknowledge the possibility of both. The slightly manic substitutions in midfield in the home championship—four in all—were hardly compatible with an attempt to create stability.

Revie now planned to fly in the opposite direction to his team—more literally than we knew at the time. He was to go to watch Italy against Finland in Helsinki, while the team flew to Rio for the opening match against Brazil. In fact Revie travelled via the Middle East to negotiate his defection (*the subject of the next chapter*). He rejoined the team in Buenos Aires, having seen Italy win 3–0 and arranged for himself a disloyalty bonus of stupefying proportions. In his absence, England held the transitional Brazil side to a goal-less draw, and the only change in three games was when Revie omitted Francis, impressive against Brazil, for the second game against Argentina, recalling Channon. Two more draws followed, England playing containing, unadventurous football in which the only gleam of light came from Wilkins. Brooking missed all three with injury; the goal-less draw with feeble Uruguay was the nadir, roundly condemned by those Uruguayans who could remember the days of style—theirs and England's.

It was ironic that in the moment he chose to desert the ship, Revie should make the fewest changes—one in three matches—of his entire spell as manager, and belatedly achieve some continuity. Yet the team remained unadventurous, scorning the advice of Helmut Schoen, manager of the West German team which was also on tour. He said, as the two squads found themselves in the same hotel in Rio: 'Play possession football by all means—but attack. There used to be a time when we came to South America trembling, but no longer. Football here is not the force it was; they do not like being attacked at home.' Germany had just beaten Uruguay and Argentina, but on this England showing—one goal in their last five matches—Italy would not be trembling as they marched towards the sound of English gunfire in November. Revie was asked after the draw in Montevideo, by a disenchanted Uruguayan journalist: 'What kind of a game was that?' Revie ducked the answer, ignoring the fact that for 20 minutes in the second half England had not hit a single penetrating pass, just deluding themselves with a meaningless possession game. The sensation which was about to break was perhaps a blessing in disguise.

In the middle of July came the sudden revelation, in the *Daily Mail*, that Revie had done his deal in the shade of Dubai with the United Arab Emirates. His resignation, the *Mail* informed us, was at that very moment on its way to the FA. Truly, nothing became him like the moment of his going. The man who had preached loyalty from players allowed his employers to read of his departure in the press. All credit to Jeff Powell, the *Mail* correspondent, for his scoop. But there were those who questioned whether they would have wanted to be privy to such a tale of duplicity. Meanwhile, as Revie braced himself for the task of showing the Arabs how to lace their boots, the FA had to find a leader for the forlorn job of trying to salvage a World Cup place. Sir Harold Thompson, chairman of the FA, said:

'The recent events have been quite disgraceful. We're in the right; the public know we are. I think it could be, I hope it will be, the moment for restoring dignity, decency and loyalty. The future is difficult . . . we're not going to plunge [*in a hurry*], but we want to get near to something I believe the public really wants. Revie has behaved very badly. What we do has got to be done with 100 per cent clear, clean distinction.'

Sir Harold, creator of Pegasus, the last great amateur club, was anxious to find a man who would restore to England not merely dignity, but a spirit of adventure in their play for so long missing. Such a man, he believed, was Ron Greenwood. His problem was to convince the rest of the International Committee, one of whom, Dick Wragg, the former chairman of Sheffield United, had rushed into a statement that England would be looking for 'another Revie'. By the beginning of August, Sir Harold had set up Greenwood to take over until the end of the year, that was, until England's World Cup qualifying programme had been completed. They first had a friendly with Switzerland, then played Luxembourg away, and finally Italy at home. They had not only to beat Italy, but score a hatful of goals against Luxembourg to stretch Italy if it came to goal difference. It did . . . and they didn't.

That was hardly Greenwood's fault. To reinvigorate England in the space of two matches was a tall order. When his 'temporary' appointment was formally announced on August 24 he was, at the press conference, too relaxed and authoritative for a man who had just accepted odds of a kick in the teeth to nothing. I was convinced then that he had unofficially been offered the full-time job, subject to his own willingness. In January he duly became full-time manager, with a brief at least until the end of the 1978–80 European Championship. Much speculation had preceded the appointment.

The FA advertised, and drew up a short list of candidates for interview. Leaks to the press revealed that these included Bobby Robson of Ipswich, Jack Charlton, formerly of Middlesbrough, Dave Sexton (Manchester United) and Brian Clough. There was an enormous public clamour for Clough, whose Nottingham Forest team was currently taking the First Division by storm, in their first year of promotion. In polls in the *Daily Express* and *The Sun*, Clough was the runaway winner. Yet it was not publicly clear whether the FA were looking for someone to replace Greenwood, or to work with him as assistant. My own view, stated emphatically in the *Express*, was that while Clough made an outstanding club manager, for Derby and then Forest, it was doubtful whether he had the right temperament for national manager.

The two jobs are totally different—a point lost upon many of the FA committee and one of the reasons why Revie failed so disappointingly. The club manager has to motivate a small fixed pool of players in a daily routine. The international manager must have a concept of the kind of team which will, with very little practice, blend into a unit ten times a year. His most vital function is not motivation but selection. I doubted whether Clough's disciplinarian, slightly patronizing attitude would work in an 'occasional' relationship with the established stars from several clubs.

Gradually, with further leaks, it became obvious that the FA, or at least Sir Harold, were looking for a team to work with Greenwood at all levels: Senior, 'B' XI, Under 21 and Youth. A small faction on the committee was still rooting for Clough—and failed. When the details were revealed, this was Greenwood's coaching team:

Senior XI: himself and Bill Taylor (Manchester City); **'B' XI:** Robson and Don Howe (Arsenal); **Under 21:** Sexton and Terry Venables (Crystal Palace); **Youth:** Ken Burton (full-time), Clough and his assistant, Peter Taylor.

Some people viewed the offer to Clough as an insult, but it was in fact a deft move by the FA, probably advised by Greenwood. It was an offer he could not refuse if he really cared about the future of England, it put him in touch with exactly those players who would come to the front if he ever succeeded Greenwood—and it neatly silenced one of the FA's most vociferous critics.

For Greenwood it was the apotheosis of his career. For years he had advocated a more continental approach, based on the same principles of passing and the use of space by players moving off the the ball in the manner of the Hungarians and, more recently, the Dutch and Germans. He had produced three of the key players, Moore, Peters and Hurst, for the team which won the World Cup in 1966—not forgetting Byrne, signed from Crystal Palace, and possibly the most talented of the four but in decline by '66. Greenwood had patently been an international manager in charge of a club side; the accusation constantly levelled against him was that West Ham lacked conviction, fight, motivation. If that was true, it was also certain that they suffered, in domestic competition, from the physical excesses of other clubs, unchecked by referees which, while expedient in the pursuit of trophies, directly contributed to the failure in producing mature players ingrained with skill for the national team. At every level but the summit of European competition, English sides thrived because of their superior fitness, organization and 'professionalism'. But, until Liverpool in 1977, only Manchester United had won the European Cup. West Ham, be it noted, reached the Cup-Winners' Final on the two occasions when they competed. When Liverpool won in Rome, beating Borussia, they did it with many of the basic, non-physical qualities extolled by Greenwood—and he recognized the fact by including seven of them in his first team against Switzerland.

1977-8

Sadly, Liverpool failed to deliver the goods for England, stifled by man-for-man marking by the Swiss in both attack and midfield. A goal-less draw gave no encouragement for the requirement in Luxembourg. Clemence, Neal, Hughes, McDermott, Callaghan, Kennedy and Keegan, with 'outsiders' Cherry, Watson, Channon and Trevor Francis, could not penetrate the tenacious Swiss. The dilemma for Greenwood was this: whether to use Liverpool's 4–3–3 system, or go for a bolder 4–2–4, with two wingers, using Keegan up front in conjunction with another, conventional central striker. After the Swiss miss, Greenwood admitted: 'You would have to be tremendously brave to risk that (*4–2–4*). If I had two years, I might say damn the results, let's have a go.'

Mistakenly, perhaps, he refused to take that gamble against Luxembourg. Keegan was unfit, and Neal was omitted from right-back in a 3–4–3 formation, with Wilkins, McDermott, Callaghan and Kennedy in midfield, Francis, Mariner and Hill up front. Francis and Hill were being asked to do what Bobby Charlton and Jimmy Greaves had done 17 years previously—score a hat-trick each. The truth was that the front three for this match had scored one goal between them in 13 collective appearances. Now was the winter of England's inexperience. When England hit nine past Luxembourg in 1960, they scored 44 goals in a run of eight matches with only three team changes. The present team had scored only nine in eight matches, with 25 changes!

On the night, England scuffled two goals from Kennedy and Mariner, the flank players Francis and Hill rarely got to the bye-line; Luxembourg packed their defence, fouled regularly and stayed more or less intact. One of the nonentities of the World Cup had played a significant part in determining the composition of the finals. Three days later Bettega showed what wing play should be, lashing four past Finland in Turin as Italy ran up six—and all was over bar the shouting. Even defeat for Italy at Wembley would leave them with a comparative stroll in their final game at home to Luxembourg. Back home there was the usual stream of banal comments about 'too much coaching'; when what England had suffered from for so long was too much *bad* coaching at grass roots level by schoolmasters more concerned with big strong boys winning cups.

It was sad to see players such as Kennedy and Mariner, who had given everything, returning home almost like convicts, when they were merely pawns in an administration bankrupt of ideas and initiative—afraid to tackle the question of better referees; too ignorant to appoint and *support* the best coaches as managers, irrespective of a few bad results; too feeble to resolve the issue of priorities in club versus country quite simply because most of them represent both League (club) and FA

Kevin Keegan congratulates Mike Channon on scoring England's fourth goal in the 5–0 win over Luxembourg at Wembley.

(country). Enzo Bearzot was in no doubt: 'What you need is not a new manager but new players. The national team is the expression of the domestic game—too physical and defensive.'

Greenwood took Bearzot's advice . . . and beat him over the head with it at Wembley, too late to affect the ticket to Argentina. Selecting for the first time 'his' team, he brought in two wingers, Steve Coppell of Manchester United and Peter Barnes of Manchester City, with Wilkins and Brooking forming the midfield in a 4–2–4 formation. Greenwood said beforehand: 'I would like to think this will be a stepping stone for the future . . . towards a situation in which our clubs will try to play like England, instead of England sides attempting to play like a club.'

Greenwood's formation confronted Bearzot with an unknown quantity—all his travels to watch nine of England's last 11 matches suddenly irrelevant. He would have to play an extra defensive marker, which would disrupt his midfield—and give England even more scope to attack. Keegan said hopefully: 'It might just happen, though it is asking a lot.' Barnes, thrust in at the deep end in his first match, was shyly anxious: 'I hope the public isn't expecting too much of me.' Greenwood reflected: 'We have to start putting our house in order. England are not bad; there's talent coming through, but other nations have overtaken us with dimensions to their game which we don't possess.'

England's splendid 2–0 victory began to correct that, and it was galling to reflect, on a night of minor triumph, that England might have been on their way to Argentina if Revie had had half the guts the players showed in this game. Greenwood's attacking gamble was not enough to erase the futility of Revie's multi-change defensive gamble in Rome. Keegan gave his greatest yet performance for England, scoring

Revenge, too late, as Kevin Keegan beats Renato Zaccarelli, to head home Trevor Brooking's cross for England's first goal in the tie at Wembley.

the first and making the second for Brooking as Italy descended into panic and finally brutality. Greenwood had written his own terms to redirect England's future, while Italy needed only a 1–0 win over Luxembourg to assure themselves of a place in the finals.

For a scratch team thrown together without practice it was a remarkable performance, against a side which had played together almost unchanged for two years. What might England have done with the same consistency of selection? Keegan produced a performance even more complete than that against Borussia in the European Cup final, while Barnes electrified the crowd with his dribbling. Those who contended that Italy were not *trying* seemed totally to overlook the manic fouling of Bearzot's team the moment England scored after only 11 minutes. The goal was perfection, the reaction ferocious. Brooking worked clear on the right, floated a near-post cross, and Keegan soared above Zaccarelli to head over Zoff.

Some of the fouls by Benetti on Barnes and Keegan were a disgrace, but England were not to be intimidated. Nine minutes from time Keegan, just before being cynically cut down by Benetti, slid the ball through for Brooking to score. Certainly Italy had lost Graziani with a head injury, but there was no doubting England's moral superiority. They had exposed serious flaws in Italy's make-up, some of them long-standing—and had opened up a new future of exciting possibilities for themselves.

The victory was built primarily on the awareness of Coppell, Brooking and Keegan; and Greenwood's vocation would be to produce a mainstream of such players. With the air of a man who has just started rather than finished a project, Greenwood spelled out his objectives for the next few years:

Trevor Brooking glides England's second goal between defenders Facchetti and Mozzini (5) and past Zoff to crown a great night for England's new manager Ron Greenwood.

'Self-expression of artistic players must be brought back into the game. A forward line with flank players is the first move towards having a good defence. I've been advocating these things for 16 years at West Ham. Why should people suddenly all start listening now? The crowds at West Ham haven't been rewarded by results, but they keep turning up because of the good football they see. Other clubs will suffer from the old bugbear that results count more than anything. This has been the ruination of English soccer. We must concentrate on practising rather than playing to win trophies.'

On December 3 in Rome Italy put three goals past Luxembourg.

CHAPTER FOUR

Revie's Defection

'Don Readies' was football's nickname for the manager who was strongly motivated, it always appeared, by money. Why else should he abandon, so furtively,
the most honourable job which English football has to offer, in order to build a
new reputation on sand for £340,000? Having observed him as player and manager
for 25 years or so, for the last three often at close quarters, I am baffled by some
of the contradictions evident in him. At different times we made three attempts
to resolve disagreements over his policies. He could be persuasive in the most
friendly way, but there always seemed to be a trace of the hustler in the background.
I thought his final departure was a pathetic capitulation to mammon, sacrificing
honour for riches in a way which made one feel sorry for him not having the guts
required for high office. My criticism of him is more factual—that over the years
he fostered attitudes with Leeds which were deeply damaging to the game at large,
and that with England he pursued policies which unnecessarily jeopardized qualifi-
cation for the World Cup. Those who have cause to resent him, even more than
his employers the FA, are those players whose international careers were disrupted
by his confused management, whose ship he deserted when it was already sinking.

Don Revie was born in 1927 in Bell Street, Middlesbrough, in a two-bedroomed
house close to the town football club. His father, a joiner, was often unemployed
in hard times. His mother died when he was 12. It is easy to see why the young
lad kicking a rag ball in the streets grew up to place a disproportionate value on
money, why he should be obsessed in his tactical attitudes with insecurity. We are
all the prisoners of our childhood. It was schoolboy days with a local club, Middlesbrough Swifts, which also established another deep-rooted approach to the game
in later life. The Swift's manager, engine-driver Bill Anderson, held regular pre-
match meetings at his council-house home to study dossiers on opponents.

Revie left school at 14 to begin an apprenticeship as a bricklayer, joining Leicester
City at 16. His lack of education bothered him in later years. He would send his
son Duncan and daughter Kim to expensive private schools—Repton in Derbyshire
and Queenswood in Hertfordshire—when the money was good. At 21 he married
the manager's daughter, Elsie Duncan, a Scots girl whose influence was said to be
considerable in shaping his attitudes. He moved clubs to Hull and then Manchester
City, where he became famous for the 'Revie Plan', a system in which he played
a deep-lying centre-forward after the manner of the Hungarians and which helped
City to win the FA Cup in 1956.

Subsequently he moved to Sunderland, and then, as player-manager, to Leeds.
From the brink of the Third Division he took Leeds to the top of the First in three
seasons. Between 1964, when they won the Second Division, and his appointment
as England manager in 1974, Leeds were League Champions twice, runners-up five

Don Revie scores one of his two goals, from a penalty, in England's 5–1 win over Denmark in Copenhagen in 1955. He scored four goals in six international appearances. *Inset* Revie, aged 22, with Leicester City in 1949.

times, FA Cup winners once and runners-up three times, League Cup winners once, UEFA Cup (then Fairs Cup) winners twice, and runners-up in three other European finals. They simultaneously managed to be the most unpopular side in England.

Without much disguise, they used physically intimidating tactics, in which Bobby Collins was conspicuous, to climb out of the Second, and continued the same way in the First. This reputation was substantiated when the FA disclosed that Leeds had the worst disciplinary record, at all levels, of any club. Yet it was not merely that Leeds were 'dirty'; they employed every ruse in the book such as time-wasting, feigning injury, and carefully studied tactics to undermine the referee, with two or more players applying incessant verbal pressure, with every decision disputed. They were booed at most grounds, and against Everton at Goodison, in 1964, referee Ken Stokes had to take both teams from the field to cool down.

In one particular collision Willie Bell of Leeds and Derek Temple of Everton had been laid out. Temple was taken off on a stretcher, while Bell attempted to get to his feet. Les Cocker, the Leeds trainer, sensing the wrath of the crowd, told Bell to stay down, and called to the ambulance men for another stretcher. To which he received the sharp reply: 'Get your own —— stretcher.' It is indicative of the Leeds philosophy that this tale was recounted often and proudly... by them. The most familiar gesture on the Leeds training ground from Cocker or Revie was the right fist smashed into the left palm, an exhortation which left no scope for subtlety, or doubt. The plaque on the dressing-room wall read: 'Keep Fighting'. When, the week before the 1973 FA Cup Final against Sunderland, I itemized the methods by which Leeds had debased the game, in the *Sunday Telegraph*, I received a solicitor's letter on behalf of Johnny Giles, complaining of my comments. Within a week the newspaper had five First Division managers willing to testify that the comments were fair. None the less, the players were barred by Revie from talking to me—a facility I had seldom wished to exploit.

Yet Revie, the Godfather to his close-knit squad of players, was conscious of their damaging image. After an infamous FA Cup semi-final with Manchester United in 1965, of which I was critical, Revie invited me to Leeds. I was met off the train from London, taken round the ground to see the truly splendid facilities which he had created out of the decaying remains he had inherited in 1961. I was introduced to almost every member of the staff, taken to lunch, returned to the train. For that half-day Revie was an attentive, proud host, with every reason to be proud of what he had achieved. How was it that such a gifted player, a man burning with energy and imagination, a coach with so much understanding of the game, could poison his own creation? It was that haunting insecurity which would never leave him, which reached a private crescendo whenever the club approached a climax, and inevitably communicated itself to the players. 'He was an utterly brilliant manager, but knotted with fear,' says Wales Captain Gary Sprake.

Too late, he realized the image could not be shifted, not even by adopting the famous all-white kit of Real Madrid, and claiming that his team were now the equals of the former aristocrats of Europe. The damage was done. Revie had presided over the most successful, and the most criticized team of the decade, in which standards of behaviour in England on and off the field had plunged to unprecedented depths. There had to be a correlation between these factors. Yet Revie was the man to whom the FA turned in 1974, having sacked Sir Alf Ramsey.

It was with a heavy heart that I drove the 30 miles out of Munich to greet Revie when he arrived in Germany for the World Cup Final. It was important, profession-

The Earl of Harewood, President of the FA, presents Don Revie with the inaugural Bell's Whisky Manager of the Year Award after Leeds had become 1969 League Champions.

The Revie family at Buckingham Palace for his OBE investiture in 1970: Don with his children Duncan 15, and Kim 10, and his wife Elsie.

ally, that I should be on speaking terms with him again. To wish him well was not hypocrisy, but altruism for the cause of England. Recognition of his faults did not blind one to his vast knowledge and efficiency. As a gesture of goodwill I gave him a detailed dossier (!) on suggestions for easy working relations with the international corps of football writers, how to utilize the press without expecting to shackle it. As far as I was concerned, he started his new, vital role afresh.

The differences between the role of club manager and international manager have been well summarized by Miljan Miljanic, the former Yugoslavia and Real Madrid coach. They are:

> The club manager selects his tactics according to his players, the international manager his players according to his tactics. The club manager is less concerned than the international manager with the creative part of the game; his concern is to motivate players at regular, short intervals, even when they do not feel like playing. The club manager can command; the international manager can only seek co-operation. The club manager selects players for their form on the day; the international manager has to have a long-term vision on little practice or evidence. The club manager is pragmatic; the international manager should be concerned with the broader development.

I doubt if the FA, when they sat down to consider Ramsey's successor, were conscious of these differences. I am certain that Revie was not, once he began the job, nor even by the time he quit. Throughout his three and a half years he was turning somersaults. When the draw was made for the World Cup qualifying competition

in 1975, Revie, poacher-turned-gamekeeper, said: 'In the last 12 months, going round to League matches, it has been increasingly obvious that skills do not have the chance to develop because of the fierce physical contact.' Surprise, surprise.

In 1975 he said: 'Some players don't know how lucky they are. They should go down on their hands and knees every night and thank God they are doing something which they love and are being well paid for.' Meanwhile Revie himself was asking £200 to speak a few words at the launching of the *Rothman's Football Annual*, the Wisden of soccer. Such a fee would be fair game for opening a supermarket, but not for a routine football event a taxi-ride from the FA. Yet he was bold enough to insist on another occasion: 'I've never taken a penny from a sports goods firm in my 15 years at Leeds, nor since I took the England job. If it had been money I was after I would have stayed at Leeds.' This was contradicted by the evidence of Richard Langridge, marketing director of Stylo Matchmakers, who claimed that since becoming manager of England, Revie, had signed a contract to boost its boys' soccer boots, following a previous contract with the Leeds players' pool.' Langridge refused to say how much money had changed hands on either deal but commented: 'Don impressed me as an astute businessman; he's got his head screwed on properly.'

However, it seems likely that Revie did not receive anything for negotiating a £250,000 deal for the FA with Cook and Hurst, the Admiral sports goods firm. This gave the FA a huge sum in sponsorship for wearing Admiral gear, where previously they had paid for their equipment. Bert Patrick, the Admiral chairman, denied that Revie was financially involved in the deal, or in advertisements bearing his name in European sports magazines. It was Revie's claim that he had in fact made a million pounds profit for the FA during his management, even if they had blanched at some of the bills which came in for champagne, cars, telephone calls from abroad. After his defection to Dubai, Revie stated he had made nothing out of his deals for the FA. But he had astounded people in the game with a circular in 1976 announcing that he was available for soccer seminars at £200 a time.

Such controversy as this was nothing compared with what was happening on the field. The players and the policies altered faster than the public could follow. He attempted to play without a conventional central striker, then changed his mind. He decided to play with wingers, then changed his mind. First of all he was against man-for-man marking, then in favour.

For the most critical of all the matches, away to Italy, the decision to employ man-for-man was abandoned *only the Friday beforehand*. Soon after his first match, at home to Czechoslovakia in the European Championship, his caution had been preparing the ground in advance, when he told the FA international committee: 'Gentlemen, it is now clear to me that despite our strength in depth, England are seriously short of international-class footballers. We will be lucky if we win this European group, let alone qualify for the World Cup.' Such a view was seen to be transparent nonsense when Ron Greenwood selected new players and a different system to beat Italy at home, then conceded nothing in meetings with West Germany and Brazil.

Revie *was* unlucky in certain aspects, and it was true that some international players had been conditioned by their clubs to play in a way which failed to exploit their international potential. The points for and against Revie can be summarized thus:

FOR
1   No-one achieved more club success (other than Liverpool) built on the modern possession game, combined with astute study of the opposition.
2   His international record, 12 wins in his first 21 matches, was the same as Sir Alf Ramsey's.
3   He was limited, as was Ramsey, by the time available for preparation, by injuries in domestic matches immediately preceding international fixtures.
4   Long-term injuries to important players—Bell, Madeley, McFarland, Beattie, Gerry Francis, Thompson—were serious setbacks.
5   Outstanding talents such as Hudson, Currie and George proved unreliable during his time as manager.
6   England were literally kicked out of the European Championship in Bratislava by the Czechs' exploitation of a weak referee.
7   Against Brazil in Los Angeles in 1976 there was a blend, even in defeat, full of promise.
8   The loss of form of Todd, an important cog, at a critical period, depleted the team.
9   He used, primarily, those players with established club records, character and experience.
10   He was limited by the fact that English clubs play to a dozen different tactical patterns, making the interchange of international players that much more hazardous.

Don Revie leaves the FA offices with Leeds chairman Manny Cussins in July 1973, smiling broadly after a nominal, suspended fine of £3000 on the club, following more than 40 first-team bookings the previous season.

AGAINST

1 His tolerance of physical excess with Leeds, together with Ramsey's with England, helped force English soccer down a blind alley of intimidation.

2 He supposed that it was possible to select differing teams for individual matches as at club level, whereas an international team needs every available chance to play together unchanged—at least a dozen matches a year.

3 Changes of policy on target strikers, wingers, and defensive marking systems confused and weakened the team.

4 The use of 52 players in 29 matches was excessive even in a period of transition.

5 Six changes against Italy in Rome, including two players not in the original squad of 22, was blatant panic.

6 If Clement and Mills, for example, were the correct full-backs to play against Italy, they should have played in the preceding match against Finland.

7 As experience showed that England regularly lost cup-ties on foreign soil trying to defend, it was worth the gamble to attack.

8 Obsession with the quality of the opposition, in the form of dossiers, was confusing and inhibiting.

9 He failed to give experience soon enough to players such as Trevor Francis, Wilkins and Coppell.

10 He defended on the 1977 South American tour, when it was imperative to produce an attacking team to meet Luxembourg and Italy.

11 He believed that international players could be controlled and manipulated minute by minute. A lion taught to jump through a hoop is no longer a lion.

12 His phobias, his 'lucky' suits, were redolent of fear.

The dossiers epitomized his thinking. Kevin Keegan has since admitted that he and Mike Channon used 'to use the back of the dossiers for keeping the score at cards'. There is the story, unconfirmed, that Keegan once telephoned Gerry Francis from the team's headquarters, when Francis was absent injured, to come over and explain what Revie was talking about. Revie's use of adolescent games to keep the players amused was another irritant with the more mature members of the squad. He once

68

even instituted a 'merit table' with the entire corps of national press on a foreign trip to Portugal, based on a bonus for booking the table for lunch, a penalty for being late down to breakfast etc. A few hard-bitten journalists, accustomed to finding their way around the world unaided, were almost anaesthetized with disbelief!

Even so, they still had no thought that he could be planning a defection *before* the return game with Italy at Wembley. That much less so when, shortly before the game against Scotland at Wembley the previous May, he said: 'I'm not a failure. I'll be disappointed if England don't qualify for the World Cup finals. But what happens to me if we don't qualify rests solely with the FA. I have no preconceived ideas of resigning if Italy beats us.' Yet, if we are to believe the exclusive story given to Jeff Powell of the *Daily Mail* after Revie had arrived in Dubai, he said he had been thinking about his defection for some weeks before the Scotland game.

When Revie flew to Dubai before going to Helsinki to watch Italy—while England were drawing with Brazil in Rio—did Les Cocker, his £7,000 a year★ assistant, know of his intentions? Seemingly not, for Cocker said before England's departure that he had dissuaded Revie from changing his mind and travelling with the team. 'I told him he should be in Helsinki to watch Italy, and finally he agreed,' Cocker said at Gatwick Airport. However Cocker—for whom the suffix 'spaniel' would seem appropriate—duly joined Revie in Dubai, so we may draw our own conclusions about the statement at Gatwick.

On arrival in Rio, Dick Wragg, chairman of the FA International Committee, was busy defending Revie with the most misplaced zeal since the Charge of the Light Brigade. Wragg, who had told me emphatically ten days before England failed to beat Poland at Wembley in the previous World Cup that Ramsey would not be sacked, now said: 'It makes me angry to hear criticism of a man who is working himself into the ground and trying all he knows to get things right for the England team. All the man needs is a break.' A break in Dubai, as it happened!

Not only was Revie busy negotiating his 'security for life' in England's time, but he had the nerve, on arrival in Buenos Aires, to attempt to negotiate a pay-off from his contract on the grounds that he could no longer stand the pressure on himself and his family. That might have been acceptable had it been true, even from a man who preached loyalty.

Wragg, and the other members of the committee, including Sir Matt Busby and Peter Swales of Manchester City, were shocked by Revie's request—even not knowing the truth—and told him to see out his contract, at least until after the Italy game. Frankly, I do not wholly believe the talk of the pressures on his family. His daughter Kim had been singing previously at a night club in Luton—an assignment for which the public position of her father had presumably not been a disadvantage, and one which required a disposition hardly compatible with a publicity-shy schoolgirl.

Having failed to persuade the FA to pay him off, Revie now looked for a different channel of remuneration. It was said that the *Mail* paid him in excess of £15,000 for his story. If not, then why should he exclude from such a 'scoop' Frank Clough, the chief soccer correspondent of *The Sun*, a close acquaintance for many years? Clough, like Revie, is a Yorkshireman, from Cleckheaton, and they had shared

★ Not £12,000 as widely reported.

A man prey to anxiety. Don Revie and his skipper Billy Bremner dejectedly watch Sunderland collect the FA Cup after the Second Division team's sensational 1–0 victory in 1973. In the background Allan Clarke, David Harvey (*kneeling*), Eddie Gray and Johnny Giles. *Inset* Revie, now England manager (1974), unimpressed at Highbury.

many long hours during Revie's climb with Leeds over the years. It was Clough who had first introduced Powell to Revie, who had been one of Revie's staunchest supporters. Only a short time before his 'resignation', Revie had written to Clough, thanking him for his support, without a mention of his intentions. The conclusion must be that the *Mail* paid for the story. It certainly must be the first time that an international manager's resignation from his national association has carried a newspaper's 'copyright' line.

Across a million breakfast tables the crocodile tears must have rolled as *Mail* readers learned that Revie 'sat down with my wife Elsie one night, and we agreed the job was no longer worth all the aggravation. It was bringing too much heartache to those nearest to us.' There was some heartache at the FA. After deliberation, they suspended Revie indefinitely from all football in England until such time as he presented himself to them to explain his breach of contract—and possibly also to answer questions concerning allegations of attempts to 'fix' matches during his time at Leeds, published by the *Daily Mirror*.

Revie took out a writ for libel against the *Mirror*, but by July 1978 it had still not been served. Meanwhile, attempting to justify his failure with England, he had told Powell: 'As soon as it dawned on me that we were short of players who combined skill and commitment, I should have forgotten all about trying to play more controlled, attractive football, and settled for a real bastard of a team.' Well, at least England were spared that.

Perhaps the last word on this sorry episode in English football should rest with Jack Charlton, one of Revie's strongest allies in the Leeds era, centre-half for England when they won the World Cup with Ramsey. In an interview with Terry McNeill in the *News of the World*, Charlton said: 'I like Don Revie. I had 12 great years with him at Leeds, and I think I understand him. But it's my belief that if you sign a contract, you should see it through to the end. Revie's players must feel they've been let down. He always demanded that players should be loyal, dedicated and aware of their responsibilities. These same players might well feel he hasn't practised what he preached.... What will upset him deeply is criticism from people whom he knows and trusts, people like Billy Bremner and myself. I'm trying to be fair to the man. He has always been close to his family, not just those who live under the same roof, but aunts, uncles and cousins. But I have to say that his resignation at such a time can hardly help England's cause. The new manager, whoever he might be, just hasn't the time to get his ideas across.'

Revie, the poor boy from Middlesbrough, had, in the words of Wilde, learned the price of everything and the value of nothing.

CHAPTER FIVE

Scotland's Luck

	W	D	L	F	A	Pts
Scotland	3	0	1	6	3	6
Czechoslovakia	2	0	2	4	6	4
Wales	1	0	3	3	4	2

Scotland made a bad start in the 1974–76 European Championship, losing their first tie at home to Spain, the eventual group winners. Billy Bremner scored in a 2–1 defeat, and although a goal by Joe Jordan earned a 1–1 draw in the return in Valencia, Scotland could not make good the loss of these three points, in spite of two draws with Romania, two victories over Denmark. Beating England 2–1 at Hampden to win the Home Championship, Scotland were confidently ready for their World Cup campaign, following a six-goal friendly spree against Finland, in which Andy Gray scored twice.

Czechoslovakia were the new European Champions, having won the final against West Germany in Belgrade on penalties at the end of extra-time, Uli Hoeness missing the decisive kick. Willie Ormond picked a 4-4-2 formation for the opening

Scotland's early World Cup ventures were unspectacular. In 1954, in Switzerland, they let in seven against Uruguay. Goalkeeper Fred Martin—now a whisky salesman—has a good view of the third.

tie in Prague, with Andy Gray and Jordan as the spearhead in front of a middle line of Rioch, Dalglish, Masson and Gemmill. But in a tough game, with five booked and two sent off, Scotland crashed 2–0. Yet ironically it was the game which probably decided the group in Scotland's favour, because the Czech sent off, Anton Ondrus, the key to their defence, was suspended for the remainder of the group matches. He was the backbone of their team; without him they lost away to both Scotland and Wales.

Scotland, in fact, started well in Prague, and should have been two or three up in the first half-hour. There were some explosive fouls, notably one by Gordon McQueen on the Czech left-back Gogh, for which he was booked. Although Scotland had one or two chances, the front pair, reinforced by Dalglish, were not linking smoothly; Masson was being close-marked and pushed deeper and deeper into his own half. Then two minutes before half-time came the incident which turned the game ... and the group. Ondrus tackled Gray from behind, Gray punched him, and Italian referee Michelotti, on the evidence of his linesman, sent both men off. Two goals in two minutes immediately after the interval left Scotland with a daunting task in their remaining games, it seemed, especially without Gray.

In the 46th minute McQueen, who had returned to the team following an Achilles injury, missed a cross, Rough parried a volley by Nehoda, and Panenka smashed in the loose ball. Two minutes later Petras, the dazzling right-winger, scored a spectacular second, and before the finish Scotland had disintegrated. In addition to McQueen, they had Gemmill, Buchan and Donachie booked; Mike Smith, the Wales manager, thought that the Czechs had looked really impressive, for it was Scotland's first defeat in nine games. The team was: Rough, McGrain, McQueen, Buchan, Donachie; Rioch, Dalglish (Burns), Masson (Hartford), Gemmill; Jordan, Gray.

A month later, in November 1976, Scotland met Wales at Hampden—and won by an own goal by Crystal Palace defender Ian Evans. Before the game there had been talk of Ormond's position being at stake—all part of the hazard of international management. He was considering replacing Masson with the volatile Kenny Burns from Birmingham—and did. Smith had reservations about his star winger Leighton James of Derby, decided to play him—and James slumped, being substituted at half-time by Alan Curtis.

The goal came after 15 minutes. McGrain made a sprint up the right, Dalglish back heeled and confused the Wales defence; and Evans, with a desperate lunge, turned the ball into his own net. That should have set Scotland up for the kill, but they failed to build on their advantage. Wales might well have drawn but for a superb save by Rough from a header by John Toshack, hammered from eight yards from a cross by Mike Thomas. Dalglish hit the post for Scotland, but faded; Flynn, Yorath and Mahoney nearly saved the game for Wales. If James had produced anything like his best, Wales would have won, but Ormond could claim: 'We are in a better position than England in their group. I would have liked more goals but we are now back to square one. We will beat the Czechs here, and then we must win in Wales. Kenny Burns gave us a lot of stability; it was a team performance.' Smith simply reflected on the winger who didn't deliver. The team were: SCOT-LAND: Rough; McGrain, McQueen, Blackley, Donachie; Rioch (Hartford),

73

Scotland were the only unbeaten team in the 1974 finals. If Billy Bremner (4) had not missed this one against Brazil (Rivelino and Leao watching), Scotland would have reached the second round.

Burns, Gemmill; Dalglish, Jordan, Gray E. (Pettigrew). WALES: Davies; Page, Phillips, Evans, Jones, J.; Griffiths, Flynn, Yorath; Thomas, M., Toshack, James (Curtis).

The following March, Wales thumped Czechoslovakia 3–0. Smith had decided to drop James, but was obliged to recall him when Toshack cried off with an achilles injury. Smith had told James he was out of the game, but the Derby winger gave the phone number of his mother-in-law—just in case, he explained!—and was with the squad in North Wales within an hour of Smith's SOS. He was told in uncompromising terms by Smith that he had got to 'make things happen this time', and rewarded the team with a brilliant solo third goal.

Wales were one up at half-time through a free-kick by James, Sayer of Cardiff misleading the Czech keeper Vencel with a dummy run across the flight of the ball. Then, at the start of the second half, Wales were almost overpowered by a breathtaking burst from the Czechs—'as good as anything I've ever seen,' said Smith. Had the Czechs scored then, they would probably have won; but they did not.

Wales sorted themselves out, Yorath marked man-for-man on the dangerous Pollak, and Wales went two up through Nick Deacy, playing his first match. James gave the final flourish, and the Czechs, badly missing Ondrus, had conceded their

74

first defeat for 23 matches—since losing to England in the opening game of the European Championship at Wembley. After three matches, each of the three countries had two points; suddenly Wales were serious contenders for the finals. Their team was: Davies; Thomas, R., Evans, Phillips, Jones, J.; Mahoney, Yorath, Flynn; Sayer, Deacy, James.

The psychology of the group altered two months later with the resignation of Willie Ormond. Reduced to a state of near-exhaustion by the 1974 finals, hurt by rumours of approaches behind his back by the Scottish FA to Jock Stein of Celtic, he jumped at the invitation to join Heart of Midlothian in his beloved Edinburgh. He had not lost a match in 1974, but the job was always slightly alien to this essentially quiet, friendly, domestic-minded man living in his Musselburgh council house, drinking with the local fishermen. Leaving the SFA may well have been his most satisfying moment as Scots manager.

Ormond had already named a squad for the home championship. Stein was the obvious target for the SFA, but there were complications. Scotland's most famous, most experienced manager was still lame from a serious car accident, and his contract with Celtic involved the pay-off of a testimonial match, a handsome golden handshake which he would forfeit if he switched seats. So the choice was Ally MacLeod, formerly with Ayr United on the West Coast for 10 years—struggling to stay in touch, with a team of part-timers—and then Aberdeen. MacLeod later told me: 'Deep down I knew from the start that I could do the job. When I took over, Scotland had lost in Czechoslovakia and had only beaten Wales with an own goal at home. I said to my wife: "What have I let myself in for?" But we qualified. All those years while I was at Ayr I thought privately that I was good enough to make it at the top. When I moved to Aberdeen, where there was a bit of money and we won the League Cup, people said: "Oh yes, they've got resources", rather than giving any credit to me.'

MacLeod was nothing if not confident. He took over the squad selected by Ormond, and within a month it was '*my*' team rather than '*our*'—Scotland's—team. Thanks partially to continuing fluctuation by Don Revie, Scotland won the Home Championship, beating England 2–1 at Wembley with goals by McQueen and Dalglish—the Scots supporters digging up the pitch afterwards and wrecking the goals. Like England, the Scots were afterwards bound for South America to gain experience. A sub-standard Chilean side was beaten 4–2 and the performance hailed by MacLeod as 'world class'. Like England, Scotland ran into a brutal reception from Argentina, drawing 1–1, with a foul count of Argentina 41, Scotland 14. Willie Johnston and Vincente Pernia were sent off; Martin Buchan had to be dissuaded from leading the rest of the team off. The Buenos Aires papers were unanimous in condemning their own team for squalid tactics. Subsequently Brazil defeated MacLeod's men 2–0 in Rio—a tour which should have taught MacLeod that he needed more penetration from midfield, provided in Chile by Lou Macari with two goals.

Scotland's luck, if in this instance it can be called that, continued in the home qualifying tie with Czechoslovakia, who found the fates sickeningly stacked against them. Arriving in London during an air strike—late—they had to travel to Glasgow by train, only to find their sleepers had not been booked. They sat up all night,

Gordon McQueen (5) beats Czech keeper Vencel to this corner-kick in Prague in 1976, but Scotland lost 2–0. Andy Gray (*background, left*) was later sent off.

there was no bus to meet them when they arrived in Glasgow, and in vain they applied frantically to FIFA for a 24-hour postponement. So they went into the match tired, and afraid ... with some justification.

Scotland hit them in the first half-hour like a wave of marauding commandos. The Czechs had suffered a wretched run since losing to Wales, failing to score against Switzerland, Hungary and Austria, and winning by a single goal against Turkey. Not only did Scotland now blast them with one of the most sustained spells of co-ordinated soccer by a British team for several years, but the physical challenge of the Scots was intimidating and often illegal.

Marian Masny, the Czech right-winger who had troubled England so severely, was crushed by McGrain under the benevolent eye of Belgian referee Rion. 'I thought they exceeded reasonable bounds,' commented Mike Smith, 'but I knew we wouldn't be a soft touch when it came to our turn.' An 85,000 crowd merely revelled in the destruction of the Czechs, chanting with ever-increasing confidence 'Scotland will be there' as Jordan, Hartford and Dalglish rammed home the goals in a 3–1 win.

Once Masny, had been softened, Scotland were in almost total command. In the 20 minutes leading up to half-time, they played with a collective penetration and variety which surpassed anything Billy Bremner's team had produced in Germany four years before. As in 1973, it was a goal by the towering but so often ineffective

76

Jordan, against the same opponents and on the same ground, which sent Scotland surging towards the finals. From a corner by Johnston, he rose to head into a gaping hole on the far post. How the loss of Ondrus had been crucial!

Scotland had to survive one brilliant dribble by Masny, centre-back Capkovic bursting into attack to glance the cross wide with a plunging header. But in the 36th minute the Czechs were stunned by a seven-pass move. Rioch, Masson and Hartford set it in motion; Johnston pitched a cross from left to right. I thought that the Czech's reserve keeper Pavol Michalik was fouled by Jordan as the pair went up together for the ball. Both fell, the referee's whistle stayed silent, and Hartford tapped the ball into an empty net from eight yards.

The victory was sealed nine minutes into the second half as Dalglish back-headed another header driven in by Jardine from the edge of the penalty area. Scotland were there indeed—though the late, swerving drive with which Gajdusek scored for the Czechs could have proved vital had Wales taken three points from their remaining two games. In this particular match the Scots middle line of Rioch, Masson and Hartford, criticized towards the end of the season, reached its peak. The team was: Rough; Jardine, Forsyth, McQueen, McGrain; Rioch, Masson, Hartford; Dalglish, Jordan, Johnston.

And so the scene moved, for the climax, strangely to Liverpool—as Smith put it, 'a saga of incompetence'. The new ground-safety regulations introduced by the government had meant reduced capacities at Cardiff (to 19,000) and Wrexham (to 16,000). It was said that the cost of improvements to get Cardiff ready for a worthwhile crowd—say 30,000—would be too great. Yet the irony was that later in the season (1977–78) Wrexham were granted a special licence for 25,000 for the FA Cup tie against Arsenal. Such a crowd, at their own ground, would certainly have suited Wales more than Anfield, which in the event was bulging with three times as many Scots as Welsh! The FA of Wales had been offered Wembley, as well as Villa Park and Anfield, but Smith chose Anfield 'because I wanted to prepare in Wales, and Anfield is the nearest to our headquarters; the team gets a psychological lift from coming home to Wales'.

Once the decision was taken, the rabid Scots fans just about acquired the leasehold of Anfield by every ruse imaginable. It was stipulated that only a third of the tickets should go to the Scots, the rest to Wales. But bus-loads of Scots travelled to North Wales to apply for tickets; they used accommodation addresses, and succeeded in soaking up much of the Welsh allocation. On the night some 35,000 of the 50,000 spectators, it was estimated, were from Scotland. When the first, controversial goal went in, and the crowd was baying its delight, Smith turned to his assistant, Cyril Lea, on the bench and exclaimed: 'Where are our boys on the terraces?'

The dice had seemed loaded against Wales all along the line. For this vital game they were without James, who was injured, but Smith said defiantly beforehand: 'If you say that without James we are nothing, then look at the facts. We reached the quarter-final of the European Championship, better than either England or Scotland, we were the first team to beat Hungary in Budapest for 60 years, we beat the Czechs at Wrexham, and England at Wembley. Of course the Scots are strong, and have fine players. But we know that we need not be afraid, or desperate; we are a team which has achieved a few things.'

It was a night of perpetual motion ... and emotion. Before the kick-off, the band of the Royal Welch Fusiliers was drowned by the Scots hordes, a bad omen; and for the first 15 minutes it seemed that the Welsh team, too, would be swamped. Scotland could easily have been three up, but Davies in goal made one superb save from Dalglish. Scotland's only changes from the team against Czechoslovakia were Donachie for McGrain at left-back and Macari for Rioch, and Macari was soon troubling the Welsh with his intelligent forward thrusts. Scotland forced three corners, but somehow Wales scrambled the ball clear. The game grew increasingly physical, but the French referee Wurtz was firmly in control, so much so that his involvement in the most controversial moment of the whole qualifying group was that much more bizarre. Wales at last began to get a grip on the game when Flynn began to shackle Masson.

Toshack, in his duel with McQueen, was more than breaking even, but he was unable to extend Rough in the Scots goal. Wales' best chance of the first half was when Phillips put Sayer through and his shot, in full stride, went just wide. In the second half Scotland had to replace the injured Jardine with Buchan; Deacy replaced Sayer; Donachie and Yorath were booked. Then, on the hour came Wales' great moment—the split second when they were within an inch, perhaps, of a place in the finals. Toshack beat the off-side trap, clear of the defence but put on-side by Forsyth. From just inside the penalty area Toshack cleverly lobbed Rough. It was a goal all the way. But somehow Rough, climbing upwards and backwards as the ball curled over him, just managed to get a touch and turn it onto the bar.

That save was almost immediately matched by another at the other end by Davies, who beat out Dalglish's close range header from a corner. And now came the incident which decided all. Willie Johnston took a long throw into the penalty area, a bunch of players went up, a hand was seen to punch the ball. The referee ruled that it was David Jones, but it was conclusively proved by television that it was Jordan. As the Welsh stood numb, Masson hit the penalty which took Scotland to Argentina.

Smith said afterwards: 'I think that if anything the referee was too close for that incident. He had otherwise been magnificent throughout. I thought at first that it was one of our boys, but the fact is that it settled the game. We never really got going again after that.'

Dalglish added a second, from a position ahead of Buchan's cross, which may have been off-side. It hardly mattered. Wales were out, having conceded only three goals, one an own goal, plus a wrongly awarded penalty. But they had not scored enough—three in one match against the Czechs and none in the other two. They had badly missed the midfield drive of Arfon Griffiths, who previously had notched six in a 12-match spell. But those were reflections for Wales, not Ally MacLeod and his Tartan Army, now dancing on the terraces or busy breaking up the suburbs of Liverpool. The teams that night were: WALES: Davies; Thomas, R., Jones, D., Phillips, Jones, J.; Mahoney, Flynn, Yorath; Sayer (Deacy), Toshack, Thomas, M. SCOTLAND: Rough; Jardine (Buchan), McQueen, Forsyth, Donachie; Macari, Masson, Hartford; Dalglish, Jordan, Johnston.

In the final match in the group, sad Wales went down by the only goal to Czechoslovakia in Prague. Scotland, with a mixed 2–1 win over Bulgaria in a friendly at Hampden in the new year, advanced on the Home Championship in a flamboyant mood that was not in keeping with some of the factors at work within their squad. The regrettable loss of Danny McGrain following an operation deprived them of a most dependable full-back and one of their genuinely world class players. The loss of club form of Masson and Rioch, following their transfers to Derby from Queen's Park Rangers and Everton respectively, did not augur well for the balance of the team. And Jordan, transferred as was McQueen from Leeds to Manchester United, was still not the goal-scorer needed at the highest international level.

These factors apart, there was the question of temperament, individual and collective, which when unchecked was a potential threat to any Scots venture, not to say to any competition in which they took part. The stability of the squad was further disturbed by the volatile pronouncements of the manager, who was rapidly acquiring the nickname of Mohamad Ally. Not only was he outrageously over-confident—'when we win the World Cup on June 25 it should be made a national "ally-day"'—but whether or not he realized it, he kept contradicting himself.

In January he was busy telling James Mossop of the *Sunday Express*: 'I was pleased with the way the lads reacted on last summer's tour of South America. They grew up with the experience, and they know that if any one of them reacts to provocation he will be out. I cannot afford, and will not have, anyone who cannot behave himself on and off the field.' This was in marked contrast to subsequent comments in the

Daily Express when interviewed by me, and in articles published under his own name.

In a series I wrote in March, I quoted MacLeod as saying: 'I want Scotland to play with fire—the way they know how. That's what I told them before we beat the Czechs. People say this style won't succeed in South America. We'll find out. The situation is made, I believe, for a European team to win for the first time on the other side of the Atlantic. But you have to have the right temperament to win, and you don't win without what Scotland have got.' And in a later interview with John Mann of the *Scottish Daily Express* he said: 'I don't want angels in Argentina. We Scots have built our style on our national characteristics. We're aggressive. We play to win. That is the style which has taken us this far, and we must not abandon it now.'

His series with John Mann was rich in rash assertions for a man who had never yet played a cup-tie outside Britain, who had experienced only a handful of friendlies. 'I believe in letting the opposition worry about us, not the other way round.' Now that is fine, so long as you don't ignore the qualities of the opposition. Over the years Scotland had a history of squandering their possibilities precisely through ignoring the fact that the other side might be able to play a bit. And the most foolish statement of all was: 'This year the home internationals must be treated as glorified practice matches.' Even if he believed it, and there is sense in such an attitude, it could only magnify the pressure on his team if, in the event, they were beaten. However much MacLeod tried to play down the importance of Scotland *v* England, there would be no possibility of the fanatical fans taking the same view. In the past it has been the English who mocked the Scots for believing that if they beat England they were champions of the world. But there was no prospect of MacLeod changing the emotions of a nation overnight. I had travelled to the Czech

Scotland's path to the 1978 finals was opened by the 3–0 defeat of the Czechs by Wales at Wrexham. Here Deacy (PSV Eindhoven, on right) slides home the second on his international debut.

80

Joe Jordan (9) climbs high above the Czech defence to head Scotland's first goal in the vital 3–1 win at Hampden.

cup-tie on the local train from Glasgow Central Station. It was packed to bursting for a game against a foreign side which would determine whether Scotland took part in the World Cup finals, yet the whole way to Hampden all that the fans were chanting was: 'If you hate the f—— English, clap your hands?' MacLeod had misjudged his public, and convinced a lot of rational people that he tended to say things for effect without weighing the consequences . . . and that he underestimated the size of the task.

That feeling was reinforced when he announced his squad of 22. Excluded were Andy Gray, the Villa striker whom many regarded as Scotland's most potent central attacker, and Leeds keeper David Harvey. 'These are the 22 who can play tactically the way I want,' insisted MacLeod, but they hardly displayed this in the Home Championship. Against Northern Ireland, MacLeod picked two big centre-forwards, Jordan and Derek Johnstone of Rangers. They failed to blend, though Johnstone scored in a 1–1 draw against what was the weakest of the four teams. Instead of facing the music, Ireland called the tune. If this was practice for Scotland, it was less than helpful. Against Wales things were even worse. Johnstone, with a superb header, gave Scotland the lead following a bad error by Phillips. But instead of taking charge, Scotland stuttered. Carl Harris hit the bar for Wales, Flynn missed a penalty, and in the last minute Willie Donachie put a back-pass wide of Blyth into his own net.

Ally MacLeod, Scotland manager for only nine matches, relishes the moment of qualifying for the finals at the finish of the last tie against Wales at Anfield, Scotland winning 2–0.

Dalglish had replaced Jordan, but for the crunch against England, MacLeod recalled Jordan, who had scored only twice in four years for Scotland and had not reached double figures in the league season; and left out Johnstone, scorer of 41 goals in all matches, including two in Scotland's last two. Souness, schemer of Liverpool's European Cup triumph, and Archie Gemmill were dropped in favour of Rioch and Masson. England played poorly, Coppell and Barnes never got going on the wings, and Scotland dominated most of the match. But they failed to take their chances, which were few; Masson played too deep, and to the profound irritation of everyone north of the border, Coppell sneaked a late win with the only goal. Did Rough drop the ball on the cross from Barnes or was he nudged? It was a question which would disturb Scotland's more objective critics, bearing in mind the South American ability to make the ball move in the air.

But even more disturbing was the conduct of Jordan. Four times the big centre-forward was on target, but his target was not the goal so much as England defenders. He was booked, Rioch was lucky not to be, and Scotland's blatant physical intimidation was suddenly once more a matter for sharp anxiety.

One of England's most experienced players said afterwards: 'If the Scots play like that in Argentina, they will finish up with seven men on the pitch.' And one of the Scots squad—not in the team—having watched a television recording of Argentina–Peru a few days beforehand, admitted: 'If we give away as many free-

82

kicks as we did today, we will put tremendous pressure on our defence, because the Latin Americans are so skilful with their free-kicks.' McQueen missed the match because of an injury received when clearing off the line against Wales; it was touch and go whether he would be fit to travel to the finals. The 22 who set off for what ought to be the formality of a group including inexperienced Iran and ageing Peru were:

		Age	Caps
Goalkeepers:	Alan Rough (Partick)	26	18
	Jim Blyth (Coventry)	23	2
	Bobby Clark (Aberdeen)	32	16
Defenders:	Sandy Jardine (Rangers)	29	33
	Martin Buchan (Man. Utd.)	28	27
	Willie Donachie (Man. City)	26	30
	Tom Forsyth (Rangers)	29	18
	Stuart Kennedy (Aberdeen)	24	3
	Kenny Burns (Nott'm Forest)	24	10
	Gordon McQueen (Man. Utd)	25	20
Midfield:	Don Masson (Derby)	31	16
	Bruce Rioch (Derby) captain	30	22
	Archie Gemmill (Nott'm Forest)	30	25
	Asa Hartford (Man. City)	28	24
	Graeme Souness (Liverpool)	24	6
	Lou Macari (Man. Utd)	28	22
Forwards:	Joe Jordan (Man. Utd)	26	30
	Derek Johnstone (Rangers)	24	13
	Kenny Dalglish (Liverpool)	27	53
	Willie Johnston (WBA)	31	21
	John Robertson (Nott'm Forest)	25	1
	Joe Harper (Aberdeen)	29	3

CHAPTER SIX

Brutal Brazil

Hosts—Argentina

In spite of not having to qualify, Argentina's preparations were more troubled than most, with manager Cesar Luis Menotti riding a series of setbacks. A wise man, he announced that win or lose, he would quit when the finals were over! Rumours beforehand suggested that he would be replaced at the last minute by the Machiavelli of South American football, Juan Carlos Lorenzo, former national manager during the infamous scenes of 1966, and subsequent violent incidents involving Racing of Buenos Aires against Celtic, Lazio against Arsenal, and Atletico Madrid against Celtic. But Menotti survived, to be Argentina's longest serving manager since the war!

His problems began when the Argentine FA delayed imposing a ban on the transfer abroad of star players—the cause of anaemia for half a century—until the most valuable scorer, Mario Kempes, had already been sold to Valencia of Spain. It remained uncertain to the last moment whether, in addition, Piazza of St Etienne and Wolff of Real Madrid would be released in sufficient time to join the final training.

The captain, Jorge Carrascosa, walked out over a domestic issue and goalkeeper Hugo Gatti was sacked for refusing to train. Midfield players Galvan and Larrossa of Independiente were suspended for 20 months for an attack on a referee, then reinstated, with the resultant resignation of members of the disciplinary committee. Defender Tarantini was left without a club when Boca Juniors refused to renew his contract. In spite of the sideline criticisms of Lorenzo, Argentina had the players to mount a formidable bid for the title—especially remembering their performance in 1977 against European teams in Buenos Aires, with only one defeat in seven matches—Poland 3–1, West Germany 1–3, England 1–1, Scotland 1–1, France 0–0, Yugoslavia 1–0, East Germany 2–0. This was followed in 1978 with warm-up victories over Peru, Romania, Republic of Ireland, Bulgaria and Uruguay.

Clearly, the hosts were a force to be reckoned with, even excluding the influence of their demonic fans. They, by the time the finals arrived, had a growing confidence in the leadership of Menotti, who had played with Pele for Santos for a time, and as manager had won the Argentine championship with unfancied Huracan.

Holders—West Germany

Strongly backed to retain their title in Buenos Aires and become the first European winners on the 'wrong' side of the Atlantic, West Germany ran into rough water in the months beforehand. Lucky to beat England 2–1 in Munich, after being behind until 11 minutes from the end, they then lost at home 1–0 to Brazil in Hamburg, for the first time since the defeat by the same score in the same stadium against East Germany in the first round of the 1974 finals. This was immediately followed by a 3–1 defeat in Stockholm, and suddenly Helmut Schoen was floundering.

'We are a team without a leader,' claimed Gunter Netzer, their former midfield star, before the game against England. The retirement of Gerd Muller, the departure of Beckenbauer to New York Cosmos, the rift between Schoen and Paul Breitner, combined to reduce the champions to average proportions. Klaus Fischer, restored to favour after a ban over the Schalke bribery affair, was not scoring goals, the muscular Rainer Bonhof, a key figure in 1974 following the East Germany defeat, was less than commanding. Heinz Flohe, now 30, was less effective for Schoen than for the Bundesliga champions Cologne, and the decline of Berti Vogts, 31, was evident in the European Cup semi-final between Borussia and Liverpool. Only Sepp Maier in goal, survivor of two World Cups and two European Championships, had sustained his level of performance—at 33.

Europe

GROUP 1—POLAND

	W	D	L	F	A	Pts
Poland	5	1	0	17	4	11
Portugal	4	1	1	12	6	9
Denmark	2	0	4	14	12	4
Cyprus	0	0	6	3	24	0

Poland, third in 1974, when they reached the finals by holding England 1–1 at Wembley, dropped only one point, at home to Portugal in their final tie. Jacek Gmoch, succeeding Kazimierz Gorski as manager, remained faithful to the nucleus of the team which had won the 1972 Olympics—and was now in danger of being too old. That was the fear for the finals. All the familiar names were there—Tomaszewski in goal, Deyna in midfield, Lato and Szarmach in attack ... plus Lubanski, now 31 and a professional with Lokeren in Belgium. Lubanski missed the finals in Germany having been injured in the home qualifying tie with England. Also recalled was the huge defender Jerzy Gorgon, following a long suspension for revelries on a club trip, and a cartilage operation. Missing from the 1974 line-up would be defender Musial, victim of a serious car crash, and Maszczyk (midfield) and Gadocha (left wing), both in France and over the hill. The return of Lubanski gave great hope to the romantic Poles—but could their ageing team maintain the same attacking impetus as in Germany? Would expediency require a less physically demanding, more defensive approach? The key to the qualifying group had been the 2–0 win away to Portugal in their first tie, and in five warm-up victories before crossing the Atlantic, against Luxembourg, Greece, Republic of Ireland, Czechoslovakia and Bulgaria, they had a goal tally of 15–3. They would have to be respected.

GROUP 2—ITALY
(See Chapter Three)

GROUP 3—AUSTRIA

	W	D	L	F	A	Pts
Austria	4	2	0	14	2	10
East Germany	3	3	0	15	4	9
Turkey	2	1	3	9	5	5
Malta	0	0	6	0	27	0

Austria qualified for the finals for the first time since 1958 at a time when the game, as measured through the turnstiles at league football, was in the doldrums. Shortly before the decisive draw, 1–1 in Leipzig, which saw them through, the five First Division games drew fewer than 20,000 . . . in all!

In the thirties, under the guidance of Hugo Meisl, Austrian football was the envy of the world, but they have never really recovered from the wartime 'amalgamation' with Germany; their semi-professionals are mostly no match for powerful neighbours, yet . . . Not only did the national team qualify, but FK Austria were challenging for a place in the European Cup-Winners' Cup final. Since finishing third in 1954 in Switzerland, there had been little to celebrate, but now, under the leadership of Helmuth Senekowitsch, there was new impetus.

The key to the group—in the same unsatisfactory way which marred others— was the performance of a minor team, Turkey, in holding East Germany to a draw away, in the second game. That proved critical, Austria finishing with a one-point lead over the 1974 finalists. Yet Germany were fortunate when Austria's ace scorer Hans Krankl had a winning goal disallowed in Vienna by Welsh referee Tom Reynolds. Austria led through Willy Kreuz of Feyenoord, one of five 'exiles'. Hoffman equalized from a free-kick when goalkeeper Koncilia took too many paces. Four minutes from time Krankl, of Rapid, headed the winner, but a fringe player was given off-side. In the following protest Reynolds sent off Krankl; subsequently the Austrians claimed it should have been defender Eduard Kreiger. But without Krankl, Austria drew the return in Leipzig, to the delight of 10,000 supporters from home.

Hattenberger (Stuttgart) gave Austria the lead, Lowe equalized. Besides exiles Kreuz and Hattenberger, Austria called on Jara (Duisburg), Hickersberger (Fortuna Düsseldorf) and Kreiger of European Cup finalists Bruges. With half the team playing abroad, their preparations were difficult, but they now had eight points. Germany could not qualify—but Turkey could if they won their last three matches. They lost at home to both Austria and Germany. A blow to Austria was the serious ligament injury to Innsbruck striker Stering, the most powerful partner for Krankl, who over two seasons averaged almost a goal a game. The other key figure had been Kurt Jara in midfield, formerly with Valencia, but released by the Spanish club when they bought Johnny Rep from Holland, under the two-foreigners-only rule.

GROUP 4—HOLLAND

	W	D	L	F	A	Pts
Holland	5	1	0	11	3	11
Belgium	3	0	3	7	6	6
N. Ireland	2	1	3	7	6	5
Iceland	1	0	5	2	12	2

Northern Ireland began with a bang, and went out with a whimper. Under the new management of Danny Blanchflower, their captain in 1958, they went to Rotterdam in their first match and held Holland, the 1974 runners-up, to a 2–2 draw. McGrath (Man. Utd) and Spence (Bury) scored the goals in reply to Krol and Cruyff. George Best was back in harness in a midfield role, and there was under-

Northern Ireland, under the new leadership of Danny Blanchflower, their inspiring captain of 20 years before, held Holland to a draw, but then slumped 2–0 in Liège, where Raoul Lambert is seen heading the second past Allan Hunter (5) and Pat Jennings. Holland won the group.

standable optimism in the camp. But a month later all that faded in Liège, Belgium winning 2–0 with goals by Van Gool of Cologne and Van der Elst of Anderlecht. With Best once more disappearing from the scene, hope vanished when, in Iceland six months later, Ireland lost by the only goal to the amateurs coached by former Leicester defender Tony Knapp. Ireland's one remaining contribution to the group was to beat the talented Belgians 3–0 in Belfast (Armstrong 2, McGrath 1), assuring an easy passage for Holland—who had previously won in Antwerp with a devastating display of their renowned skills. Cruyff was rampant, but he was already hinting that he would not be going to the finals even if Holland qualified, an attitude which hardened by the time they did. This was bad enough, but Holland's prospects were further dampened by the withdrawal of Ruud Geels, the Ajax striker.

There was pressure by the Dutch show-biz world, and by a number of newspapers and individual journalists, to persuade other players to boycott the tournament in protest against Argentinian political extremism, but the Dutch FA stood firm. Manager Ernst Happel, former Austrian international doubling with his role as manager of Bruges, found himself in the same position as Rinus Michels before the 1974 finals—with plenty of skill but not necessarily a team. Rep and Rensenbrink would again provide exceptional penetration on the flanks, Krol had become a brilliant sweeper, but where was the midfield leadership, Neeskens apart? Jan Peters had faded, but there was a new name to conjure with, Tschel La Ling, of Chinese paren-

87

tage from The Hague, a winger capable of playing on either flank. Krol's opinion was: 'We shall qualify for the second round, but then ...?' It would be surprising if Holland and Scotland did not dominate their first round group with Peru and Iran, but subsequently, for Holland, it would be a question of how serious they were. When Van Beveren of PSV Eindhoven, their best goalkeeper, joined the list of those asking to be excluded, Holland's backers began to dwindle.

GROUP 5—FRANCE

	W	D	L	F	A	Pts
France	2	1	1	7	4	5
Bulgaria	1	2	1	5	6	4
Republic of Ireland	1	1	2	2	4	3

France, like Austria, enjoyed a sudden revival which recalled better days of the fifties—of the great team which reached the semi-finals in Sweden, including Kopa, Fontaine, Piantoni. Now, as then, there were four star players in the renaissance: Platini, from Nancy-Lorraine, hailed as the greatest since Kopa, and Bathenay (St Etienne) in midfield, plus the St Etienne striker, Rocheteau; and Marseilles libero Tresor. Bathenay and Rocheteau plus full-back Janvion, were part of the marvellous St Etienne team which reached the 1976 European Cup Final, undeservedly losing to Bayern. But both Bathenay and Rocheteau were hit by injury prior to the finals. With both fit and in form, France would be a problem for anyone, not least the hosts Argentina in the exceptionally tough group including Italy and Hungary.

Johan Cruyff, the world's number one player since the retirement of Pele, helped Holland to qualify, but then disappointingly confirmed his decision not to take part in the finals. Here Cruyff is seen scoring Holland's second in the 1974 destruction of Brazil.

The improvement in the national team began with Stefan Kovacs, the Romanian former manager of Ajax, who developed the potential of Bathenay. When Kovacs returned to Bucharest he was replaced by Michel Hidalgo, who maintained the positive attitudes and built his team around the fluid talents of Platini, for whom Internazionale had taken a £60,000 option contract. France arrived at their last qualifying tie in the same position as England against Poland in 1973—needing to beat Bulgaria at home to overtake them by one point. They won 3–1. Platini, who had watched England win the 1966 Final on TV at the age of 11, was poised to emerge as one of the world's foremost players.

GROUP 6—SWEDEN

	W	D	L	F	A	Pts
Sweden	3	0	1	7	4	6
Norway	2	0	2	3	4	4
Switzerland	1	0	3	3	5	2

Considering that they have neither professionals nor state-sponsored 'amateurs', and a small population, Sweden's achievement in qualifying for the recent finals in Mexico, West Germany and Argentina is remarkable. Of course, the quality of their players has long been recognized, ever since winning the 1948 Olympics. In 1959 they became the second foreign team to win at Wembley, the year after losing the World Cup Final to Brazil. Then, as now, they were dependent for experience on their professional exiles in West Germany, Italy and elsewhere.

Unquestionably their group was a soft one. The threat from Norway was settled when the Swiss beat the Norwegians in the final match, allowing Sweden to stroll through. Yet even mild improvement by the Swiss, and one or two performances comparable to that at Wembley when they frustrated England in Ron Greenwood's first match, might have totally changed the outcome. As it was they lost 2–1 home and away to Sweden, whose manager Georg Ericsson was the only survivor, with Helmut Schoen of West Germany, from the 1974 finals. Sweden, like Austria, had half a dozen or so exiles, complicating their preparation. Much would depend on the performances of keeper Ronnie Hellstrom, survivor of the previous two finals; scapegoat of 1970, star of 1974, when Sweden twice led West Germany in the second round.

Sweden's other stars were the former PSV striker Ralf Edstrom, who surprisingly returned to join IFK Göteborg in 1977, and Bjorn Nordqvist, the 35-year-old centre-back, also ex-PSV, who with Rivelino of Brazil would be bidding to break Bobby Moore's record 108 caps during the finals. Edstrom was another key player nursing injury as the finals approached.

GROUP 7—SCOTLAND
(See Chapter Five)

GROUP 8—SPAIN

	W	D	L	F	A	Pts
Spain	3	0	1	4	1	6
Romania	2	0	2	7	8	4
Yugoslavia	1	0	3	6	8	2

Troubles too, for Spain, having qualified for the first time since 1966. Camacho, the winger converted to full-back for Real Madrid by Miljan Miljanic, and ever present in the qualifying matches, was subsequently injured in training, received surgery and was likely to miss the difficult group with Brazil, Austria and Sweden— as was the Real utility player Del Bosque.

It would be the swan-song for Pirri, survivor of the 1966 side, one of the most consistent and accomplished players of Europe for over a decade. When Real won the 1966 European Cup, Pirri was in midfield, but Miljanic switched him to sweeper, in 1974–75, in which position he became the club's leading scorer. A superb captain.

It had been a tense group. In the final match in Belgrade, Yugoslavia, having come back from the dead to win astonishingly 6–4 in Bucharest, needed to beat Spain 2–0 to win a three-way tie not on goal difference but, that being the same as Romania's, on the most goals scored! In the event Spain won a disgraceful game 1–0, English referee Ken Burns failing to check the violence which was precipitated by the Slavs and returned with interest by the Spaniards.

In front of a hostile 95,000 crowd in the Red Star stadium, the only goal was scored by Ruben Cano—a member of Argentina's squad of 40 for the 1974 finals.

Yugoslavia have produced more world-class players than possibly any nation, but lost their final home tie 1–0 to Spain when needing to win 2–0. Here, Karasi is seen scoring the only goal conceded by Scotland in the 1974 finals, with Jardine and goalkeeper Harvey stranded.

In 1974 Spain had lost a play-off with Yugoslavia in Frankfurt for a place in the finals. Now they had revenge, in more ways than one. Burns booked four Spaniards and one Yugoslav, and failed to send off the two or more players which might either have quelled the fury ... or obliged him to abandon the match, considering the mood of the crowd. Pirri was kicked out of the match and substituted after only a quarter of an hour.

Yugoslavia, potential winners with a host of superb players in 1974, had finished fourth in the 1976 European finals, and now fielded a young side, without Dzajic, Oblak or Bogicevic. Surjak could not inspire them, Muzinic had a goal disallowed, and Cano smashed in the winner in the 70th minute from a cross by Cardenosa. Five minutes later Juanito, the Real winger, was felled by a bottle from the crowd—but at least the Argentinians would be glad of the financial advantage of another Spanish-speaking nation arriving in June. Ladislav Kubala, ex-Hungary, Spain and Barcelona star of the fifties and early sixties—who master-minded the greatest 20 minutes of soccer I have ever seen when Barcelona blitzed but failed to beat Benfica in the 1961 European Cup Final in Berne—had pulled it off after more than 10 years as national manager. He used 25 players in the four ties, disproving theories about 'settled' sides. A settled side would hardly have mattered in Belgrade!

There had been an earlier row, prior to Spain's 2–0 win over Romania in Madrid. Stefan Kovacs, Romania's manager, had alleged, in an interview in *L'Equipe*, the Paris sports paper, that there was a conspiracy between Yugoslavia, Spain, FIFA and UEFA to oust Romania. He later claimed to have been misquoted, which was strongly denied by Jacques Ferran of *L'Equipe*, with whom I collaborated on the official West German book of the 1974 finals. Whatever the facts, Leal and Cano scored in the last 18 minutes.

GROUP 9—HUNGARY

	W	D	L	F	A	Pts
Hungary	2	1	1	5	4	5
USSR	2	0	2	5	3	4
Greece	1	1	2	2	5	3

European/South American Play-Off
Hungary 6, Bolivia 0
Bolivia 2, Hungary 3

Runners-up in 1938 and 1954—when they should have won—and quarter-finalists in 1966 (their last appearance in the finals), this would be Hungary's seventh time in the finals. It was an arduous route, which began with a 1–1 draw in Athens, and ended with a praiseworthy victory at 10,000 feet in La Paz ... leaving them to face Argentina, Italy and France in the first round.

It was, whatever the results in the finals, a triumph for the white-haired doyen of international management: Lajos Baroti, now 63, the longest serving of all, who had been in charge since the finals of 1958, 1962 and 1966, coming back from retirement three years before the present competition. Yet the vital result, in fact, was the 1–0 home win over the USSR, Hungary's hated opponents, by Greece. With

Hungary winning against the USSR 2–1 in Budapest and losing 2–0 in Moscow, the Greek result gave Baroti's potentially outstanding side a one-point advantage.

For the vital second leg of the play-off against Bolivia, Hungary were without the fulcrum of the side, Nylasi, left behind injured. The squad went first to Lima, Peru, for three days preparation. A new young player of rising reputation, Halasz, deputized for Nylasi—and he made the first and scored the second in a literally breathtaking first half. Pusztai got the second in between two for Bolivia by Aragones. Baroti said afterwards: 'Our victory here will serve as a warning. With a reasonable draw we could do well in Argentina.' It was hardly the draw he would have hoped for.

Yet this young side, based on the successful Under-23 team of 1975–76, was poised to restore Hungary's pride and prestige abroad. Three players in particular were echoes of famous, bygone days: Nylasi, rival to Platini as one of Europe's most gifted midfield players; Torocsik, hailed as Hungary's most dangerous striker for 12 years, and Varadi, who in 1977 hit 36 goals in 34 games for Vasas, to be runner-up in the Adidas golden boot award, but failed to score in any of the ties against Greece and the USSR.

South America

GROUP 1—BRAZIL

	W	D	L	F	A	Pts
Brazil	2	2	0	8	1	6
Paraguay	1	2	1	3	3	4
Colombia	0	2	2	1	8	2

GROUP 2—BOLIVIA

	W	D	L	F	A	Pts
Bolivia	3	1	0	8	3	7
Uruguay	1	2	1	5	4	4
Venezuela	0	1	3	2	8	1

GROUP 3—PERU

	W	D	L	F	A	Pts
Peru	2	2	0	8	2	6
Chile	2	1	1	5	3	5
Ecuador	0	1	3	1	9	1

Play-off

	W	D	L	F	A	Pts
Brazil	2	0	0	9	0	4
Peru	1	0	1	5	1	2
Bolivia	0	0	2	0	13	0

Brazil and Peru qualified. Bolivia played off with Hungary, and lost.

BRAZIL

There was a dramatic opening to Brazil's campaign, when they were held 0–0 in Colombia—and immediately manager Oswaldo Brandao was sacked after a 22-match spell. Claudio Coutinho, a physical training university lecturer and basketball expert, was the surprise replacement, but he appeased the public, not to say the federation, CBD, with a 6–0 win in the return match in Rio. Brazil duly finished top of the group, after two anxious games with Paraguay, then won the play-off group. Zico, suspended for the first game against Peru (1–0), then scored five of Brazil's eight against Bolivia. Brazil had not lost, at this stage, for two years, but Coutinho's reign was not proving entirely smooth. They were handicapped by the absence, with Atletico in Madrid, of Luis Pereira, their formidable central defender, whose release in time for the finals was uncertain. Additionally, the black Paulo Cesar and blond full-back Francisco Marinho were dropped from the final squad for indiscipline. Pereira had been flown home for the qualifying matches, but resented criticism, of the team and himself.

Brazil, scared stiff by an opening 0–0 tie in Bogota, duly qualified—but showed their fear on tour in Europe with brutal tactics against West Germany and England. Amaral reflects on Kevin Keegan's (7) equalizing free-kick at Wembley.

Coutinho's oft publicized intention was to make his team more 'European', by which was meant physically competitive. Just how successful he had been was discovered on the usual European tour with which the three-times winners always prepare for the finals. Losing, undeservedly, by the only goal to France, they moved to Hamburg. A crescendo of abuse had been poured on Coutinho at home. Defeat against the world champions would probably lose him his job. But Brazil proceeded to kick the Germans at every turn, hacking down their wingers Abramczik and Rummenigge. Edinho, the left-back, should have been sent off for his repeated fouls on Abramczik, was not, and Brazil won by the only goal. It was even worse at Wembley.

The same cynical attitude to opposing forwards, observed in the 1974 finals but now more blatant, angered a full house at Wembley. Dutch referee Charles Corver, one of the panel for Argentina, gave cause for concern by his failure to arrest the abuse of the laws. England's wingers Steve Coppell and Peter Barnes were regularly sent sprawling, so was Tony Currie, recalled in the absence of injured Trevor Brooking and the inspiration of the side. Gil scored a stunning early goal for Brazil, Kevin Keegan equalized with a free-kick: but Brazil had given warning that they were prepared to abandon their skill in the so-called interests of safety. It was an absurd attitude, for they had shown, in players such as Zico, Cerezo and the veteran Rivelino, the sublime technique which had made them admired around the globe for a quarter of a century. Coutinho's parting excuse, as the condemnation rained down, was that Brazil had been 'provoked' by the skill of England's attack—a new twist to international tactics. The exposed nerve-ends in the Brazil squad posed internal trouble. Returning to Rio, Dirceu, the clever little midfield player, publicly criticized Coutinho and Rivelino, and was duly disciplined. It would be an uneasy camp at Mar del Plata for the less-than-straightforward group with Spain, Sweden and Austria.

PERU

One of the more entertaining teams in 1970 in Mexico—with no defence, they had to attack!—Peru qualified again ... with several of the same players, now older and slower. Would they pose a threat in their opening match with Scotland?

Teofilo Cubillas, an explosive striker in Mexico where he helped Peru reach the quarter-finals, subsequently played in Switzerland and Portugal before returning home, to a role in midfield. At 29 he had become injury prone, as had Hugo Sotil who, following a spell with Barcelona, also returned to play for Alianza. With star defender Hector Chumpitaz nudging 30, Peru seemed physically vulnerable, and manager Marcos Calderon was, like his Latin American colleagues Menotti and Coutinho, under heavy pressure as the finals approached. They lost home and away to Argentina in friendlies, 2–1 and 3–1, while Universitario of Mexico were demanding huge insurance cover for star right-winger Juan Jose Munante—or no release. Munante, the only player with a foreign club, was said to be the best winger in Latin America.*

North America

MEXICO

Play-Off Group

	W	D	L	F	A	Pts
Mexico	5	0	0	20	5	10
Haiti	3	1	1	6	6	7
El Salvador	2	1	2	8	9	5
Canada	2	1	2	7	8	5
Guatemala	1	1	3	8	10	3
Surinam	0	0	5	6	17	0

Mexico qualified—as well they might with the final series of matches played in Mexico City and Monterrey! In their opening game they disposed of Haiti, the 1974 qualifiers, by 4–1, and from then on it was a formality, Jose Antonio Roca's team taking maximum points. The closest result was 2–1 against Guatemala, the 1970 finalists, who upset Canada 2–1. Had Canada beaten Haiti, they could have qualified by a win over Mexico, but drew 1–1, then lost 3–1.

Haiti were holding Mexico until Roca brought on Victor Rangel, his 19-year-old striker, as substitute for Jimenez. Rangel, expected to be Mexico's chief weapon in the group with West Germany, Poland and Tunisia, obliged by scoring a hat-trick. He had made his first division debut only the year before, following the Montreal Olympics. From Guadalajara, Rangel had scored more than 50 goals in international matches at all levels. Hugo Sanchez, another striker of whom much was expected, scored four in the 8–0 friendly against Grasshoppers of Zurich, after which Gunter Netzer, their player-manager, said: 'Mexico are a good side; they play more

* Interestingly, in the light of subsequent events, this was written before Scotland left for the finals.

94

of a European game than the slow Latin American style we expected.' The hub
of the side was Leonard Cuellar in midfield.

Africa

TUNISIA

Play-Off Group

	W	D	L	F	A	Pts
Tunisia	2	1	1	7	4	5
Egypt	2	0	2	7	11	4
Nigeria	1	1	2	5	4	3

Zaire, the 1974 qualifiers, withdrew from the final play-off without playing a match.
Tunisia qualified when they won the decisive final match of the group at home
to Egypt in Tunis. But drama was to follow. In the match for third place in the
African Championships, the Tunisian players walked off, claiming an equalizer by
Nigeria had followed a handling offence. In spite of pleas from manager Majid Chetali, the players refused to return; and Tunisian teams were banned from international competition for two years—Sadok Attouga, the goalkeeper who had led
the walk-off, for three years. But after 10 days of suspense, the African Confedera-
tion announced they would not ask FIFA to nominate a replacement African team
for Argentina.

Chetali, who won 68 caps, learned his coaching in West Germany under Hennes
Weisweiler, but it was not expected that this would ease Tunisia's problems when
they met the holders in the first round. A 4–0 warm-up defeat at home to Holland
was ominous—and defender Gasmi was banned from the opening game with Mexico because of two suspensions. Training was impeded by political unrest, which
forced players to remain at home for a period. Attouga, regarded as Africa's best
keeper, with more than 130 appearances for Tunisia in amateur, military and senior
internationals, was likely to be busy. Tunisia's chances of success were doubtful unless they could sustain, in unfamiliar conditions, the form of that final tie against
Egypt, when they were two up before half-time through Akid and Temim, and
ran the opposition off their feet. Temim was recalled from Saudi Arabia for the
qualifying ties.

Asia Oceania

IRAN

Play-Off Group

	W	D	L	F	A	Pts
Iran	6	2	0	12	3	14
Korea Rep.	3	4	1	12	8	10
Kuwait	4	1	3	13	8	9
Australia	3	1	4	11	8	7
Hong Kong	0	0	8	5	26	0

Iran played 11 qualifying matches—more than any other nation—and their triumph
stemmed from the two wins, home and away by the only goal, over Australia,
the 1974 qualifiers. Iran undoubtedly benefited from the coaching they received
from Frank O'Farrell, following his sacking by Manchester United, under whom

they had won the Asian Championships. A further blow to Australia's hopes was the home defeat 2–1 by Kuwait.

An even bigger blow to Iran was the threatened boycott by the national hero Parvis Gheleechkhani, who is to Iranian soccer what Pele was to Brazil. He missed the qualifying games because of his contract with San Jose Earthquakes in California, but was the talisman for the finals. Then, during political demonstrations against the Shah a month before the finals, Gheleechkhani, who can play in defence, midfield or attack, said he would not take part.

Manager Heshmat Mohajerani, deputy to O'Farrell for two years, was satisfied with a 0–0 warm-up draw against Yugoslavia, but worried about the failure of leading scorer Hassan Rowshan to recover his form following a cartilage operation. If Gheleechkhani refused to go to Argentina, it would be a severe loss to Iran, whose matches had been attended by capacity crowds, even for an April friendly with Wales. Gheleechkhani had forecast: 'In the last four years our game has made great strides. We didn't do badly in the last World Cup, and Scotland, Holland and Tunisia should not underestimate us. Our matches with them will not be a break-time bell, but a danger bell.' Few teams would have as thorough preparation for the finals as Iran, as Scotland were about to discover.

Rudi Krol, the brilliant Dutch full-back, arrives too late to prevent Gerd Muller—watched by referee Jack Taylor, Uli Hoeness and distant Paul Breitner—scoring the winner in the 1974 final: the 'qualifier' for 1978.

1 Sweden's goalkeeper Hellstrom and defender Erlandsson concede the third consecutive corner at the end of the game with Brazil, following which Welsh referee Clive Thomas disallowed Brazil's 'winning' goal because he had blown for the finish (1–1)

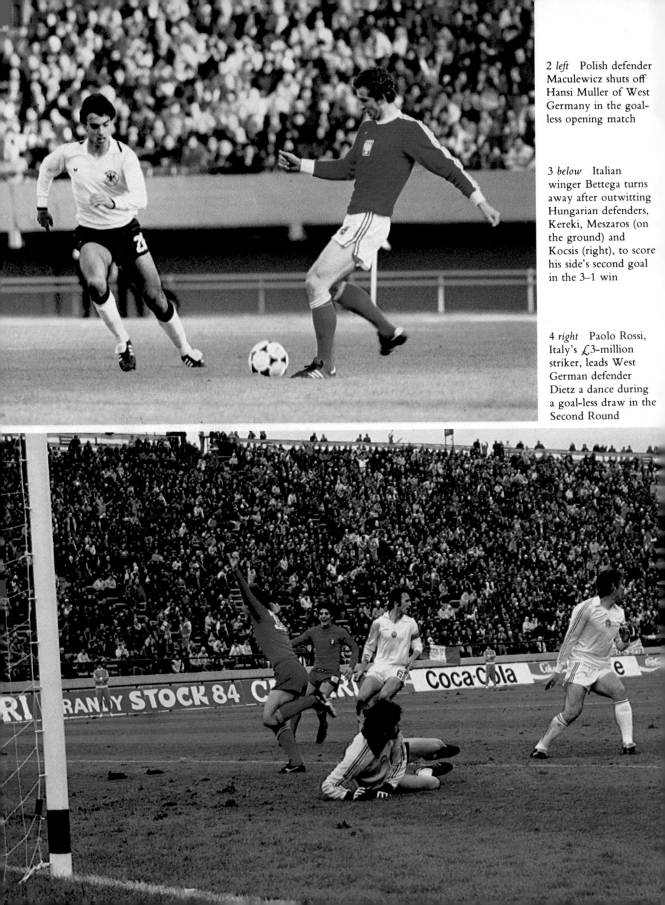

2 *left* Polish defender Maculewicz shuts off Hansi Muller of West Germany in the goal-less opening match

3 *below* Italian winger Bettega turns away after outwitting Hungarian defenders, Kereki, Meszaros (on the ground) and Kocsis (right), to score his side's second goal in the 3–1 win

4 *right* Paolo Rossi, Italy's £3-million striker, leads West German defender Dietz a dance during a goal-less draw in the Second Round

0 - R

5 *above* Brazil's
midfield pair,
Dirceu (11) and
Cerezo (with ball),
for once in
harmony against
Spain on the cut-
up Mar del Plata
pitch (0–0)

6 *left* The balding
Lato and his
captain Deyna (12)
leave Peru
guessing, but
Poland's 1–0 was
not enough to
challenge for a
place in the final

7 *right* Kenny Dalglish lashes Scotland's first goal past Dutch goalkeeper Jongbloed—the start of a stirring 3–2 victory which was too little and too late

8 *below* Scots midfield ace Graeme Souness, belatedly recalled to the team, outwits Willy van der Kerkhof of Holland during a memorable performance

9 left The towering inferno which never caught fire: Joe Jordan, Scotland's big striker, leaps above Dutch goalkeeper Jongbloed

10 right Neeskens in the 45th minute of the final, leaps above Passarella (19) and Galvan to head across the goalmouth to Rensenbrink (out of picture) for one of Holland's agonizing near-misses (see picture below)

11 below Fillol, the outstanding goalkeeper of the tournament, successfully smothers Rensenbrink's two-footed half volley from four yards out, watched by (left to right) Tarantini, Galvan, Passarella and Rep

12 *above* Dirceu, Brazil's dazzling schemer, bursts between Causio (16) and Patrice Sala in the Third Place match, won by Brazil 2–1. Antognoni is in the background

13 *below* A nation celebrates. Argentinian team in their moment of triumph: (left to right) Fillol, Kempes, Luque, Ortiz, Passarella (with trophy), Ardiles, Larrosa, Galvan

CHAPTER SEVEN

Scotland Crash

Scotland squandered their spectacular skills in almost every World Cup in which they have played. For 20 years I had watched them falling flat on their face ... in Sweden in 1958, when they stumbled against France and Paraguay; in Naples in 1965 when Ronnie Yeats, Liverpool's centre-half, kicked off wearing a No. 9 shirt and then rushed back to defend, in vain; in Hamburg in 1969; and against Zaire, in Dortmund in 1974, when they threw away the goal initiative in their opening match.

In Argentina, an expectant soccer world was waiting for Ally MacLeod's men to light the fireworks when they opened their campaign against Peru in Cordoba. Whether they could even strike a match, after their mediocrity in the British Championships, was the question many Britons hardly dared to ask. The competition was wide open: everyone knew that. And in the lull before the storm, that anxious period of a week or so when the teams have all arrived and are weighing each other from a distance, when gossip is rife and rumours abound, the one sure fact was that Scotland were strongly fancied as one of the outsiders if they could touch anything like true form.

This was confirmed when I bumped into Miljan Miljanic, a member of the FIFA Technical Committee studying the 1978 finals. Probably remembering his experiences against the Scots as manager of Yugoslavia in the 1974 finals, Miljanic was convinced the British representatives were sitting pretty. He and that other tactical eminence Rinus Michels, who took Holland through the previous finals, were agreed; and he told me over a coffee in the imposing, closed-circuit-TV-monitored Sheraton Hotel: 'Many of the coaches I have met up to now fear Scotland. Their form has not been impressive, they have lost Gordon McQueen, but everyone we have spoken to seems to think that if Scotland can find a rhythm they will be very difficult to beat, especially because other countries are lacking confidence. Wherever you look, at the Dutch, Germans, Brazilians, French, Austrians or Spanish, they have problems. Yet I feel that Scotland should be cautious. They must watch Peru's wingers Munante and Oblitas, who are two of the fastest and most dangerous in the competition.'

This last comment was especially prophetic, and was echoed by Denis Law, who was covering the tournament for Radio and TV. The famous scourge of defences a decade and more ago said: 'I tell you this: we played Peru at Hampden in 1972, and I don't care how old they are now—those fellows have such devastating control, and hit such sweet passes, we'll really have to sit on top of them to stand a chance.'

Asa Hartford, that gritty component of MacLeod's regular midfield, also agreed. He had said shortly beforehand: 'In these opening matches we've got to force an English League-type of game on the opposition. It would be a disaster if we let

97

Kenny Dalglish yawns in the sunshine at Alta Gracia after the 36-hour journey from Prestwick. He never really threw off that end-of-season fatigue.

them slow it down to easy-easy stuff. The Cordoba stadium is open, with the crowd well back from the field, and on a warm day there could easily be a lazy atmosphere. But we can't allow that. We've got to get at the other lot, build up urgency, play at a pace that suits us.'

Out at the Scots camp at Alta Gracia City, a small white-walled ranch-style town set in the foothills of the High Sierras, MacLeod was conducting press conferences with an uneasy optimism. When one of the players called out one morning 'not long till kick-off now', MacLeod was heard to murmur under his breath 'aye, and that's what worries me'.

The squad derived some satisfaction from watching the drab, opening goal-less draw between West Germany and Poland on TV from Buenos Aires, but Bruce Rioch observed: 'The result suited them both—we have to go for a victory.'

MacLeod had been bothered during the run-in by a thigh injury to Joe Jordan, but when he announced his team, sure enough Jordan was there to the exclusion of Derek Johnstone of Rangers, a striker with 41 goals to his credit in the season just ended. Confronting Peru's wingers would be the young and inexperienced Stuart Kennedy, preferred to Sandy Jardine, and Martin Buchan, deputizing for the suspended Willie Donachie and lacking the speed in a position demanding direct confrontation more than strategic intelligence. The midfield, inevitably, was Rioch, Masson and Hartford. MacLeod said boldly: 'Spurring us on is the thought of the people back home. When we go out onto the pitch, we will be thinking of the empty streets in Scottish cities and the millions of fans watching us.'

It could not have been a more inspiring motive, but in the event the motivation proved missing. One of Scotland's accepted tactical strengths, the pace of Willie Johnston on the left wing, was little seen, though MacLeod had told Johnston beforehand: 'You are the man we expect to do the business, to get round the back of Peru's defence and supply the ammunition for Jordan and Dalglish.'

It went well enough for a quarter of an hour. On a warm evening, with the mud-dust still settling in the vast new, unpaved car parks surrounding the imposing stadium, Scotland set off with encouraging urgency. In only the second minute Dalglish sent Hartford through and, under pressure, he shot close. Masson, going clear on a header from Jordan, shot at goalkeeper Quiroga. Jordan, pursued by Velasquez, was brought down on the corner of the penalty area. Peru at this stage had the air of amateurs, not quite certain what to expect.

In the eighth minute a fine move between Hartford and Rioch put Masson away and from 12 yards he again shot at Quiroga. A steady momentum was gathering, and in the 14th minute Scotland's World Cup expedition seemed successfully to have left the launching pad when Jordan put them in front. Johnston and Dalglish combined to release Rioch, his shot was parried, and Jordan bustled in the loose ball. The transformation which now took place was as total as it was unexpected.

From the 15th to the 25th minute Peru overwhelmed the Scots' defence; any one of seven pulverizing attacks could have brought an equalizer. Suddenly Oblitas and Munante were going past their full-backs like leaves on the wings of a gale; and, most sinister of all, the veteran, sumptuously skilful Teofilo Cubillas, was anni-hilating the Scots' midfield. In between his wingers, La Rosa was tormenting Forsyth and Burns; suddenly it was Scotland who looked the amateurs. Cubillas went close; Cueto, who was also surging through from midfield, had an overhead shot blocked; Munante rasped a swerving free-kick into the side netting; Rough in goal anxiously turned away a volley by La Rosa, then saved from Oblitas.

Joe Jordan (9) is congratulated by Tom Forsyth on scoring the goal which gave Scotland so much early optimism; but Peru won 3–1.

On the bench, where MacLeod sat impassively watching the damage which was being done, Archie Gemmill and others were already yelling at him to make changes. It was clear that, after the initial bright beginning, Rioch and Masson could not cope with the pace of Peru's midfield trio. For several months it had been evident, back home, that they were in decline and now the fact was being driven home like a stake into sand. Cubillas, at 29—a year or two the right side of Rioch—was totally unfettered. Those who for weeks had urged the infusion of Gemmill and Graeme Souness were being painfully vindicated.

Yet, in the 27th minute, the chance fell for Scotland to haul themselves out of the hole into which they were dropping. A flick from Jordan during a counter-attack, a lob by Dalglish, and for a split second it looked as if they would go two up. But somehow Quiroga, out on the edge of his penalty area, got his fingertips to the ball as it arched over him; the reprieve had gone. Back came Peru, Cueto blasted over the bar from 25 yards, and three minutes before half-time he equalized. Velasquez was fouled, Swedish referee Ulf Eriksson waved play on, Cubillas and Oblitas rippled through, Cueto beat Rough. Demoralized and disorganized, Scotland retired to the dressing-room.

The team looked to MacLeod for advice, for tactical adjustment. But none was forthcoming. His only concession, it seems, to the gathering crisis was to tell Rough to kick the ball further upfield to 'bypass' the Peruvian midfield. But the battle was being fought on the ground, not in the air. What was required was a player who could shut down Cubillas, but MacLeod baulked at making the obvious change until Peru had taken the lead and it was too late.

Cesar Cueto (*right*) equalizes for Peru, watched by Munante, Burns and Hartford.

Early at the start of the second half Oblitas stole the ball off Rioch, impudently, on the halfway line, raced 50 yards and crossed to La Rosa, who headed wide. Still MacLeod stared out impassively. Scotland enjoyed a brief recovery; Hartford put Jordan through and he struck the ball against the stanchion at the back of the side netting. On the hour Johnston, little seen until now, switched to the right, crossed the ball to the far post where Jordan headed square, and Dalglish, taking the ball on the turn, had his shot deflected over the bar. Two minutes later Scotland were thrown a lifebelt: and failed to catch it.

Cubillas was ruled, questionably, to have brought down Rioch, and Masson stepped forward for the penalty kick which could give Scotland a firm foothold along the path to the second round. But his shot was tame, hit without power and to a convenient shoulder-height to Quiroga's right. The Argentinian-born keeper saved easily; and within moments Scotland were again in a panic as Cubillas scorched through the middle but was foiled on the edge of the penalty area.

In the 70th minute Munante and Cueto cut open the defence, Cubillas lashed the ball past Rough from 23 yards to put Peru ahead—and now MacLeod sent out Gemmill and Lou Macari to replace Masson and Rioch. Slowly Rioch walked from the field with the air of a man who reluctantly recognizes his share of responsibility in an abortive mission. In another eight minutes Peru were out of reach.

Too late, Gemmill and Macari tried to force the momentum the other way, but there was no budging the elated Peruvians. Kennedy, by now overrun, flattened Oblitas on the edge of the penalty area. Cubillas curved his kick, off the outside of the foot, round the end of the defensive wall, just over Macari's shoulder, and into the top left-hand corner of the goal beyond Rough's reach.

Bobby Charlton said afterwards: 'If I could have planned the game for Peru, I could not have done it better than Scotland. Peru want two things in a match. They want to play one-twos going into the penalty area and they want to win

Tom Forsyth (14) is too late to block this studied drive by Teofilo Cubillas which puts Peru 2–1 in front.

free-kicks just outside. In that position, to South Americans, a free-kick is as good as a penalty.' The passionately cherished hopes of a brave soccer nation had perished primarily because MacLeod had misread the situation. He had stated beforehand, 'We know what to expect from them', but it was glaringly obvious that this was not so. The study of TV videotape had given insufficient warning of the scorching speed of Peru's wingers, against whom makeshift full-backs were destined to struggle. The loyalty to Jordan, the omission of Andy Gray from the squad, the exclusion of Johnstone from the team, the persistence with a doubtful goalkeeper, Rough, and a fading midfield pair had combined to undermine Scotland's chances before they took the field.

Worse still, MacLeod compounded his errors the following day by breaking the first rule of management—laying the blame on his players. Twelve hours after his blunders of selection and tactics, he seemed to remain ignorant of the root cause of the defeat, claiming: 'Eight of the team just didn't play.' At the morning press conference at Alta Gracia he offered not a single coherent explanation, and his re-action to the setback only further exposed a limited grasp of international tactics.

On Scotland's worst day for 24 years he said: 'It was just one of those things. I can't put my finger on it. If you play as we did yesterday, you won't beat anyone.' On his selection: 'On the day, I didn't think it was a mistake.' On why Scotland were swamped in midfield after leading 1–0: 'Cubillas didn't chase back when we attacked, so when Peru won the ball they had five attackers.' (No mention of Rioch never chasing Cubillas.) On Masson's missed penalty: 'I thought he hit it reasonably well, but it let Peru off the hook (!), and they played pretty well after that.' (And before?) On Peru's wingers, Munante and Oblitas: 'I always said they were good going forward.' (So why play two inexperienced full-backs?)

Scotland were almost out of the World Cup at the first hurdle because they had hired the local blacksmith instead of an international architect as manager. He was left with two matches in which to rescue a bleak situation, made none the better by Holland gaining a comfortable 3–0 win over Iran the same evening in Mendoza. Heshmat Mohajerani, Iran's manager, had been worried beforehand by the expected absence of Hassan Rowshan, saying: 'It's a very serious blow to us. He is our best goal-scorer and we rely on him greatly.' Rowshan, in fact, came on as substitute for Faraki five minutes after half-time, with Holland leading by Bobby Rensen-brink's 38th minute penalty. Holland's slow, cautious opening against the modest Iranians had itself been moderate enough. Parvin, their captain, playing in his 80th international, had organized the Iranians well enough, and Faraki had almost put them in front with a shot which flew just wide. The Dutch seemed con-tent with possession; their attacks often foundered on the powerful Nazari. Iran were more than happy to give away 15 free-kicks: but the 16th was inside the area, when Abdollahie brought down René van der Kerkhof, for Rensenbrink to send Hedjazi the wrong way from the spot.

Rensenbrink added two more, a far-post header and a second penalty, and although the Dutch would continue to moan about the spongy state of the Mendoza pitch, their problems were nothing as compared with Scotland's. MacLeod had asked the Scottish director of coaching Andy Roxburgh to send a report of Holland–Iran; but it subsequently became apparent that Roxburgh's advice had been little heeded. In the interval, the drug-storm had burst on Willie Johnston, and against Iran he was replaced by John Robertson, the Forest winger who had been an unexpected inclusion in the squad in preference to Arthur Graham of Leeds. The drug scandal had put additional pressures on a manager and a squad whose self-confidence was seriously dented. The selection for the second match did little to repair the situation. Martin Buchan and Kenny Burns were named as central defenders, never having played together before, and although Gemmill replaced Masson and Macari deputized for the injured Rioch, there was still no place for Souness—or Derek Johnstone. Roxburgh had advised MacLeod that Iran employed a most orthodox 4–4–2 formation, with two big men, Faraki and Jahani, up front. The bold move for MacLeod would have been to play two markers on the Iran strikers with Buchan as sweeper, four men in midfield and three strikers. But he scorned this, and continued with four men across the back. Sandy Jardine replaced the unhappy Kennedy, had no one to mark, but seldom provided that extra width in attack which would have been valuable down the right flank.

SCOTLAND 1, IRAN 1   HOLLAND 0, PERU 0

Scotland began nervously, Willie Donachie, back after his one-match suspension, putting the ball out of play with his first touch. Early on, Macari hooked a shot from close in against goalkeeper Nasser Hedjazi, from a clever little curling cross from Dalglish, but Scotland were getting little out of Robertson on the left. After a quarter of an hour Faraki and Jahani, combining intelligently, nearly created a chance in spite of Scotland's four defenders, but for the most part Iran were happy to defend—successfully.

After 20 minutes Gemmill sent Hartford away; he was brought down 20 yards out; Jordan took a quick free-kick, Hedjazi plunged full-length to turn the ball away for a corner, following which Dalglish arched a back header close over the bar. Jordan, switching from wing to wing, was putting some pressure on Iran's defence, but there was no pattern or rhythm to Scotland's build-up, and when a goal came a minute before half-time, it was by courtesy of the opposition. Jordan followed through to make a challenge on Hedjazi as he gathered the ball; centre-back Eskandarian attempted to protect his keeper by getting in Jordan's way. The outcome was a collision, the ball bounced free and a desperate Eskandarian, sticking out a leg, struck the ball 15 yards back into his own empty net.

The sun continued to shine, but there was little feeling among the 20,000 crowd, although the small Scottish contingent loyally continued to give what encouragement they could from high in the stands.

The pattern continued in the second half, with Iran's midfield quartet—Parvin, Ghasem-Pour, Sadeghi and Danaie-Fard—successfully smothering the Scots in midfield. In the 50th minute Abdollahi felled Jordan in the 'D' dangerously close to the penalty area. Shortly afterwards Scotland lost Buchan with a cut head—the blow inflicted inadvertently by Donachie. Scotland were in command, but MacLeod wasted his chance by replacing Buchan with another defender, Forsyth. This did not prevent Iran equalizing shortly afterwards. Danaie-Fard took the ball off Gemmill, went away from Jardine, and beat Rough from an angle cutting in from the left, vainly pursued by Gemmill. In the very next minute, with Scotland anxiously

Lou Macari (16) nearly gives Scotland the lead after five minutes, but his shot strikes Iran goalkeeper Nasser Hedjazi, watched by Dalglish (8), Parvin (7) and Nazari (*on line*).

pressing forward, Ghasem-Pour counter-attacked rapidly from the halfway line, breaking clear on a lone run, but approaching the penalty area, he knocked the ball too far in front and Rough, coming out 16 yards or so, was able to gather it.

Just under half an hour remained for Scotland to ease themselves from the jaws of a second successive disaster, but MacLeod's only reaction to the continuing lack of thrust was to send out tubby little Joe Harper, with only 15 minutes to go, in place of Kenny Dalglish: a decision which appeared strange not least to Johnstone, still sitting on the bench. Scotland's only chance of a desperately needed winner came nine minutes from the end when Hartford's free-kick was met by Robertson's head—the winger's most positive contribution to the match—only for Hedjazi to make a fine save. Dejectedly, Scotland stumbled out of the World Cup, discredited on all counts: lacking leadership, tactics and technique in this depressing, negative shambles of a match. Statistically, there was still a remote possibility that if they were to beat Holland by at least three goals in Mendoza four days later, they could qualify for the second round on goal-difference. But for the moment they had looked as if they would struggle to defeat the Isle of Man. Those valiant supporters from home, some of whom had mortgaged their incomes for the next few years, who had come overland down through Central America and the West coast of Peru, now vented their wrath. As the team departed afterwards by bus, they were booed, jeered and spat at, with cries of 'You only want the money.' Whether this was directed at the players or the manager, one could not be sure. Certainly they

104

Archie Gemmill (15) beats Dutch goalkeeper Jongbloed from the penalty spot to put Scotland 2–1 ahead. They won 3–2.

had all been to some extent preoccupied with the financial tactics of their appearance in the world's premier sports tournament. MacLeod had said at the press conference after the game: 'The team could not play as they can because of the pressures they have had to endure.' Did they not expect pressure? England were not exactly free of pressure when they reached the quarter-final in Mexico amid a sea of local hostility. MacLeod should have perhaps asked Claudio Coutinho about pressure. Mohajerani, Iran's manager, said: 'We may lack experience, but we have given little away in the encounters so far, even though this is our first World Cup. We did better today than against Holland in spite of the supposed class of the Scottish players—and we even gave them their goal.' The next morning in the Cordoba press centre a notice on the board stated: 'The Scottish squad has no activity programmed for today.' Just like yesterday, we all mused.

Peru had tightened their grip on the second round place which everyone had assumed would belong to Scotland by holding Holland to a goal-less draw in Mendoza. The Dutch continued to blame their listlessness on the pitch, though it was clear that at this stage manager Ernst Happel was not succeeding in motivating a team which was supposed to be more of a unit temperamentally, not less, in the absence of Johan Cruyff.

The result dealt Scotland a nasty blow from behind, putting Peru level on three points with Holland; though the Dutch had done their homework and gave the South Americans little chance to exhibit the effervescence which had routed Scot-

105

land. Peru's stars were once again Quiroga in goal and Cubillas in midfield. They went on the defensive, forced Holland to do most of their shooting from outside the penalty area; and Quiroga was equal to that. There was evidence of Holland's uncompromising tackling which was to become a feature of later stages of the tournament.

Scotland were out of the World Cup unless they could produce a major tactical transformation and a victory of unlikely proportions against the Dutch—who had three hours experience of the Mendoza pitch to which the Scots had now to move. Before the game against Iran I had advocated that the players should take over the selection and tactics of the team from the manager: and by all accounts this is what now happened before the final encounter. Players such as Rioch, Buchan and Gemmill possessed sufficient international experience, for club and country, far in excess of the manager, to know what was required. The first essential was to get control together with flexibility, in the department in which the Dutch were strongest—midfield. In consultation with the players, MacLeod nominated a midfield of Gemmill, Souness and Hartford, with Rioch having a non-marking free role to move forward. Probably only Rioch's position as skipper preserved his place at the expense of Macari, who had shown himself more adept at getting into the penalty area.

Lamely, MacLeod apologized for the previous exclusion of Souness, which he conceded was a mistake—a mistake of such proportions, as proved by Souness's competence, that alone it probably cost Scotland their place in the second round. There were four changes, with Jardine, Burns, Macari and Robertson losing their places, Kennedy, Forsyth, Souness and Rioch returning. But could they gain the necessary margin against the Dutch? It seemed about as improbable as them winning the Boat Race—the more so when, on a quick trip to Mendoza two days beforehand,

Scots goalkeeper Alan Rough takes off in a vain attempt to reach the drive by Johnny Rep (*inset*), which made it 3–2 and cut Scotland's goal-difference.

I encountered the mood in the Dutch camp. The difference between the approach of Holland and Scotland to the World Cup was that while Scotland had employed as manager a man who had spent the greater part of his career in the remoteness of the Scottish second division, Holland had offered Happel—one of Europe's most experienced coaches whatever his instinctive caution—£60,000 for six weeks of expertise during their campaign in the finals. Happel, capped 54 times for Austria and manager of European Cup finalists Bruges, had temporarily taken charge, with full-time manager Jan Zwartkruis relegated to second-in-command. Happel, having employed a 3–5–2 formation in defeating Austria 1–0 in Vienna immediately prior to the final, had proceeded with caution in the first two games, but now warned me: 'We have been accused of being in bad shape, of being excessively careful. But on Sunday we will prove to the world that Holland are still a great team. We will attack Scotland in an open game. We do not underestimate them. They are British professionals; they are never finished. But it is their last opportunity to show they can play football, and we will exploit this.'

Johan Neeskens, one of Europe's foremost players throughout the 70s, as formidably hard as he is skilful, echoed Happel's strategy: 'There is more chance for us, more danger for Scotland, in an open game. They have to attack or they are finished. This will give us more openings than usual.' Neeskens had been troubled by a rib injury and, on the day, stretching for and missing a tackle on Rioch after only eight minutes, he further tore the painful rib muscles and had to be replaced by Johan Boskamp—a factor which undoubtedly helped turn the game Scotland's way but was largely overlooked in the wave of euphoria which greeted an exciting but vain victory.

SCOTLAND 3, HOLLAND 2   PERU 4, IRAN 1

The extent of the loyalty and zeal back home for an expedition already doomed, bar some startling reversal of form, was demonstrated by the 3000 telegrams from well-wishers received by the Scots before they kicked off, more in desperation than hope. The fact that Souness converted them into a slick, fighting force, two matches too late, was a matter more for anguish than celebration. What if he had been there from the start? After five minutes, it was from a cross by Souness that Rioch, ghosting forward, headed against the angle of the posts. Immediately after Neeskens went off, Dalglish had a goal disallowed, Jordan having fouled Rijsbergen on a long clearance from Rough. Scotland were making the running; Dalglish went close again; Jordan was brought down riskily by Willy van der Kerkhof inside the penalty area. For five minutes around the half-hour the Dutch flourished briefly, Rensenbrink missed a reasonable chance from a cross by Jansen, getting too far under the ball and directing his header upwards, Rough saving.

In the 34th minute Scotland's defence was caught pushing forward, Kennedy brought down Rep, and Rensenbrink hit the 1000th goal in World Cup history from the penalty spot. But a minute before half-time Souness worked through on the left, pitched a perfect cross to the far post, Jordan headed square and down, and Dalglish thrashed the ball past Jongbloed from close range. The Dutch were to complain bitterly afterwards that a foul charge by Jordan a short while earlier had injured centre-back Rijsbergen, who was replaced in the second half by the 20-year-old Wildschut.

The goal had imbued Scotland with real confidence for the first time in the competition. At the start of the second half Jongbloed had immediately to turn away a dangerous cross from Souness. Inside two minutes Scotland had taken the lead. Willy van der Kerkhof brought down Souness, and Gemmill scored from the penalty spot. Holland responded with a spell more representative of their true ability; Rough had to save from Rep and for 10 minutes it seemed as if the Dutch might take charge. Then Souness worked through on the right, crossed the ball and Dalglish sent a glancing header over the bar. On the hour Jordan went close with a header across the face of the goal, from Souness's free-kick. And now came one of the really great goals of the finals—from Gemmill. Setting off on the right on a memorable run, he went past Wildschut on the inside, veered away from Suurbier on the outside, then flicked the ball between Krol's legs, raced onwards, drew Jongbloed from his goal, with a dip of the shoulder sent the goalkeeper to his right and simultaneously curled the ball away to the left and inside the far post.

For three glorious, giddy minutes it looked as if Scotland would reach that three-goal margin which would carry them, clear of all their errors and misjudgements, into the second round. But then Johnny Rep, who throughout the finals seldom touched the same level of excellence as four years before, came storming through the middle on a solo run, with the defence caught off guard, to beat Rough from 27 yards and stifle the roar hanging on every Scottish throat back home.

Before the finish Rensenbrink might twice have equalized, once catching Rough horribly out of position. Rioch and Hartford faded badly and while Scotland pressed

Cubillas hits Peru's second from the penalty spot past Iran's keeper Hedjazi to assure Peru's Second Round place.

in vain for the goals which might still achieve the impossible, Johnstone and Macari remained idle on the bench.

Any hope that Iran might do Scotland a favour disappeared with the news that Peru had won 4–1. Cubillas, the man who had first put the skids under the Scots the week before, hit a hat-trick in Cordoba to become the tournament's leading scorer at that stage with five goals . . . and encourage a bid of a million dollars from New York Cosmos. Velasquez put Peru in front after only three minutes with a near-post header from Munante's cross, Cubillas got his first from a penalty after 36 minutes when Oblitas was brought down by Nazari; and a second penalty followed three minutes later. Rowsham made it 3–1. Cubillas hit his third near the end, and the nation regarded by the 'heavies' of South America as a bit of a joke, a team of jugglers, was through to the second round at the expense of Scotland— a team with a sad, recurring aptitude for self-destruction.

CHAPTER EIGHT

Merci, France

Group 1

At the Hindu Country Club 20 miles out of Buenos Aires—a restful, low oak-panelled retreat set in a green oasis amid ugly tumbledown suburbs—France and Italy prepared side by side for their opening match against each other down on the coast at Mar del Plata. While France remained relaxed and carefree, Italy were all too clearly on edge. In spite of it being their first appearance in the finals for 20 years, France with justification had confidence in their ability. Not so Italy, who crossed the Atlantic in low spirits after a dismal goal-less draw in their last warm-up against Yugoslavia, criticized with a spitefulness which only the Italian press knows. Everything which Enzo Bearzot had been attempting to achieve for four years was again in question. When the team played another practice match against a local club side in Buenos Aires, Paolo Rossi was substituted for the experienced Franco Graziani in the second half. The improvement was immediate; Italy responded to Rossi's wonderfully fluid running, so that Bearzot knew he must sacrifice the striker who had previously been so central to his tactical concept.

Michel Hidalgo, who had steered France through the qualifying round, had been happy to let the pressure lie on Italy, and said: 'It suits us that we are regarded as the underdogs in our group. I want the players to take the field relaxed. I believe Argentina have already claimed one of the second round places from Group 1, so the fight is between ourselves, Italy and Hungary for the other place. It is important that we beat Italy.'

Patrice Rio was given the job of holding down Rossi, but France would be weakened by the absence of injured Dominque Bathenay in midfield, Jean Guillou of Nice taking over from the St Etienne star. As with Scotland, the soccer world was eagerly awaiting a can-can from the French, from men such as the acclaimed Michel Platini of Nancy and superb Marseilles libero Marius Tresor. France, certainly, were expected to have the edge over Italy in this group where every game would be vital if they could first resolve their internal squabbles over money and boot contracts.

ITALY 2, FRANCE 1

It was an electric start for France, with Bernard Lacombe, their centre-forward, scoring after less than a minute. For the Italians it was a wretched, unimaginable goal. Henri Michel, from the kick-off, slipped the ball out to the nimble little left-winger Six, who darted past right-back Gentile, evaded the libero Scirea as he moved in to cover, and swung the ball across. Lacombe rising above Bellugi, headed firmly past Zoff. With the tournament hardly begun, three Italian defenders had

Paolo Rossi, Italy's £3-million striker (*right*), equalizes against France at Mar del Plata. Antognoni (9) and Causio (*centre*) rejoice; Janvion (4), Rio, Guillou (10) and Tresor (8) protest. Italy won 2–1.

made consecutive errors in the space of a few seconds, and all that avalanche of criticism back home seemed valid. Yet the effect of this goal, as Bearzot was later to claim, fundamentally conditioned Italy's attitude to the tournament—for the better. Now they were obliged to go out and attack, and for half an hour or more they produced some of the best football of the finals. With devastating accuracy, they kept the ball to themselves for long spells, so that although full-back Bossis should have scored from a free-kick by Michel after eight minutes, the French were pinned down. Tardelli, who would emerge as one of the physically most tenacious players in the finals, subdued Platini, Benetti gave Michel little scope; and after 27 minutes Italy were level. Rossi had already begun to pose problems for Rio and Tresor, when a long centre from Italy's left-back Cabrini caught the French defence off-balance. Bettega headed against the angle of the bar and post; as the ball rebounded a second shot by Causio was blocked, and Rossi was there to put the ball away. Now Italy really opened out, and before half-time Rossi might twice have scored again. At the other end Scirea did well to cut off a lilting run by Platini, but it was obvious the drift of the game was now to Italy.

For the second half Bearzot replaced the disappointing Antognoni with Zaccarelli, and in the 52nd minute it was Zaccarelli, moving ahead of his attack, who scored the winner from a cross by Gentile, with goalkeeper Bertrond-Demanes probably at fault—though he may have been unsighted on Gentile's cross. Once in front, Italy fell back on their familiar game of *what we have we hold*. There were some fearsome fouls, notably by Tardelli on Platini and Gentile on Six. Lacombe headed narrowly over the bar, turning beautifully in the air to get to a cross from Michel: but the French flame died.

111

Karoly Csapo (13) is congratulated by Pinter (10), Torocsik (9) and Nagy after giving Hungary the lead against Argentina. Argentina won 2–1; Torocsik was later sent off.

France had not beaten Italy for 58 years, and Tardelli's grip on Platini had proved the decisive factor as 20,000 Italian-Argentines cheered home their adopted team at the tranquil seaside resort, which in so many ways was like Bournemouth or Scarborough in winter. We hurried, bitterly cold in the biting wind coming off the South Atlantic, back to the airport for the short flight to the capital and with expectation of another absorbing encounter that evening between Argentina and Hungary. The hairy taxi-ride from the domestic airport bordering the rust-red Plate estuary, and the final sprint into the 'River' stadium through the hordes of flag and peanut sellers, proved well worth while.

ARGENTINA 2, HUNGARY 1

A little-publicized incident which radically affected this critical opening game for Hungary had occurred in London during their visit for the friendly match with England. The wife of Laszlo Fazekas, the team captain, had been convicted of shop-lifting—a comparatively trivial matter of a T-shirt, by someone with only £3 spending money confronted with the enticement of the West End's consumer galaxy—and the resulting shame had seriously affected one of Hungary's more experienced players. Manager Lajos Baroti felt obliged to leave Fazekas on the substitutes' bench, and one can never know how much this reduced their effectiveness. They were already denied the injured Varadi.

What is certain is that Argentina quickly revealed that only the very best of teams was likely to block their path to the final: and that only the most assertive of referees, with inflexible nerve, would withstand the pressure of the home crowd, which many of us had always supposed would be so. Hungary led after 10 minutes,

112

played some outstanding football, received no protection from Portuguese referee Antonio Garrido in the face of ceaseless minor provocation from the Argentinian defence, kicked back with interest—and had their two best players, Andras Torocsik and Tibor Nyilasi, sent off in the last few minutes, thereby effectively terminating any remaining chance they might have had in subsequent matches.

It was, as with all Argentina's seven memorable matches, a tingling occasion. The blizzard of ticker-tape cascaded down through the floodlights at the start, to an explosive roar of encouragement from the 75,000 crowd; but it was Hungary who drew first blood. Zombori from left midfield hit an away-swinging cross shot, goalkeeper Ubaldo Fillol got to the ball, but with possibly his only serious error of the whole tournament, failed to hold it; and Csapo was on hand to inflict the punishment.

The silence of a tomb momentarily fell on the vast, tiered stadium, but not for long. Five minutes later we had the first glimpse of the man whose influence was to prove such a compelling, exciting force on the story of the finals. Mario Kempes struck a free-kick round the end of the Hungarian wall, goalkeeper Gujdar could not hold it; and there was the swarthy Luque lunging to slide the ball just inside the post as he collided with a desperate Gujdar. The noise seemed to proclaim that Argentina had as good as won the cup already, but Hungary instantly jolted them with some fluent counter-attacking all the way up to half-time.

Torocsik flitted through the uncertain Argentinian defence time and again, and was repeatedly obstructed by either stopper Luis Galvan or libero Daniel Passarella. Gujdar once had to dive bravely at Luque's feet, but twice just on half-time Toroc-

Luque equalizes for Argentina in the 14th minute, goalkeeper Gujdar gets his neck bent. Houseman (9), Kereki, Kempes (10) and Torok (2) look on.

sik, who like the great ballet dancers appears to move without any impeding contact with the ground, almost deceived Fillol from positions right under his nose.

Into the second half Hungary still attacked; Torocsik was booked for excusable dissent after the Argentinians had yet again fouled him without rebuke. With 20 minutes or so to go Cesar Menotti, worried by the lack of penetration on the right from Houseman—so dynamic in 1974—replaced him with Bertoni, that brooding winger with both explosive feet and fists. Yet Bertoni, like the rest of his colleagues, was to show during the next month that Menotti's revolutionary regime of self-discipline was far-reaching.

Two minutes after Bertoni's arrival, Hungary had a golden chance to inflict the wound which could have altered the whole course of the finals, not least for themselves. Their right-back Martos, substitute for Torok at half-time, burst away on a galloping run down the touch-line. All the while Csapo was keeping pace through the middle and when Martos, level with the penalty area, hit his centre across, Csapo was there to dive full length on the near post. But his header flew just the wrong side: and in such moments is the history of every sport fashioned. Although Passarella was belatedly booked, this time for a cynical foul on Pinter, Argentina had a decisive edge, with the crowd now at their backs. With six minutes to go, Bertoni shot the winner when it seemed that Gujdar had been fouled in one of Argentina's surging attacks involving Tarantini and Luque.

The frustration was too much for some of Hungary's youngsters, who began to lash out at any passing object in blue-and-white stripes. Torocsik hung out a foot, more as a gesture than a direct blow, as Galvan went by, and absurdly was shown the red card. Two minutes later Nyilasi ran full tilt into Tarantini with no attempt to play the ball, almost as if asking to be sent off to underline the prolonged prejudice of the referee. His slow walk to the tunnel, head high, was the perverse, symbolic end of Hungary's World Cup adventure.

Afterwards Menotti, never less than realistic, conceded: 'I am satisfied with the victory but not with the performance. I don't think we played as well as we can because of the huge psychological responsibility in our first match. I'm sure we will play better.' Said Baroti sadly: 'I want to ask to be excused for the conduct of my two players. I think they were carried away by the enthusiasm of their youth. Our remaining matches will now be very difficult because we have lost two key men. Our tactics were to use rapid counter-attacks because we knew Argentina would dominate the middle, and this nearly worked. We missed our great chance with 20 minutes to go, and I believe the score should still have been 1–1, because when Bertoni scored there might have been a free-kick in favour of our goalkeeper.'

ITALY 3, HUNGARY 1

Dejected and depleted by a couple of injuries in addition to the two automatic suspensions, Hungary moved camp to Mar del Plata for their second match and the attempt to salvage some prestige. In fact they ran headlong into one of the most lethal individual attacking displays of the tournament from Roberto Bettega. On the wretchedly cut-up seaside pitch, new and almost rootless, the Juventus left-winger scored one goal, made another, and rapped the Hungarian bar three times as Italy masterfully became the first country to reach the second round. Having demolished Hungary, an enthusiastic Bearzot declared: 'We are ready for anyone: Brazil, Argentina, the lot.' Certainly they were too compact, too slick for Hungary, and a team which had been condemned before the start as wasting its time bothering to come was now emerging as a major threat to the most fancied sides. The combination of Bettega and Rossi, the power of Tardelli and Benetti in midfield, the assurance of the back four, had suddenly given Italy a collective confidence unmatched at this stage in any of the four groups.

The irony for Hungary was that the most clear-cut early chances again fell to them; and again they were undermined by a referee who appeared to favour the opposition. On another freezing day, Hungary were booed at the start by a crowd encouraged to believe, by Argentinian press and TV, that they were the villains and not the victims in that first match at the River Plate stadium. In the sixth minute Tardelli was wickedly late in a tackle on Pinter, but received no admonition from Uruguayan referee Ramon Barreto. Minutes later Bellugi committed an equally cynical foul from behind on Fazekas, now restored to the team. It was Fazekas who could and should have opened the scoring after 13 minutes. Feinting past first Bellugi, then Scirea, he came in on goal dead centre with only Zoff to beat from 14 yards—but shot over. Seven minutes later from a near-post cross from Pusztai, Fazekas nicked the ball on the half-volley under Zoff's dive and Csapo, following up behind, knocked his shot into the side netting.

Now Bettega took a hand, hitting the bar on the underside from close in as Rossi flickered through on the left. Just after the half-hour Hungary were sunk by two goals in three minutes. A cross from Causio from the left was headed out, Tardelli drove the ball back in from the edge of the penalty area, but his shot was deflected; Rossi, with goalkeeper Meszaros helplessly out of position, scored the kind of close-range goal which used to be the hallmark of Greaves. Almost straight from the kick-off Antognoni threaded the ball through, two defenders hesitated, and Bettega pounced. The second-half was almost all one way—Hungary's taste for battle steadily ebbing. Bettega hit the bar twice more, Benetti rasped home a 20-yard drive from Rossi's neat back heel; and when Andras Toth, second-half substitute in attack, scored from a penalty with 10 minutes to go, Italy were already dreaming of the final, Hungary contemplating the disillusionment of an early plane home. It was no consolation to them for Sir Walter Winterbottom, chairman of the FIFA technical committee, to point out that Hungary had made 42 penetrative attacks to Italy's 43. The scoreline, as ever, tells its own story.

ARGENTINA 2, FRANCE 1

Another mad dash back to the capital—and to another seeming instance of glaring injustice as Argentina collected their passport to the second round at the expense of buoyant, at times brilliant, unlucky France. The game turned on a penalty for Argentina in the 45th minute, a critical stage in any match; a penalty, moreover, given on the word of a linesman at least 40 yards from the incident and arguably unsighted; a penalty given against one of the most accomplished players in the finals, the gifted Tresor from Guadeloupe, so much admired by television viewers around the globe.

115

As the tigerish Kempes came striding through on the left of the penalty area, Tresor moved smoothly, with his usual faultless timing, to intercept. As he tackled, the ball rebounded off Kempes's shins and at the same time Tresor lost his foothold on the uneven pitch. As he fell, his arms spread instinctively to cushion the fall; Tresor's right hand may or may not have struck the ball. Certainly there was no possibility that, with a view at that instant of nothing but the floodlights and the night sky, he could have seen and deliberately controlled the ball. Swiss referee Jean Dubach, all of a dither, ran to consult linesman Werner Winsemann of Canada. To the incredulity of the French and anyone in the stadium other than an Argentinian, Dubach pointed to the spot; Passarella scored.

There was not even the slim justification that Argentina had been dominating the game and exerting the kind of pressure from which penalties often derive. The return of Bathenay in midfield, and St Etienne's winger Rocheteau, had invigorated the French; so that although Kempes had struck a shot against keeper Bertrand-Demanes from four yards in the 21st minute, and seen another drive parried in the 37th minute, France were anything but overawed. It was just reward when, on the hour, they equalized—Rocheteau crashing a shot against the cross-bar, Platini knocking home the rebound. Now France really turned on a show. Fillol saved nervously from little Six, who was everywhere. From a free-kick by Tresor, Fillol only just managed to hold a volley by Six, taken with incredible skill with the left foot as the ball dropped diagonally over his right shoulder. Three minutes later, and with 20 remaining, Platini rippled through the middle, going past two men as though their ankles were chained, to send Six clear of Passarella. Moving into the penalty area, squirming in search of the angle, Six went round Fillol—only to

Michel Platini, French midfield wizard, equalizes for France against Argentina, with Lacombe and Houseman in attendance. Argentina won 2–1.

shoot wide of the post and an empty net. When Passarella fouled Lacombe, Platini's free-kick was only inches wide.

France were playing with the kind of élan we had not seen since the halcyon days of Kopa, Piantoni and Fontaine, all three now spectators in the stand. The wizardry of the French at this moment was not Argentina's only problem. Valencia in midfield had been substituted, just after Platini's goal, by Alonso, who was himself almost immediately injured and replaced by Ortiz. France, too, had lost Bertrand-Demanes earlier, when colliding with a post in making a fine save from Valencia. Menotti, observing Baratelli taking over in goal, had glanced meaningfully at his trainers; and in the 73rd minute Baratelli, on the first occasion he was seriously called into action, was caught off-guard by Luque's stunning drive, taken on the turn in the 'D' and rifled low into the corner.

Still France were not finished. Fillol had to make a breathtaking save from Six, and minutes later there was a further, monstrous injustice when Galvan brutally brought down Six in the penalty area without reaction from the supine Mr Dubach. Argentina anxiously played out the last minutes with 10 men, Luque receiving treatment for an injury off the field. Right at the death—which for France it literally was—a delicate, hanging little chip by Rocheteau dropped just too far for Bathenay as he hurled himself forward in a vain attempt to equalize. Possibly the most accomplished side in the finals had been eliminated in only their second match. An objective Argentinian journalist was heard to remark, when asked whose hand had touched the ball for the controversial penalty: 'The Hand of God'.

FRANCE 3, HUNGARY 1

France bowed out of the World Cup with another superb but by now irrelevant display of fluid attack against Hungary; kicking off 40 minutes late in Mar del Plata because of a confusion over shirts, which set the television moguls back a few bob in squandered satellite time. It was with mixed feelings that one viewed France's elegant control at the expense of a Hungarian side which, in three matches, had never been able fully to demonstrate the extent of its own skill.

France had seven changes. Lopez, their reserve stopper, maintained a growing trend for accurate shooting from long-range with the opening goal after six minutes from 25 yards which had Gujdar beaten all the way. Berdoll and Rocheteau scored the other two, Zombori got one for France, Platini hit the bar—and the competition bid goodbye to two colourful sides. All that remained to be determined in Group 1 was who would finish top, with the advantage of playing all their second round matches at the River Plate stadium, who would be second and obliged to move to Rosario.

ITALY 1, ARGENTINA 0

For the first time Argentina now found themselves confronted not only by opposition as compact as a lighthouse in defence, but by referee Abraham Klein of Israel, who was unwaveringly insistent on applying the laws as they are written—with a resultant hail of abuse from the home country, when they lost, and widespread acclaim in Europe. Ironically, his brave, conspicuous performance robbed Klein of his rightful claim to the final.

Not the least significant aspect of this fascinating match was Argentina's commendable refusal to respond in kind to the calculated intimidation of Romeo Benetti, renowned hit-man of Italian football. Benetti pulled a stiletto on the hosts—and amazingly Argentina backed off. In the very first minute, stepping over the fallen Gallego in midfield, Benetti dropped his foot short and discreetly screwed his studs in the Argentinian's thigh—a gesture which left Gallego and his colleagues in little doubt as to Benetti's reading of the priorities. Scirea followed this with a calculated trip on Kempes a yard outside the penalty area; and Italy were in no way disconcerted by losing their stopper, Bellugi, after six minutes, Cuccuredu replacing him.

Italy were controlled, positive and direct; and apart from a few isolated, solo bursts by Kempes, Argentina gave their followers no thrills in the first half. Tardelli, Benetti and Antognoni stifled Argentina's midfield of Ardiles, Gallego and Valencia, with Causio dropping deep to make doubly sure of the lock-up.

By the time Benetti was booked after an hour, flashing his studs somewhere up around Gallego's neck, he and the others had successfully done what they set out to do—limit the supply to Argentina's volatile front men—Bertoni, Kempes and Ortiz, Luque being out with an injury. In the 67th minute Bettega scored the only goal. It was one of the outstanding tactical goals in the tournament. Benetti took a throw on the left, Antognoni found Bettega on the inside, away from his wing, Bettega worked a rapid one-two to deceive four defenders and Rossi's perfectly angled return sent the big winger clear to shoot past an advancing Fillol as Tarantini's tackle arrived too late.

Italy's midfield now faded; Argentina emerged, and soon Cabrini was lucky not to concede a penalty when bringing down Gallego. Zaccarelli, for the third time in three games, replaced Antognoni; Valencia went close with a speculative 20-yard shot. But Argentina were obliged to transfer the emotional centre of the World Cup up the Parana river to industrial Rosario.

Group 2

West Germany, the champions, picked up in the opening game of the finals, against Poland in the River Plate stadium, where they left off in their series of unsatisfactory spring friendlies against England, Brazil and Sweden: edgy, disorganized, lacking punch. They, and Poland too, epitomized throughout the first and second round, the tactics of caution if not naked fear. Helmut Schoen, the old fox of international soccer, had a nervous tic about his team, ringing the changes but to little effect. Into his defence for the opening game came Zimmermann of Cologne in place of Dietz at left-back, to mark Lato; while the central midfield position went to diminutive 31-year-old Beer of Hertha, Berlin. The defeat in Stockholm immediately prior to the finals had seriously confused Schoen's plans, convincing him privately, and fairly soon publicly, that his squad was nowhere near strong enough to retain the title.

Out went his Bayern winger Rummenigge, for a two-man attack of Fischer and Abramczik, with Hansi Muller in a withdrawn position on the left flank. Jacek Gmoch, Poland's manager, recalled the veteran Vladimir Lubanski, 31, who missed the 1974 finals with the injury sustained against England the previous year. Poland had waited four years to settle a score, after losing 1–0 to the Germans on a water-logged pitch in Frankfurt and missing a place in the Final. 'We are ready mentally and physically to gain our revenge,' said Gmoch. 'This is as good if not a better Polish side than four years ago.'

WEST GERMANY 0, POLAND 0

Yet for 90 minutes the two teams eyed each other across a no-man's-land while the rest of the soccer world yawned: the fourth time in succession that the World Cup had opened with a goal-less draw. To some extent one could blame the pitch: a patchwork affair hurriedly laid when the original grass was scorched brown by the wrong treatment—or salt water?—only months previously. Yet the further West Germany went in the tournament, the more obvious it was that a croquet lawn would have brought only marginal improvement to their play. After another of those artificial, contrived opening ceremonies, in this instance graced by some pleasingly natural formation-gymnastics, the enthusiastic crowd was quick to vent its displeasure on two cautious European formations. Poland, certainly, were the more fluent side—Lato, Szarmach and Deyna providing the rare moments of real class. Germany's man-for-man marking was made to look laborious; the weakness of the massive, blond Russman, Schalke's centre-back, putting intolerable pressure on Hamburg's libero Manny Kaltz. Poland had 12 penetrating attacks inside the penalty area to Germany's three—and were desperately unlucky not to score in the 60th and 75th minute.

First, with Germany on the ropes, Deyna was brought down by Russmann 25 yards out. Deyna bent the free-kick round the wall and across the face of the goal. Szarmach, sliding in on the far post, just failed to make contact, with Maier frozen

Stalemate. Nawalka of Poland is guarded by West German defenders Maier, Kaltz, Flohe (10) and Zimmermann in the opening goal-less draw.

in mid-goal. Then Lato, cleverly delaying his centre after breaking clear for the 20th time, pitched the ball just inches too far in front of Deyna as he swept through the middle. Deyna at times overran the usually faultless Rainer Bonhoff, for whom the World Cup was a sombre conclusion to a sombre season. With Flohe and Beer also ineffective in midfield, Schoen had a really ailing team on his hands. On this evidence they had no chance whatever of retaining their title or even reaching the final and Schoen admitted: 'This was a very poor game.' His former midfield star, Gunter Netzer, now general manager of Hamburg, went further: 'It was a shocking performance. Germany are without a leader, without ideas, even without skill.'

TUNISIA 3, MEXICO 1

The next day in Rosario unheralded Tunisia, African qualifiers, proudly took their place at the top of Group 2, with a surprise, runaway win over the more fancied Mexico. Abdel Chetali, Tunisia's manager, had said beforehand: 'Our goal was to reach the finals. We can't expect to win anything.' But the 1000–1 Arab outsiders, one down at half-time to a penalty by defender Vazquez, stormed back with three in the second half. Playing with a self-assurance which belied their inexperience, they were unlucky with the penalty, a speculative shot by Torre striking Jebali on the arm. Kaabi equalized 10 minutes after half-time with a shot from outside the penalty area; Gommidh put them in front 10 minutes from the end with Dhouib, their full-back, getting a third. Mexico, expected possibly to mount a challenge for a place in the second round, were outplayed and their manager, Antonio Roca, could only say: 'I knew Tunisia were dangerous, and today they were outstanding. We had our chances but didn't take them. I think our status was maybe overestimated by our own followers.' Chetali confided: 'We had studied Mexico throughout their tour of Europe; we knew all about them.' Please note, MacLeod.

WEST GERMANY 6, MEXICO 0

Whether or not Germany had much advance information on the Mexicans, they swept them aside in Cordoba in the only match in which Schoen's team approached the form demanded of it. Even then, with Germany leading 4–0 by half-time, the Mexicans had contrived to pose many problems for the German defence, and were less outclassed than the score suggests. The factor most strongly in Germany's favour, more than any matter of skill, was their physical superiority. Mexico's defence was fragile in extreme, especially in the centre, and Germany were able to score every ten minutes or so.

Following the draw in Buenos Aires, Schoen had replaced Abramczik with Rummenigge, and recalled Dieter Muller, the Cologne striker who had been such a success in the European championships two years previously. It was Dieter Muller who opened the scoring after a quarter of an hour—Germany's 101st goal in World Cup football. He took it well, on the turn with a left-foot drive, and soon Hansi Muller from Stuttgart, now playing in a more conventional midfield role down the left side, added a second from a cross by Flohe. The third by Rummenigge was the best of the six, the blond winger sprinting 50 yards, holding off a challenge on the edge of the penalty area and sliding the ball under the advancing Reyes—who had to go off, injured in the attempt to stop him. Flohe (2) and Rummenigge scored the others, but though Germany had it nearly all their own way it was evident that Bonhof, on whom they relied so heavily for midfield drive, was still out of touch. Roca was merely attempting to ease the intensity of criticism at home when he claimed: 'We were beaten by a side who played like world champions.' Tunisia would shortly have something to say about that.

POLAND 1, TUNISIA 0

The most underrated side in the finals were unlucky not to go through to the second round and thereby strengthen Africa's claim for a larger slice of the World Cup cake. Certainly they were Africa's most accomplished team to date, as they clearly demonstrated against both the Poles and the Germans. With no sense of inferiority against Poland at Rosario, they deserved at least a draw. Poland were hanging on desperately at the finish as Tunisia pressed for an equalizer. Lahzami hit the Poles' cross-bar as the balance of world soccer power temporarily shuddered. With four minutes to go Tunisia forced a corner, and from only four yards Dhiab headed wide. This was not the Poland of 1974.

In the early stages only a fine save by Tomaszewski prevented Tunisia from taking the lead, when he smothered the ball as Gommidh broke clear. This attack was the culmination of a spell which found Tunisia, unbelievably, dictating the play as Dena and the Polish midfield failed to assert themselves. The only goal came three minutes before half-time. Earlier Szarmach had squandered a fine chance, shooting weakly at Naili from just inside the penalty area. Now Lato was swift to punish a blunder by defender Kaabi, who swung at and missed a long cross from Lubanski.

WEST GERMANY 0, TUNISIA 0

That the result against Poland was no fluke, that Germany were on the blink, was established when Chetali's team held the champions to a goal-less draw. Chetali, who had studied coaching in Germany, was not surprised by his team's performances, and said: 'By 1982 or 1986 we shall have nothing to prove, and if we can qualify, those countries in our groups will no longer regard us as the outsiders but as a team to fear. The pressure on us is perhaps greater than any other team, because we are playing not for a country but a continent. The rest of the world has laughed at Africa, but now the mockery is over.'

Germany got the point in Cordoba which they needed to qualify for the second round; this was achieved only after some near escapes, the nearest when Rehaiem, eluding Russmann's challenge on the left of the penalty area, hooked a high, dropping cross-shot which cleared Maier and dropped just wide of the far post. Germany dominated much of the game, but Tunisia's goalkeeper Moktar Naili was outstanding against an attack lacking the killer-finish of a Gerd Muller. Fischer had the best chance when he broke clear in the second half, but Naili came off his line to narrow the angle and managed to get a foot in the way of Fischer's shot. With excusable glee the Tunisians leapt in the air at the final whistle, after a result which would be hailed throughout Africa. Schoen denied that his team had played for a draw,

Tunisian defender Kaabi frustrates West German centre-forward Fischer in the surprise goal-less draw.

but conceded: 'We did not play as I had planned. I was disappointed in spite of the fact that we controlled much of the match.' The disappointment would continue.

POLAND 3, MEXICO 1

Mexico, the most outclassed team of the finals, bowed before Poland in Rosario and headed home to a hostile reception. Yet Poland were little more convincing than they had been against Tunisia; Mexico at last showed some spirit and organization and came back to equalize after being one down. Mexico were marginally the better side in the first half, but three minutes before half-time Boniek put Poland ahead. In the 51st minute Rangel, of whom so much had been expected prior to the finals, levelled the score. Soon Deyna, picking up a lucky rebound off a defender, regained the lead, and before the finish Boniek, with a tremendous drive from 25 yards, had removed any hope of another Mexican revival. Soto, Mexico's goalkeeper, was seriously substandard, but could not be blamed for Boniek's first goal, the result of a fine move between Deyna and Lato. Poland continued to give the impression that they were possible finalists if only they could find a spark of inspiration, and break out of their rather dull routine of mechanical efficiency.

Group 3

BRAZIL 1, SWEDEN 1

Sweden's comprehensive recent defeat of West Germany, and the reputation of Ronnie Hellstrom in goal, suggested in advance that Brazil might have difficulty

122

in their opening match—unless they switched from the zealous intimidation, in friendlies so-called against Germany and England, to their more traditional skills. Sweden were troubled by an injury to Ralf Edstrom, their key forward four years previously; but they remained confident. Bjorn Nordquist, their 36-year-old defender, was poised to pass Bobby Moore's world record of international appearances with his 109th match.

In the event, six months' preparation by Brazil fell flat. Their attack never functioned; Rivelino and Batista were bickering in midfield; the dreadful Mar del Plata pitch, laid only a few weeks previously, was a severe limitation on Brazil's touch game. Sjoberg put Sweden ahead seven minutes before half-time after they had dominated much of the first half. Gil had proved an occasional threat to Sweden's defence, but Brazil were without co-ordination and, worse still, confidence. Just on half-time Reinaldo equalized from a cross by Cerezo, and early in the second half Rivelino was unlucky not to score when a drive was deflected by Roy Andersson just past his own post. The crowd, anti-Brazilian to a man, began chanting 'Suecia, Suecia' as Brazil failed to master the Swedes. Six minutes before the end Zico, picking up a loose ball, should have scored, but Hellstrom made a great save diving to his left. Edstrom, coming on as substitute 11 minutes from time, missed a cross from Wendt, with only Leao to beat; Brazil's safety was wafer-thin, and the match ended in high controversy.

Brazil's substitute right-back Nelinho delayed taking the third of three consecutive corner kicks, with time running out. As the third came over, Zico headed into the net, but the goal was disallowed by Welsh referee Clive Thomas, who had already blown for time. Brazil protested furiously, and lodged an official complaint with FIFA that evening—but were inevitably overruled. Thomas explained: 'Normal time was up before the corner was taken and there were 32 seconds of

Zico (8) heads the disallowed Brazilian goal at the end of the 1–1 draw with Sweden. Also in the picture: Hellstrom, Muller (1), Erlandsson (5) and Reinaldo (9).

injury time to play. The ball was in flight when I blew the whistle. I saw the header but I didn't see the ball go into the net. As far as I was concerned the game was over. The Brazilians have only themselves to blame for wasting time over taking the corner.' Technically correct, but naïve, Thomas did not referee another match.

The result was as disappointing for Brazil's millions of worldwide admirers as for themselves, but as England manager Ron Greenwood said: 'It's been a long time since Brazil have had a great side—eight years anyway. They have been living on their reputation. It's time people stopped thinking of them as they used to be. They are playing to a style that was effective when they had great players, who are no longer there. If Sweden had believed in themselves a little more, they might have won. Brazil have the same slow build-up they used to have, but no longer the explosion in attack.'

AUSTRIA 2, SPAIN 1

Austria, underrated by FIFA, who had placed them among the four weakest teams when making the draw for the finals, showed themselves to be a force when beating Spain at the Velez Sarsfield stadium in Buenos Aires, to the consternation of the local crowd, wildly pro-Spanish. Spain controlled much of the match, but threw it away with tactical blunders. Austria grabbed the lead after 10 minutes with a fine goal. The admirable Pezzey, Austria's central defender, broke up a Spanish attack and sent a long ball through to Schachner. Dribbling past two defenders, Schachner drove a high shot into the top corner of the net beyond keeper Miguel Angel—and shortly afterwards Kreuz might have made it 2–0 in another lightning counter-attack, Angel this time making a fine save. Within 10 minutes Bazan equalized for Spain, controlling a cross from Marcelino close in and beating Koncilia.

Cano had a second goal for Spain disallowed for a foul on the goalkeeper; Sara headed off the Austrian line from Rexach; Austria hit a post at the other end. Spain were clearly on top, but an injury to Cardenosa, who had not put a foot wrong in the first half and controlled the middle, robbed Spain of their authority. The

Europe's top scorer, Krankl of Austria, hits the winner past Angel in the 2–1 victory over Spain, under pressure from veteran Real defender Pirri.

substitution of Leal, and then Quini for Rexach, disrupted Spain's rhythm; Koncilia handled everything thrown at him with fine confidence. Eleven minutes from time Krankl scored the winner, compensating for two earlier misses. Ladislav Kubala, Spain's manager, admitted: 'We made two very bad mistakes which gave them two goals. I thought Prohaska was outstanding for them in midfield.' Helmut Senekowitsch insisted Austria would continue with their defensive, counter-attacking game.

BRAZIL 0, SPAIN 0

The continuing lack of form of central striker Reinaldo, the rutted Mar del Plata pitch, the fading of Zico, conspired to impose on Brazil their second unsatisfactory result. Arriving in Argentina as 9–4 favourites with the London bookmakers, they were now not certain even of reaching the second round. All would depend on their final game with Austria. Spain squandered glaring second-half chances which would have threatened instant revolution in Rio. As it was, Admiral Helenio Nunes, president of the Brazilian sports federation CBD, divested Claudio Coutinho of his sole authority over selection from now onwards.

Spain made five changes from the side beaten by Austria: two because of injuries, another because the players themselves demanded of Kubala that he replace the Argentinian-born Cano (one of Argentina's squad of 40 before the 1974 finals) with Santillana of Real Madrid. But Brazil remained inept. The only time Angel was beaten in the first half was by his own libero Olmo, who headed against the underside of his own bar. Spain should have won the match a quarter of an hour from time, but Cardenosa had a weak shot cleared off the line by Amaral after Santillana had beaten Leao in the air to a cross from Uria. It was a sad reflection of Brazil's panic that Coutinho had been reduced to playing an attacking full-back, Toninho, on the right flank in place of the brainless Gil. A ploy which failed totally.

AUSTRIA 1, SWEDEN 1

A penalty by Hans Krankl three minutes before half-time put Austria into the second round, but after the comparative elegance of their performance against Spain, this was a flat, dull encounter. The main excitement was provided by Krankl's willingness to shoot almost every time he got within range, which developed into a virtual duel between the Austrian striker and Sweden's goalkeeper Hellstrom. Yet the penalty itself was harsh, for Krankl appeared to have lost control of the ball when brought down by Nordquist. At the other end Koncilia was always the equal of anything Sweden could produce in attack—Edstrom again being confined to the substitutes' bench until the 60th minute. The return of Krieger in midfield after suspension, the reversal of Kreuz to out-and-out attack, had substantially strengthened the Austrians.

SPAIN 1, SWEDEN 0

Both teams knew that they must win to retain any chance of qualifying; but even that would be insufficient if Brazil beat Austria. So Spain's deserved victory was of academic interest only. Too late, they gave the kind of performance which could have taken them far, Cardenosa impressive in midfield, Juanito and Santillana fluid and sharp in attack. Edstrom, now fully fit, played his first full game for Sweden, but with nothing coming through from midfield, with his confidence at a low ebb, he had little chance to threaten a Spanish defence unimpaired by the absence of the vast Migueli through injury.

The only goal came a quarter of an hour before the end when a shot by Asensi, the Spanish midfield player, was deflected by right-winter Juanito. Spain's margin would have been far larger but for the performance of Hellstrom. In another duel, this time with Juanito, the big blond keeper again came out on top. It was a dignified though none-the-less disappointing conclusion to an international career for the incomparable Pirri, Real Madrid's ageless libero—dropped for the game against Brazil, now brought on as substitute for the second-half in place of Olmo. Sweden might have snatched a draw but for the agility of Real's keeper Angel.

BRAZIL 1, AUSTRIA 0

Brazil scuffled into the second round with their selection-by-committee, following the partial overthrow of Coutinho. But just how disinterested were Austria, already assured of a place in the second round? There were the usual wild rumours—from the scurrilous *Bildzeitung* on Germany that Austria had been persuaded to take a dive by some clandestine emissary from Rio, more simply that Austria wanted to lose by two goals to play in the easier second-round group. The truth, more probably, is that the Austrians merely lacked motivation for their third game in eight days.

With Brazil finishing, in fact, second on goal-difference*, they were obliged to

Ansensi (*left*) hits the only goal past Roy Andersson and keeper Hellstrom; but Spain fail to qualify for the Second Round.

* The same goal-difference, but Austria had scored one goal more, 3:2 compared with Brazil's 2:1.

Roberto drives home the 40th-minute goal which takes anxious Brazil into the Second Round. Pezzey (5) arrives too late; Prohaska (8) watches.

go into the same group as Argentina—quite the reverse of what FIFA had hoped and thereby preventing any possibility of an all-South American final against Argentina.

Brazil dropped Reinaldo, Zico and Edinho, introducing Roberto—the big centre-forward who scored the winning goal against England in Los Angeles two years previously—plus Mendonca and, at left back for Edinho, Rodrigues Neto. With Roberto scoring the only goal five minutes before half-time, the Admiral's revolution from above could be said to have been successful: up to a point. This was more great escape than memorable victory; we had still seen nothing of the old Brazil. The only warmth was the sun belatedly shining down on windswept Mar del Plata. Roberto, ironically, is the antithesis of everything you expect in a Brazilian player—big and awkward. But when Gil crossed the ball in the 40th minute, Austria's defence reacted as if moving thigh-deep in water; Roberto lumbered past Pezzey and, head down, pummelled the ball past Koncilia from 12 yards. It was just enough, sufficient to render even more pathetically pointless the death at home in Rio, by suicide poisoning, of a distraught fan after the first two matches. Brazil were still short of ideas, short of their own high standards, short of a really incisive finisher; but Coutinho insisted he was satisfied with the outcome, as well he might be after all the burning of effigies in Brazilian streets during the previous few days.

127

CHAPTER NINE

Too Late, Brazil

The smoke of unrest coming from within the West German camp thickened with the approach of their opening Second Round match against Italy. As in 1974, as in 1970 indeed, there was friction between Schoen and some of his senior players. Following the failure to dispose of humble Tunisia there was now a move, led by Rainer Bonhof and Sepp Maier, to force Schoen's hand on selection. Bonhof, seeking, as any professional will do when having a bad time, for reasons outside his own performance, was unhappy with the constitution of the midfield, blaming young Hansi Muller from Stuttgart for not giving him defensive cover. Maier, the veteran Bayern goalkeeper, fancied himself to take over the role of Franz Beckenbauer as unofficial player-selector. Certainly there was friction among the players, between the factions from Cologne, Frankfurt and Berlin, as well as between some of the players and the manager. Now the pressure was on Schoen to drop both Mullers, Hansi and Dieter—which he did, recalling Zimmermann and the ageing, experienced Holzenbein, survivor of the 1974 Final. Italy had no such problems, Bearzot fielding his now regular side, with Antognoni again preferred to Zaccarelli at the start, again substituted in the second-half. The previous autumn Germany had whipped Italy in Berlin in a friendly, after being behind, but now Italy, with the advent of Rossi, were a more compact, more threatening side.

It was ironic that, in a match likely to be decisive in determining the finalists in Group A, it should be Germany rather than Italy who resorted to a 4–4–2 formation—the first time ever that one could recall the Germans taking the field with such caution in 20 years. A two-man attack of Fischer and Rummenigge, a full-back (Zimmermann) in midfield in a side already goal-shy, promised little against the solid Italians, overflowing with confidence after their defeat of Argentina.

The mood in the German camp was not improved by the inopportune criticism of chairman Hermann Neuberger, vice-president of FIFA, always a man with an eye on the political temperature, with a tendency to interpret success as *We* and disappointment as *They*.

ITALY 0, WEST GERMANY 0

Buenos Aires, which had shivered for so much of the first two weeks, was shrouded in a thick sea-mist fog and shortly before the kick-off in mid-afternoon you could not see clearly from one side of the River Plate stadium to the other. The fog seemed to have crept into the rifle-sights of Roberto Bettega, and the story of this match was the string of missed chances by the Juventus winger, two in ten minutes before half-time, another early in the second-half. Had Bettega been on target, Italy would have been able, possibly, to take a different tactical attitude to their two subsequent matches. Twice before half-time he had the chance to put Germany in perspective—

RIVER PLATE
ITALIA: 0 - R.F. ALEMANIA   AUSTR   0

Bettega (*2nd right*), supported by Gentile, appeals for a penalty when West German sweeper Kaltz (*with ball*) appears to have blocked the winger's shot with a hand. Maier, Russmann, Dietz and Holzenbein (*on ground*) bolster Germany's defence in the goal-less draw.

a frightened, fading team which had forsaken many of its principles of positive football. Twice he failed to put the ball past Maier from close in, so that Germany survived for the draw they wanted, a draw which shabbily preserved a route to the final. Their more faithful followers might claim that it was a rearguard action of considerable skill and control, a view to which I cannot subscribe. If this was the behaviour of champions, what price the outsiders?

As the teams fenced for openings and the fog lifted slightly, we learned that Holland were already ahead against Austria in Cordoba, after only six minutes. During this early spell, though Italy controlled the tempo, the chances mainly came in German counter-attacks. Kaltz was attempting to reinforce the front line with sorties up the right. Fischer went close with a far-post header from Bonhof's corner, Zoff saved from Holzenbein, Bonhof glanced a near-post header over the bar from Flohe's corner. But Flohe was being given little space by Benetti, and after half an hour Italy began to emerge. Vogts conceded a corner under pressure from Tardelli, and now came the first of Bettega's openings. Rossi back-heeled on the edge of the penalty area, Vogts slipped and fell trying to turn with Bettega, who raced diagonally to the right evading Dietz, then Maier too. From an angle not too far to the right of the goal Bettega had an empty net at which to aim, but by the time he shot, Kaltz had somehow flung himself back into the goalmouth to block the ball in mid-air.

Two minutes from half-time Scirea—imagine it, an Italian *libero* linking in an attack on the edge of the opposition's penalty area!—knocked across a high centre to the far post which cleared a straining Vogts. Bettega brought the ball down from chest high just behind his 'marker', and from close in stabbed the ball wide. Although Antognoni had had a measure of success in his duel with Bonhof, Zaccarelli appeared for the second half, and soon Schoen replaced Zimmermann with Konopka. Italy were still calling the tune and after 55 minutes again had Germany in real trouble. Cabrini, pushing forward from left-back, hit the crossbar with Maier groping; from the rebound Bettega hooked the ball hard. Did Kaltz, once again admirably covering his goalkeeper, handle the ball? It looked suspiciously as though he did, but Yugoslav referee Duksan Maksimovic was probably unsighted.

Germany at this point were on the ropes, pinned almost in their own penalty area, Russmann bellowing at his colleagues to push out and give some depth between the back line and Maier. There was a moment when Germany had only nine men on the field, with both Fischer and Flohe receiving treatment. Beer, fresh and adventurous, replaced Flohe and over the last 20 minutes Germany began to find equilibrium, might even have scored. They should have had a penalty when Bellugi fouled Fischer quite clearly a yard inside the area, and 10 minutes from the end Fischer missed badly when put through by Beer. Yet Germany had deserved no better from their initial attitude. Italy could count themselves genuinely unlucky, though Bearzot claimed afterwards: 'We did not come here solely to win the championship, but to show how Italy had progressed. We qualified for the Second Round; everything else is a bonus.' Schoen doggedly defended his team's defensiveness, while Causio observed: 'Germany rebuilt the Berlin Wall in Argentina.'

HOLLAND 5, AUSTRIA 1

Austria, surprise package of the Second Round, were possibly thrown out of their stride by the arrival of their wives—a 'treat' from the Austrian Federation for having qualified. It is not unreasonable to assume that this sudden and somewhat odd concession to domestic life in the middle of a championship had something to do with Austria's rout by the Dutch, who for the first time produced a performance in keeping with their reputation. They would claim that the switch to the Cordoba pitch was half the story. One cannot be dogmatic about the reason for Austria's slump. The Dutch themselves had contrived a semi-conjugal existence in 1974, when their camp Hiltrup was just over the border from Holland and it was easy for their wives to travel back and forth from home. Now the Dutch were again on song and although they were without the injured Neeskens and Rijsbergen, although there was alleged to be a rift between the rival elements of Ajax and PSV, they now quickly buried the Austrians, going three up in half an hour.

A steady drizzle just before the start made the pitch a nightmare for defenders, who found themselves sliding in all directions against the pace of Rep and Rensenbrink. But it was a newcomer, the young PSV stopper Erny Brandts, who opened the scoring after six minutes, when he was allowed time and space for a header on the edge of the six-yard area, from a free-kick by Haan. Austria hit back strongly, Jara causing problems for the Dutch defence down the left wing, Krankl seeing a couple of chances slip by. But any hope of an Austrian upsurge was smothered

130

by two goals in a minute. Jansen was pulled down by Prohaska and Rensenbrink calmly hit his fourth penalty of the tournament. Then, almost straight from the kick-off, Rensenbrink went past full-back Sara on the left, centred, and Rep with marvellous dexterity lobbed the ball over the advancing Koncilia.

This was more the real Holland instead of yesterday's men we had seen in the First Round. Nine minutes into the second-half, after Prohaska had missed a fine chance for Austria, the Dutch sliced open the opposition, again the two wingers combining in sweet unison : Rensenbrink going through on the right, pulling the ball back for Rep to do the rest. Obermeyer scrambled one for Austria, Willy K. hit Holland's fifth—and even the stonefaced Ernst Happel could afford a half smile. They were in fine shape, it appeared, for their repeat of the 1974 Final in their next match : not least, they had established a priceless advantage in goal-difference over rivals Italy and Germany.

BRAZIL 3, PERU 0

With the burden of a nation's near-hysterical ambitions weighing them down, Brazil travelled uneasily from one difficult pitch at Mar del Plata to another at Mendoza ; but at least their opponents at the start of the second round, Peru, were generally regarded as a South American soft touch. With Rivelino injured—and probably dropped had he not been—with Zico and Reinaldo on the bench, Brazil duly won a somewhat flattering match, their third victory over these rivals in just over 12 months. If Peru had had their luck in the First Round, it now turned against them.

A spectacular free-kick by Dirceu (*centre-background*) beats Peru's wall and keeper Ramon Quiroga, for Brazil's first goal in the 3–0 win at Mendoza.

Navarro had to replace full-back Diaz after only four minutes when he pulled a muscle and before half-time Oblitas was injured and replaced by Rojas. Marcos Calderon claimed afterwards: 'These early injuries obliged us to change our whole pattern.' But no pattern could have influenced Brazil's first goal.

In the 15th minute Dirceu took a free-kick from 23 yards and scored with such a wickedly curving shot that, had it not gone into the net, it seemed it would have curved right back on itself like a boomerang. The ball screamed over the defensive wall and though Quiroga had it covered, it bent out of his reach, hitting the inside of the side-netting even though having been struck from a position wide of the left-hand post!

Shortly afterwards Peru might have equalized when Oblitas, still threatening at this stage, cut in from the left and shot just wide; then again when Munante struck the ball against a defender from 14 yards. Just on the half-hour, Dirceu scored a second, accelerating through a gap and letting fly a low shot which found Quiroga at fault. But even though two up, Brazil were not safe. Before half-time Leao had to save expertly from La Rosa and then Cueto; and for 20 minutes at the start of the second-half Brazil were on the rack as Cubillas, emerging from a quiet first-half, wrested the midfield from Dirceu. Oscar and his *libero* Amaral were at full stretch, twice La Rosa beat Leao but saw the ball flash wide; and it was not until the 65th minute that Brazil again forced Peru back, Roberto shooting just over the bar from a good position on the left of the penalty area. Peru's hopes were crushed five minutes later when Duarte fouled Roberto and Zico, who a few minutes earlier had replaced Cerezo, scored from the penalty spot. Coutinho said afterwards: 'It was hard work, but for the first time we have found our rhythm, and the collective spirit which has always characterized Brazil's play.' True, but they were still a long way off their own previous peaks; and besides, they had only ever lost twice in history to Peru, whose advance they had halted at the same stage in 1970.

ARGENTINA 2, POLAND 0

Argentina's still hesitant progress towards the Final hinged on two vital moments in their opening game in Rosario: a brilliantly taken goal in the 16th minute by Kempes—one of the best in the competition, by him or anyone else—and the wretchedly missed penalty, 20 minutes later, by Poland's captain Kazimierz Deyna in his 100th international.

Poland, in fact, might well have had a penalty a minute before the stunning opening goal by Kempes, Tarantini bringing down Boniek a stride inside the area. The goal at the other end was perfection. Bertoni, from wide on the left, drifted a dipping cross towards the near post. Kempes, coming from the right-hand side of the penalty area on a diagonal run, escaped his marker, Zmuda, and met the ball with timing which the great Hungarian Kocsis could not have bettered 20 years before.

Poland hit back. A dangerous cross from Lato was just too far for Szarmach; Fillol saved at full stretch from Boniek and was hurt in the process. At the other end Bertoni, with a three-quarter turn near the penalty spot, was just wide. The penalty came as Fillol failed to hold a free-kick by Deyna, Tarantini partially cleared, Lato headed back: and Kempes, defending on his own goal line, fisted the ball away. Deyna hit the kick weakly and Fillol, blatantly moving early, was able to save comfortably. Poor though the kick was, Swedish referee Ulf Ericsson should have ordered a re-take.

In the second-half Menotti replaced Valencia with Villa, but it was Poland who should have scored, Boniek twice missing good chances from close range, Lato squandering another. With 20 minutes to go, Argentina moved out of reach with a second goal. The dapper Ardiles weaved his way past a trail of Poles, found himself cut off by Zmuda and slipped the ball left to Kempes. With lightning change of stride on the edge of the area, Kempes went round Maculewicz and swept the ball wide of Tomaszewski for his second goal of the match and the tournament. Poland lost heart and their last chance died when a free-kick by Lato was brilliantly saved by Fillol. Only poor finishing by Bertoni and Houseman, and even once by Kempes when clean through, denied Argentina a wider margin. Menotti admitted afterwards: 'I don't want to dramatize our performance. We made mistakes in the first-half. I introduced Villa in the second because he has been so impressive in training. I am convinced we can play better still in our remaining matches. We shall continue to use defenders to attack whenever possible.' Jacek Gmoch reflected: 'We failed to take our chances in the first-half, and Tomaszewski was undoubtedly affected by the proximity of the crowd behind the goal. Without our own errors, we would not have lost.'

ITALY 1, AUSTRIA 0

After the first phase of Second-Round matches in both Groups A and B, the position remained wide open for any two of five teams to reach the Final. Italy substantially strengthened their position by defeating Austria, but it was a tired and laboured team compared with that which had dominated for most of the time against Germany. Once Rossi had scored in the 13th minute, Italy forgot all their newly acquired notions of positive attack, and reverted to a more familiar containing game, dull and efficient, closing down the middle of the field. Gentile marked Kreuz out of the game; Krankl was allowed hardly a shot in the whole match. Senekowitsch, inevitably, had made changes after the collapse against Holland, but the newcomers, Strasser in defence and Schachner in attack, steadied the team rather than inspired it. And in fact it was Strasser who presented Italy with their goal. A move down Italy's right wing began with Rossi back-heeling to Causio, who accelerated clear. Rossi sprinted wide for the return pass, but though Strasser got to the ball first he failed to control it; Rossi dispossessed him, cut into the penalty area with Strasser in pursuit, and shot across the front of the advancing Koncilia just inside the far post a split second before Strasser's sliding tackle brought him down.

From now on, a lack of commitment going forward from both sides led to stalemate. Koncilia was outstanding in the Austrian goal, Prohaska a sharp disappointment in midfield. Graziani, brought on as substitute for Bettega for the last 20 minutes for his first taste of action, undermined any possibility of permanent re-instatement when he squandered a chance from eight yards as Koncilia cleverly put him under pressure. The River Plate crowd whistled and jeered, impatient for

action—not to say for events in Rosario later that evening involving a small question with Brazil.

A smile from Paolo Rossi as he beats Strasser and Austrian keeper Koncilia for the only goal at River Plate.

HOLLAND 2, WEST GERMANY 2

To defend their title, and their pride, against the Dutch, Schoen made further changes in the German line-up for the match in Cordoba which was to prove one of the most absorbing of the 38 played in Argentina. Beer remained in place of Flohe, already on his way home with a bad injury. Zimmermann, also injured, made way for Abramczik and a return to 4–3–3; Dieter Muller replaced the off-colour Fischer. Holland were still without the injured Neeskens, and Schrijvers was preferred to Jongbloed in goal, so that they had only five of the side which lost the 1974 Final, and Germany only four.

This time it was the Germans who scored an early goal, Abramczik diving forward to head home the loose ball as Schrijvers failed to hold Bonhof's hammer-blow free-kick after only three minutes. Holland proceeded to throw their all at the opposition in sweet unison and were rewarded when Arie Haan equalized in the 27th minute with a shot which would not be bettered in the whole tournament. Charging at the defence through the middle like an angry bull, Haan let rip from 25 yards and Maier was almost motionless as the ball flew past his left shoulder—the first time he had been beaten in the tournament. Earlier, to his credit,

134

Maier had made a superb save from Rensenbrink. Soon afterwards, Rep, from close range, volleyed wide as Rensenbrink caught the defence going the wrong way with a header across the goalmouth. Two free-kicks by Bonhof at the other end had Schrijvers shaking in his boots. It was anybody's game, but with Vogts, Kaltz and Russmann more stable than they had been against Italy, Germany seemed at this stage well capable of repeating their victory of four years earlier. The Dutch, in fact, had not beaten them since 1956.

Holland continued to dominate the game, morally, in the second half, sailing in on Maier with the wind at their backs. The van der Kerkhofs were shaking off their chains, René shooting just over the bar from 25 yards; and now the Germans were on the ropes for a while. But it was they who regained the lead again in the 70th minute, little Beer working free on the left, crossing the ball just in front of the penalty spot and Dieter Muller, eluding Brandts, heading down and back towards the near post, forcing Schrijvers to twist vainly in mid-air. Five minutes later Rep hit the bar and, just when Holland seemed to be heading for another totally undeserved defeat, they were rescued by a second superb goal. René K. put them back not only in the game but in the World Cup with seven minutes to spare. Cutting in from the left he went round Kaltz and hit a swerving shot which bent past Maier out of reach. Russmann, lunging back in a vain attempt to usurp his keeper's privilege, got a hand to the ball, but could only help it into the net.

It was a tremendous climax. Just beforehand Beer had hit the crossbar at the other end; now Krol smacked a free-kick against Maier's post—but the kick had to be re-taken. A superb duel of European skills and tactical wits ended with Dutch substitute Dirk Nanninga being sent off two minutes from time: for laughing! Finding himself about to be booked by Barreto of Uruguay for a less than severe clash with Holzenbein, he reacted with that slightly superior, amused attitude with which the Dutch tend to view authority—and found the yellow card substituted by a red one. Schoen agreed afterwards that his team was not up to its previous standard but insisted: 'We have not yet lost a match.' They had not yet won one that mattered. He and Happel were agreed it was one of the best matches so far, but Happel warned: 'Whatever the state of our team, I consider that Argentina are improving all the time.'

POLAND 1, PERU 0

No one seriously supposed that either of these teams were still in contention for a place in the Final, but Poland kept their chances alive, marginally, in a match at Mendoza which they dominated but which could have gone the other way. The decisive influence was probably the hold exerted by full-backs Szymanowski and Maculewicz on Peru's wingers Oblitas and Munante. Not the least significance of the result was that it enabled Argentina to know that a draw with Brazil later in the evening would be satisfactory.

Early on, English referee Pat Partridge booked Peruvian defender Manzo for a foul on Szarmach—following which Deyna went close with the free-kick. Szarmach had a goal disallowed; Quiroga saved from Boniek; a diving header by Lato went two feet wide, as Poland controlled the first half. In the second the Poles always had a slight edge yet, as in almost every match, remained reluctant to take risks. Gorgon was booked for a foul on Cubillas but finally, in the 65th minute, Szarmach scored a superb goal. Lato robbed defender Navarro, hit an early centre and Szarmach, sprinting forward level with the far post, flung himself headlong to connect with a diving header nine yards out. A minute later Deyna hit a post, Lato struck the rebound straight at Quiroga—who saved again full length from Lato at the end of a five-man move. But with five minutes to go Cubillas was just too high with a 19-yard free-kick which singed the crossbar; and the game ended in a desperate onslaught by Peru, with Quiroga booked for grabbing an opponent out near the halfway line as he took on the role of *libero* behind a defence desperately surging forward—in vain.

ARGENTINA 0, BRAZIL 0

The prelude to the clash of South American giants at Rosario was highlighted by the thinly concealed row between Coutinho and his ageing, moody genius Rivelino. As Pele had stated for some months, Brazil's main shortcoming was the lack of somebody up front to put away the chances. All too conscious of this fact, Coutinho had wanted to use Rivelino in a striking left-wing position. But the chain-smoking, brooding star of 1970 preferred to see himself as the great 'game-maker' in midfield—where his loss of speed and disinclination to work made such ambition out of the question. His conceit apparently exceeding his patriotism, Rivelino refused to make the compromise which might have saved Coutinho's neck—and found himself merely on the substitute's bench, in spite of asserting: 'I have not come to Argentina as a tourist; I have come as a player.' It was not certain whether the ankle injury which had kept him out of the previous three games had been an ailment of convenience, while Menotti had stated patronizingly before the announcement of Brazil's team: 'If he is the same Rivelino I knew in 1974, he is dangerous. If he is the same as we have seen him here, it does not worry me.'

It was eight years since Argentina last beat Brazil, who had won five of the last six encounters. On a night of over-loaded tension, Argentina were more than happy to settle for a draw. The opening exchanges were so hostile, so charged with emotion that it at first seemed that the referee, Karoly Palotai of Hungary, would be swamped: six fouls in the first three minutes, 14 in the first 12; and no booking. Within only ten seconds Luque, returning after injury and the death of his brother in a road accident, went clattering into Batista, a wild assault which was quickly repaid by Oscar, Brazil's stopper. The players were doing no more than respond to the frenzy in the streets, which had been jammed with every inhabitant of Rosario from midday onwards, chanting, whistling and banging kettles with an expectation which flooded all sanity. Every wizened, black-shawled granny, every flag-waving bemused two-year-old was caught up in the great surge of nationalism which was now distilled into the vulnerable skills of 22 men and an umpire.

Menotti decided this time to play Luque between wingers Bertoni and Ortiz, with Kempes attacking from a midfield role on the left; but Kempes, on this occasion, was seldom in the game, and Luque too, perhaps still troubled by his arm injury, was rarely threatening. Brazil, needing to win, desperate not to lose, cleverly slowed the game, yet regularly released Gil on spectacular runs down the right flank where he had the beating of Tarantini. After a quarter of an hour or so Palotai had begun to achieve some authority with the whistle; and the next busiest man on the field was Fillol. His save from Gil in the 16th minute was one of the sharpest and certainly the most critical in all the finals. Dirceu beat two men and put Gil clear of Argentina's back line. Pounding through, with a clear gap visible between Fillol and the right-hand post, Gil struck a powerful shot from 16 yards, low and close to Fillol's legs, the most difficult of all spots for the 'keeper. Yet somehow he dropped on the ball and held it, and the dense crowd growled with relief.

Brazil, emerging as a unit for the first time—still masters of angle and weight of pass—played most of the football in the first half, controlling the middle of the pitch. But it was Argentina who had the next, glaring, opening. Bertoni scorched past Edinho and raced 40 yards, Edinho in pursuit, before cutting the ball square across the middle of the penalty area to where Ortiz had arrived from the opposite flank. Taking the ball on the outside of his left foot from only eight yards, with Leao caught still covering the other post, Ortiz steered it well wide; the whole country groaned. Just before half-time Ardiles was hurt, twisting an ankle, and was replaced by the venomous Villa. Moments later Chicao, a player of equally severe appearance and even more severe reputation, was booked for a foul on Kempes.

At the start of the second-half rain began to fall; Edinho chopped Villa, who was almost immediately booked for a foul on Batista. There was little more space on the pitch than there was on the terraces. Edinho was booked for time-wasting, though on that basis Palotai might have booked all 22. Zico came on for Mendonca, and soon created a good chance for Roberto, who delayed his shot and finally hit the ball against Galvan. Brazil still had the whip hand, and must have wished they had anyone but Roberto, when he hooked wide a glorious chance with four minutes

Erny Brandts (*on ground*), under pressure from Bettega (*right*), strikes the ball past his own keeper Piet Schrijvers to put Italy one up. Schrijvers collided with Brandts and went off injured; but Holland won 2–1.

to go. Just before that Leao had dived courageously at the feet of Luque to cut out a cross from Bertoni.

Italian keeper Dino Zoff floored by Arie Haan's long-range winner for Holland.

A draw had always been the most likely result: now, in the remaining matches in Group B, to reach the final on goal-difference Argentina had to beat Peru by one goal more than Brazil's score against Poland . . . *if* Brazil beat Poland. Coutinho expressed his dissatisfaction with the arrangement—FIFA being more concerned with finance and TV than a fair competition—by which Brazil would have to kick off two and a half hours before Argentina, to Argentina's great advantage. Menotti, reasonably, pointed out that Brazil's result against Poland could make Argentina either calm or really nervous. He politely offered the opinion that Brazil's chief qualities were defensive, and that the best team Argentina had so far played was France!

HOLLAND 2, ITALY 1

Enzo Bearzot had told me, after Italy's fine exhibition against Germany: 'Holland have expressed the best football so far; they have a tactical vision ahead of most teams.' He would not be in such a generous mood after the defeat by the Dutch which crushed Italy's dreams of the Final. Holland were of the opinion, when I spoke to them out at their training camp at Moreno—where there was another dreary process of having your press accreditation re-identified—that this game would be harder than the comparable 'semi-final' against Brazil in 1974. Neeskens

138

said: 'Italy have everything—technique, finishing power, strength, experience.'
Ernst Happel and his skipper Rudi Krol agreed that Holland would have to go for
a win. Even though a draw would see them into the Final, barring some goal
explosion by Germany against Austria, 'to play for a draw will be too risky.'

Happel planned to drop young Piet Wildschut and recall Wim Jansen for a marking role, with Neeskens returning in midfield after injury. What was not apparent
out at Moreno, as the Dutch played tennis, conducted their multi-lingual press conference and sipped lager, was the growing streak of ruthlessness. It was seemingly
not apparent to Spanish referee Angel Martinez, who allowed Holland the licence
to do much as they pleased. 'Mr Martinez was slow to realize that the Dutch in-
vented the clog,' observed the admirable David Lacey in *The Guardian*.

Frankly, though, no side boasting Benetti and Tardelli in midfield will glean too
much sympathy as the recipients of strong-arm stuff; and the fact is that Holland
gave Italy a goal start and then beat them with more switches than a telephone
exchange. For half an hour there was only one team in it as Italy held every ace
from one penalty area to the other. The Dutch midfield of Jansen, Willy K. and
Haan was nowhere to be seen; Krol was working overtime to shore up breaches
in the dyke; Bettega was pouring past young Brandts as if he were not there. Holland's only counter-strike in that first half-hour was a header over the bar by Rensenbrink from the penalty spot from a cross by Willy K.

In the 18th minute Benetti forged through, beating the offside trap, and presented
an open goal to Causio—who was himself a foot offside. A minute later Italy were
in front. Benetti freed Bettega past the stricken Dutch defence, Brandts made a
despairing lunge from behind in an attempt to nudge the ball back to Schrijvers
. . . and knocked it past him into the goal, the pair colliding and Jongbloed having
to come on as substitute in goal. Rossi, twice, and Benetti both had good chances

Victory sign from
Arie Haan, who
scored the winner
against Italy,
together with two-
goal Erny Brandts
(one own-goal!).

soon afterwards. Still Holland struggled. Rep was booked for putting his boot in Benetti's stomach; then Benetti was booked for a foul on Rensenbrink, his second yellow card which would put him out of either the Final or third-place match.

For the second-half Bearzot replaced Causio with Claudio Sala, a decision he defended on the grounds that the physical state of the game demanded it. The fact was that Italy were never again the same fluid force, but this could not be attributed exclusively to either the substitution, or Holland's burst of renewed intimidation. Three minutes after the interval Zoff turned the ball over the bar from Brandts, and was unmercifully battered simultaneously by Rensenbrink and Neeskens—who had now switched from his surprise role in the first half, marking Rossi, to his normal position in midfield.

Zoff was still shaken two minutes later when Brandts gave Total Football a new twist by scoring the second goal of the match . . . to equalize! Krol hit the ball hard into the penalty area, Gentile lost it, and Brandts, lashing out without even a glance at goal, was as astonished as anyone to see the ball flash into the net. A minute after that Haan was booked for the most shameful foul of the match, on Zaccarelli, and should have been sent off. But Neeskens now had the Italian midfield on the run, attacking them at every turn, sapping their already draining strength with burning runs, which made them wince as if with the approach of the dentist's drill. Rossi had a goal disallowed for offside, and a huge roar greeted the scoreboard revelation that Germany and Austria were level 2–2.

A draw, Holland now knew, was good enough; and Happel's acceptance of this was plain when he replaced Rep with Van Kraaij, the PSV *libero*. As Italy's nerves frayed, Tardelli was booked; he too would miss the third-place match. And Haan,

Austrian centre-forward Krankl moves between Kaltz (5) and Russman, to hit the winner in a 3–2 win—Austria's first against Germany since 1931.

to close the match on a flourish, took a short free-kick from Neeskens, galloped at the Italian goal, and beat Zoff with another of those blistering 30-yard specials. In vain did Bearzot protest afterwards: 'To contain our superiority in the first half the Dutch fouled us, and the second half was even worse. The referee encouraged them. Haan's foul on Zaccarelli was the worst I've seen in the World Cup, unspeakably spiteful.' Bearzot, clearly, had been looking the other way when Tardelli cut down Pinter of Hungary. It was no use Bearzot, who had tried so diligently to civilize the Italian leopard, now crying 'wolf'.

AUSTRIA 3, WEST GERMANY 2

Germany finally surrendered their title in their first defeat by Austria since the Wunder-team of Hugo Meisl won 5–0 in Vienna, in 1931. In 12 subsequent matches there had, indeed, been only three draws, but now the Austrians were spurred to one last flourish by the dismissive previews of the match in the German press. On the day, in Cordoba, it was the Germans who were without personality and leadership, Krankl sealing his imminent transfer to Barcelona with the winning goal three minutes from time.

Long before the finish there were cries of 'Bonhof out' from the German supporters, and even Schoen was moved to say afterwards: 'This tournament would have been better for us if Bonhof had played as he did in 1974.' But there was more to Germany's failure than merely Bonhof. In six months, Schoen had seen his team suffer more defeats than in the previous six years.

In spite of an inept opening, Germany took the lead after 19 minutes when Rummenigge ran into a gap for Dieter Muller's return and placed his shot wide of Koncilia. Yet although Prohaska controlled the midfield for Austria with his most authoritative display so far, they did not draw level until the hour; and then with an own goal when Vogts, under pressure from Kreuz, deflected Schachner's header past Maier. Soon Krankl scored his first with a firm volley from Krieger's cross, only for Holzenbein to equalize with an unopposed header from Bonhof's free-kick. Prohaska, Sara and Abramczik were booked as play became frenzied, but Krankl was calm enough as he weaved through for the winner. In his final press conference as a World Cup manager, Schoen said sadly, tongue in cheek: 'I thank the press for their suggestions, but it is my belief that we would not have achieved better results by changing the players. Austria's victory came as no surprise to us, because we knew they would be very difficult. We were not guilty of euphoria.'

BRAZIL 3, POLAND 1

Though they struggled at times against Poland, Brazil precipitated a night of high tension for themselves and Argentina with a victory of sufficient margin to put real pressure on the hosts when they kicked off against Peru shortly afterwards. A full house in Mendoza, cheering the Poles to the echo, was plunged into dismay when the burly Roberto smashed in the two goals in five minutes around the hour which temporarily gave Brazil a ticket to the Final.

Zico, who had been impressive as substitute for the last 20 minutes against Argen-

tina, was back in the Brazilian front line, and it was a blow when he was injured early on in a tackle by Kasperczak, and carried off. Although returning, he soon limped off again to be replaced by Mendonca. Undeterred, Brazil went ahead in the 13th minute with a devastating free-kick by full-back Nelinho, who curved the ball round the face of the defensive wall, diagonally from left to right, and into the net before Kukla, Poland's deputy goalkeeper, could move. Poland were undeterred, and fought back with spirit and clarity, but it was not until a minute before half-time that they drew level. The move began deep in Brazil's half, Boniek and Deyna combining cleverly, Boniek bursting into the penalty area, being blocked, and Lato squeezing the ball home through a crowd of legs. After half-time Poland continued where they had left off, attacking strongly. A perfect move between Lato and Szarmach ended with Deyna flashing a shot only just wide of the post. Brazil were rattled; Mendonca and Cerezo were booked within minutes of each other. Poland seemed poised to do Argentina a sizeable favour. The crowd in the beautiful pine-surrounded stadium was heaving with glee.

Suddenly they were silenced by a goal out of the blue. With a speculative shot from a position of comparative innocence, Mendonca crashed the ball against the post. From the rebound Roberto, reacting with more co-ordination than usual, knocked it home. Five minutes later, with Brazil's own supporters now raising a frenzied samba-beat beneath their green and gold banners in the stand, Roberto scored again. It was, in its way, one of the most remarkable goals in the competition. Dirceu, the mainspring of almost all Brazil's success during four nerve-racking weeks, pulled the ball back from the line. First Gil and then Mendonca hammered the ball against the woodwork, and finally it was Roberto who was on target as Poland lurched about like ninepins.

Which way did it go? Polish defenders reel as Brazil right-back Nelinho blasts a free-kick for the first goal. Gorgon (6) prefers not to look, skipper Deyna (*far left*) winces.

142

Soon afterwards Cerezo struck a shot against Kukla, the game having now turned on its head. With ten minutes to go, Leao was a hero as he preserved Brazil's essential goal-difference with a plunging, full-length save from Lubanski. In the closing moments Oscar cleared off the line; Gorgon shot wide as the Poles flung in everything; Nelinho eased the pressure on Brazil with another free-kick which Kukla turned over the top. It was a nervous celebration which Brazil now began for the next hour or so. Jacek Gmoch said firmly: 'I wish to stress that Brazil did not beat Poland; it was Poland that lost the match. I cannot understand how Gorgon could miss from three metres.' Coutinho, scarcely able to endure the anxiety of the next couple of hours, deferred questions on Brazil's performance to his captain, Leao.

ARGENTINA 6, PERU 0

The rumours, the slander, the innuendo, were thick in the air long before Argentina went dive-bombing into their 'Pearl Harbour' annihilation of hapless Peru. At the centre of the smear campaign, of course, was Peru's goalkeeper, Argentinian-born 'El Loco'—the crazy one. Up to this moment Quiroga had rather caught the imagination of a worldwide public with his many fine saves, his antics, his sorties to the halfway line. It is possible that Brazilians deliberately set in motion the rumours that Quiroga would leave his door on the latch for Argentina, simply to sting him into the game of his life. The keeper himself said beforehand: 'It has always been my dream to come back and play international football against Argentina, but I am sorry it had to happen under these circumstances. I know that if I do my job well I will become the most hated man in the country.'

Forecasters of Peruvian perfidy were of, course, overlooking an obvious factor—that Peru, without a point from their first two Second Round matches, had little incentive plus an inborn sense of inferiority whenever they met Argentina or Brazil. Seldom was there a more ready-made invitation to capitulate. The mathematics as the game began were that, with a goal-difference of 2–0 compared with Brazil's newly acquired tally of 6–1, Argentina now needed to win by 4–0 or 5–1. Though 3–0 would give them the same goal-difference, Brazil would qualify by having scored one goal more.

There was no suspicion of a Peruvian sell-out; for 20 minutes they attacked like fury. In the 11th minute Munante roasted Tarantini on the outside and blazed the ball against Fillol's left-hand post. Shortly afterwards Oblitas cut in from the other wing, and from an angle sent a cross-shot scudding wide of Fillol and just past the far post. Tarantini revealed Argentina's anxiety as he went clattering into Munante without any rebuke from French referee Robert Wurtz. (Another factor overlooked by the cynics was that if Mr Wurtz could be expected to show leanings they would be, one supposed, towards Peru, since he enjoyed a long-standing and friendly relationship with the CBD.) The truth, I am convinced—together with the majority of my international press colleagues with whom I discussed the question—is that the result on this tumultuous night in Rosario was determined by natural forces: by the psychological factors which drive, or undermine, any team.

After a quarter of an hour it was clear that Peru had moved into a dangerous phase of false security, indulging in their favourite, fancy short passes, even around their own penalty area. They were the tactics of doom. In the 21st minute Bertoni and Kempes combined with Passarella, whose final pass sent Kempes clear of Manso to sweep the ball low into the corner, with Velasquez giving vain chase. The floodgates were open.

For the next 20 minutes Peru were torn apart; but had they been party to some conspiracy they would surely not have held out for even that long. Luque and Olguin both hit a post; Quiroga dived this way and that, flinging himself at the feet of galloping forwards; Ortiz and Bertoni both went close. Menotti, dead-pan gambler, had moved Passarella in front of a back line of three, to reinforce the middle and give Kempes greater freedom to stream forward. With Ardiles still injured, Larrosa partnered Gallego. Approaching half-time, Passarella headed just wide from six yards under pressure, Quiroga saved superbly from Larrosa. In the 43rd minute, from Bertoni's corner, Tarantini, unmarked 12 yards out, headed home as Kempes, Gallego and Chumpitaz all jumped and missed.

The issue was put beyond doubt, and Argentina's margin achieved, when Kempes and Luque scored twice in three minutes at the start of the second half. The first was a superb goal. Peru, refusing to sink without a fight, gave away a succession of free-kicks. From the third by Olguin, Kempes chested the ball down and took a short wall-pass from Bertoni. Deceiving three defenders, Rojas, Manzo and Velasquez, with his devastating pace, Kempes lashed the ball wide of Quiroga. Then, from a cross by Larrosa, Passarella headed square from beyond the right-hand post back over Quiroga; and Luque, diving forward only a yard from the line, headed into a gaping goal. I had thought initially the goal was offside, but pictures in *El Grafico* magazine showed conclusively it was not. Houseman, with his first touch after coming on as substitute for Bertoni after 64 minutes, scored the fifth as Ortiz accelerated powerfully between Duarte and Manzo. Luque knocked in a sixth: and for the sixth time in a month the streets of the whole country throbbed till dawn with wildly excited humanity. Menotti said after the match: 'We played as we should have done on previous occasions—all or nothing. If Brazil could score three goals against Peru with two strikers, it was easy for Argentina to score twice that number with five attackers.'

Third-Place Match

BRAZIL 2, ITALY 1

Disgruntled if not bitter, Brazil for the second time in four years found themselves disputing the match for third place: an indignity by definition. The accusations of corruption between Peru and Argentina rumbled on, so that the great Pele was driven to complain: 'My people are losing their dignity. They should consider themselves fortunate to reach the last four. Must we, as Brazilians, sink so low as to allow a smoke-screen to hide the real reason for Brazil's failure to reach the final? The truth, quite simply, is that we were not good enough.'

Pele had maintained for some months that Brazil lacked the necessary striking power. Yet in the most entertaining match for third place in memory—so superior to previous encounters, Poland–Brazil ('74), West Germany–Uruguay ('70), Por-

Italian winger Franco Causio heads opening goal past Leao in Third Place match, which Brazil won 2–1.

tugal–Russia ('66), Chile–Yugoslavia ('62)—Brazil demonstrated clearly that, had they scored the goals they earned against Argentina six days before, they would have contested, and quite possibly won, the Final against Holland. The last half-hour, after Rivelino belatedly took the stage as substitute for Cerezo following Nelinho's equalizing goal, fleetingly recalled Brazil's former glories. Even Rivelino unfit was something to make the pulse race, especially that moment of sublime vision in which he set Brazil in motion for the winning goal. Here were Brazil playing once again in their own unique style, the way they know how—the style to which their supporters and their own skills spontaneously respond. The question mark over Coutinho's controversial attempts to reform Brazilian tactics was never larger than in their most satisfying performance of, for them, a wretchedly unsatisfactory tournament. The defeat of Italy was more than a matter of two bull's-eye bullet-shots from Nelinho and Dirceu.

Brazil were booed onto the pitch at the River Plate stadium, hardly surprisingly, and there were cheers when Mendonca shot wide from a good position after a quarter of an hour. Yet as Brazil's football slowly gathered momentum like violins in symphony, the instinctive humanity of the Argentinian people warmed sufficiently to applaud the men who are their direst rivals. Italy, their capacity for mental concentration already spent, their cohesion disrupted by the suspension of Benetti and Tardelli, began the game more with an eye on survival than prestige. When they scored after 38 minutes it was against the run of play. Roberto, at the other end, was twice fouled inside the penalty area, and twice Abraham Klein ignored the foul. Often uncharacteristically far behind the play, Klein gave the impression that he was merely going through the motions; that, like Brazil, he considered the Final was his rightful platform. Straight from the second foul on Roberto, Antognoni broke clear and put Rossi away on the right wing. The dark, quicksilver striker went round Amaral—a rare achievement—and floated a high, hanging cross over to the far post where Causio, inexplicably unchallenged, headed a simple goal. Given this encouragement, Italy might have scored twice more before half-time. Rossi and Causio cut the defence open; Leao failed to hold a header by Causio, who smacked the ball against the crossbar from the rebound. When Cuccureddu put Rossi clear, the centre-forward went round the advancing Leao, but his momentum had taken him too far wide and, from an angle, he missed an empty goal.

It was a different tale in the second-half. Now Italy were on the retreat, all too evident in bad fouls by Scirea and Gentile on Mendonca and Roberto; both again were ignored by Klein. In the 63rd minute, from a position of no apparent threat way out on the right wing, full-back Nelinho hit a storming, swerving drive which Zoff saw all the way but never looked like reaching. Now Rivelino began to conduct

Dirceu leaps high after hitting the winner to give Brazil Third Place, from cross by Rivelino (11), who receives hug from Amaral. Inset (*top left*). The pain of beaten Italian keeper Zoff.

the orchestra and eight minutes later laid Italy bare for the kill. With a glorious side-step over the ball, which sent two defenders lurching the wrong way, and without even a glance upwards, he swept the ball from the left, in a wide curve to Mendonca, who chested the ball down and back for Dirceu to pounce and belt in the winner. Italy reacted angrily to the spectre of defeat; Gentile was booked. Brazil's tackling also became ferocious. With two minutes to go, Bettega made a final gesture as he hit the bar from Causio's chip.

CHAPTER TEN
Man of Vision

ARGENTINA 3, HOLLAND 1 (after extra-time)

It is, in prospect, one of the most fascinating finals ever: the confrontation of Argentina's irresistible yet vulnerable, compulsive yet suspect policy of attack, against the tactically most sophisticated team on earth, Holland. Argentina, the team with the tournament's most exciting player, volcanic Mario Kempes; Holland, without Johan Cruyff but with a side containing half a dozen other players capable of scoring great goals. Cesar Luis Menotti, a man with vision of rare glory carrying a nation on his back; Ernst Happel, the mercenary, pragmatist, as unemotional as marble, fired by the *idea* of victory more than by the smell of gunpowder.

The days of anticipation are almost as gripping, it seems, as the match itself—until the match begins. Out at Argentina's encampment at José C. Paz, behind an armada of security guards and police, where every tree in the car park camouflages an automatic machine-gun, the mood of the players carries something of the mission of their manager. Passarella and his team have not the same urbane, relaxed, men-of-the-world air which pervades the Dutch at Moreno. Ardiles, sleek, small-boned, more a cross between tango-dancer and jockey than a world-class footballer, treads lightly on his injured ankle through training, nervously evades direct questions about his chances of playing. Left-back Tarantini voices the fears latent in his colleagues when he says: 'The traditional gap between European and South American concepts of the game makes me worry. Holland are hard. They are very strong and tackle powerfully. I'm not saying they have evil intent, but we are worried about what we saw in the Italy–Holland match.'

Luque, still mourning his brother, is quiet and withdrawn, arms folded, matter-of-fact, but shifting edgily from one foot to another. Kempes, for all the swarm of photographers and microphones besieging him, seems to have a happy acceptance of the colossal responsibility thrust at him. Passarella, dominating his crowd of interviewers, has if anything even more of a captain's aura off the field than on.

In an open barn, behind a counter where ample Argentinian ladies of middle-age are somehow coping with the impossible demands of serving coffee to 300 journalists out of one kettle and a dozen cups, Menotti stands surrounded by more microphones than Nixon at his capitulation. Tension hangs in the air like the thunderstorms which have rumbled round Buenos Aires for the last week, rendering hazardous these journeys out of town by flooding the underpasses on the motorways, so that four-lane streams of traffic are suddenly confronted by buses and lorries lumbering towards them in the wrong direction because ahead the road is impassable. Patiently, Menotti handles his interrogation; it is on his terms, not his interrogators'. He has a natural, theatrical presence—an obvious leader, not easily sidetracked. Drawing heavily on his 2000th cigarette of the 1978 World Cup, he makes the unequivocal promise: 'We will attack flat out.' So the fuse is lit for Argentina to take their place alongside the other truly original teams of the past 25 years: Hungary, Brazil and Holland. Menotti says: 'Holland have superior physical strength, but we will continue to take the same risks, to go straight for victory. We have achieved more than I dared hope for three months ago. The Final will be decided by possession. Holland's total football is probably unanswerable at its peak—but they have to get the ball first! I'm scared because of the way Holland played against Italy, but in spite of this we will attack from the start.'

At Moreno, Happel faces the media with a kind of half-suppressed intolerance, an attitude somewhat akin to Sir Alf Ramsey's which used to say, I am a professional, what do you amateurs understand of the intricacies of the modern game. Yet the appeal of Holland's 'intellectual' game is as powerful for the public as the new surging excitement produced by Argentina. Happel, almost smug says: 'We are optimistic. My players do not know what the word "fear" means. We do not care which team Menotti chooses.' His players themselves are more specific.

Rudi Krol, eloquent skipper with just a trace of nervousness in the eyes, reveals the thinking which in retrospect will explain Holland's ferocious opening. He tells me: 'Four years ago in Germany we played the better football and lost. We are not prepared to accept that again. The emotional crowd factor favours them, the physical factor favours us.' The fantasy of Dutch football stumbled in 1974 against the resolute and predictable efficiency of West Germany. They know now it will require more than intellect if they are not to be swamped by Argentina's capacity for sustained onslaught.

Willy K. predicts: 'Happel will want us to lock them up in the middle of the field. South American teams must not be allowed the freedom to flow. We can make them struggle in midfield where they are less strong, and hit them hard in the counter-attack.' Haan, Jansen, Neeskens and Willy K. know all about locking up, if anyone does.

Rensenbrink, the man to whom Dutch fans looked to take over from Cruyff, says guardedly: 'It was silly for people to expect me to assume Johan's role. I do not have the personality or character to be his substitute. Besides, we must look to the future and it is pointless to lament the fact that he isn't here. The one country I did not want to face in the final was Argentina. They will have the crowd behind them. They are strong physically and mentally. Obviously it will be hard for us, but our side can match anyone for skill and we have the experience needed for such an occasion.' Back to Menotti for the last word: 'The world has witnessed through television that we are a positive side. That philosophy will not change now. Against Peru we created at least 15 chances. We will continue to go forward....'

As the Dutch came up through the trap-door from the dressing-room the prescribed 12 minutes before kick-off, for the preliminary ceremonies in front of President Videla and the bulging, screeching crowd, the tangerine of their shirts seemed to have a more than usual vividness—perhaps because they were on their own. With inexcusable gamesmanship, it was another eight or nine minutes before the Argentinians appeared, by which time Holland had broken ranks to go out on the pitch to kick about and calm their nerves. When Passarella finally led his men out, the

Italian referee Sergio Gonella leads René van der Kerkhof from the pitch, following complaint by Argentina about the Dutchman's right-arm plaster moments before kick-off. Luque (14) and Brandts (22) accompany them.

snowstorm of ticker-tape was the most engulfing yet; again the Argentinian people showed their collective sporting instinct by whistling for silence during the playing of the Dutch national anthem—an attitude not to be found these days at Wembley.

The sportsmanship did not extend to the Argentinian team, who had yet another trick to pull before the kick-off. As the players lined up in the centre-circle there was suddenly a protest to Italian referee Sergio Gonella about the protective plastic guard on the wrist of René K. This could only be a move of calculated disruption, because it was well known that the Dutchman had been wearing the shield for the past five matches. Gonella badly missed his first chance to show authority, and instead of telling the Argentinians to start the match, permitted several minutes of wrangling on the touch line. Neeskens, incensed by the incident, told Hugh McIlvanney of the *Observer* later: 'I asked Passarella what kind of regulations could allow René to play five matches with the covering on his hand and then ban him from the field a minute before a World Cup Final.' Neeskens' command of Spanish would have left Passarella in no doubt of Holland's anger. Neeskens went on: 'Gonella was listening to this nonsense, looking as if he would be influenced by it, so I said to Passarella "All right, if Van der Kerkhof goes, we all go. You can play the World Cup Final all alone." That was it. Rudi Krol called for us to leave the field and Gonella knew we meant it.' René recalled: 'When I had finally put some padding on my hand, and we were walking back to kick off, Neeskens turned to me and said: "All right, let's go and get them."'

They did just that. In the first two minutes Poortvliet and Haan committed shuddering frontal fouls on sly Bertoni and frail Ardiles—exactly as Argentina had feared, and no doubt the root cause of their psychological warfare before the start.

150

Almost immediately Holland had the first of the several openings which, if taken, would have buried the Argentinian dream. Olguin fouled Haan wide of the penalty area on the left, Haan's free-kick curved into the middle, pale Johnny Rep out-jumped Passarella and Galvan—but his header flew a yard wide.

Holland were setting out to do precisely what they had said: to stifle Argentina's flow. Consistently they had nine or ten men behind the ball when Argentina started to move forward. Brandts, young carrot-headed PSV stopper, was in difficulties against the swift-turning Luque and it was this which resulted, as much as anything, in Krol being booked after 15 minutes for up-ending Bertoni as the winger exploited Brandts' error. Gonella failed to see Bertoni's vicious jab on Neeskens, with his elbow, as the players lined up for the free-kick: a huge swipe from 23 yards by Passarella which was only just held by Jongbloed, retained in goal because of Schrijvers' damaged knee. Two minutes later Galvan deliberately handled for the first time as Haan and Rep flickered through in a counter-attack.

Soon Kempes was well wide with his first, range-finding cannon-ball after Brandts had again been turned inside-out by Bertoni. Holland's attacking was spasmodic and lacking co-ordination; they shook their heads in annoyance but did not slacken. In the 24th minute there was a searing near miss by Passarella, volleying over the bar from close range as he stole in behind the defensive wall to meet Olguin's free-kick, after Bertoni had been fouled by Poortvliet.

Three minutes later came another of Fillol's stupendous contributions to Argentina's progress. Jansen, put through by Willy K., crossed the ball to the back of the penalty area. Rep controlled and let fly, but Fillol to a deafening cheer turned the shot over the bar with nerves of steel. The aberrations of officialdom continued when the Austrian linesman, Linemayer, hoisted his flag in a panic with Rep at least five yards on-side; at the other end, after two corners forced by Ortiz, Jongbloed had to turn the ball over the bar.

Mario Kempes shoots beneath advancing Dutch 'keeper Jongbloed to give Argentina the lead in the first half. Jansen arrives too late, Luque follows up. Ardiles (*sitting, behind Kempes*) started the move.

Seven minutes before half-time Kempes, always lurking ominously on the left like some bionic 12th man behind the front three, snatched the goal which released the crowd's pent-up emotions. The architect was Ardiles, showing no signs of his injury; the execution epitomized that sharpness of reaction which makes Kempes so special. Ardiles won a tackle on the left, and slipped the ball square to Luque, who glanced it on diagonally between Brandts and Krol. The pass lacked momentum and Kempes had to nudge the ball past Krol before shooting wide of Jongbloed almost in one movement.

Now Ardiles was booked; and again Galvan handled, this time a really dangerous chipped through ball by Willy K. Again no booking. Argentina surged back, and once more Passarella infiltrated the Dutch back line to meet a free-kick from Kempes, Jongbloed saving the header uneasily. Holland counter-attacked in the last seconds of the first-half, saw another gilt-edged opening crash to the ground. Willy K. crossed from the left, Neeskens on the far post climbed high, high above the defence, and headed back into the goalmouth. Rensenbrink raced forward, lunged with both feet, met the ball on the half-volley barely three yards out—and somehow Fillol smothered the half-hit shot.

In the individual, man-for-man conflicts the Dutch had so far had the best of the exchanges ... except that Willy K. had allowed Kempes to get goal-side of him in the attack which gave Argentina the lead. In golfing parlance, Brandts was level with Luque after the first 18 holes, Willy K. two down to Kempes after leading; Haan was all square with Ardiles, full-backs Poortvliet and Jansen were one up on Bertoni and Ortiz, Neeskens was two up on Gallego; Rep and Rensenbrink would have been two up on Galvan and Olguin but had both missed short putts; while Krol had played every club to perfection and had never missed the green. Passarella had hit a couple of glorious approach shots to within inches of the hole.

Throughout the second-half the Dutch were even more in command than they had been in that desperate Final in Munich four years before. Had they equalized earlier than the 81st minute, they would surely have overrun the Argentinians. But fate, and this time the referee too, was against them. In the 56th minute, just after Jongbloed had hurled himself at Luque's feet on a cross from Bertoni to concede a corner, Galvan handled a third time and scandalously received no booking. Happel sent out burly Nanninga in place of Rep, intending to apply a more direct physical threat at the centre of Argentina's defence. Twice within minutes Nanninga was fouled without a free-kick being given. Ardiles, by now feeling the pain again, was replaced by Larrosa. Bertoni, once more beating Poortvliet, gave Luque a chance which, holding off (literally!) a challenge from Willy K., he hooked wide.

With Holland's frustration mounting to boiling-point, Suurbier replaced Jansen. In the 73rd minute Neeskens, pounding through the middle, was disgracefully tripped by Galvan four strides from the penalty area. *No booking*. You could have excused Krol if he had again called his men off the pitch, but an equalizer was just around the corner. Haan put René K. clear on the right, and his long cross was driven home with a hammer blow from among a sea of straining heads by Nanninga. Almost straight from the kick-off René K., now grinding Tarantini into the ground, was clear again but was shut off by Passarella for a corner. Neeskens was hurt, hit in the mouth by Passarella—and still Holland had the chance to seal victory in normal time. With almost the last kick Rensenbrink, stealing round the back of the defence on the left to meet Suurbier's perfect cross, stubbed the ball against the post behind Fillol from an acute angle. What agony for Holland!

For the first time since 1966 the Final went to extra-time. As with England then, Argentina had had victory snatched from them with a late goal in normal time. Like England, they wound themselves up for a final onslaught. Holland, from a position of near-total domination, now receded, their energy spent. Their running off the ball in the second-half had consumed their reserves. There was a limit to the extent to which their spirit could rise in the face of prejudiced decisions.

Early in the first period of extra-time Larrosa and then Poortvliet were booked. In the 14th minute Kempes scored the goal by which he joined the roll-call of legendary strikers. Put through by Bertoni on the left, he held off three challenges, had his first shot smothered by Jongbloed, but somehow managed to prod home the rebound as he fell. With Neeskens now a virtual passenger, even his magnificent fighting spirit doused, there was no holding Argentina in the last 15 minutes. Luque, going like a train, broke away, on and on, finally blocked by Jongbloed. With six minutes to go Bertoni, Luque and Kempes roared off together, three stallions in line, Bertoni hitting the eventual shot as Holland were swamped. The remaining time was spent in wild, ugly tackles by both teams, neither any longer having the slightest respect for the referee.

Dirk Nanninga (18) heads Holland's equalizer between Galvan and Passarella, over Poortvliet and wide of Fillol (5).

Daniel Bertoni, Argentine right-winger, smashes home the third goal with Jongbloed (8) and Brandts (22) helpless.

Overhead a jet from Aerolineas Argentinas swooped low on approach to the nearby domestic airport, dipping its wings in silvery salute. And the country was pitched into yet one more orgy of emotion in the streets. When we had to abandon our press bus, and walk the last 20 or 30 blocks back to the hotel through stationary, honking traffic an hour later, one thought of Kempes—to whom the winners, and the tournament, owed so much; and the inconvenience seemed unimportant. It may not have been a classic match, and there lingered the suspicion that Holland had been robbed. Yet it had been a great occasion; the personality of the winning team had been universally infectious. I was glad to have been there.

Argentina: Fillol; Olguin, Galvan, Passarella, Tarantini; Ardiles (Larrosa 65), Gallego, Kempes; Bertoni, Luque, Ortiz (Houseman 74).

Holland: Jongbloed; Jansen (Suurbier 72), Brandts, Krol, Poortvliet; W. van der Kerkhof, Neeskens, Haan; R. van der Kerkhof, Rep (Nanninga 59), Rensenbrink.

Referee: Sergio Gonella (Italy).

154

CHAPTER ELEVEN

A Kind of War

'*Football coaches are being subjected to a kind of terrorism by the press and TV. It has become almost impossible to do the job.*' So claimed Miljan Miljanic midway through the tournament. He should know, having in the last few years been manager of Red Star Belgrade, the Yugoslavia World Cup team in 1974 and then, for three and a half seasons, Real Madrid. We were at the Hindu Club, where Italy were resting between their Second Round matches against Germany and Austria. Enzo Bearzot was slumped in a chair, chain-smoking, staring into space as if in a sleep-walk. It was mid-afternoon. He had been to his room but could not sleep, and had come down again to have coffee and a brandy with his colleague. His eyes seemed sunk more deeply than ever in that sharply boned, heavily lined face—the face of someone enduring a trial by jury which has dragged on for weeks. Only did the eyes light up when the two men began to discuss, in purist terms, the tactics of their profession: Miljanic drawing with rapid arrows on endless sheets of paper, Bearzot becoming animated until he was almost shouting.

Miljanic told me: 'I have been talking to Michel Hidalgo of France. He's a good guy and he has done brilliantly with his team. They were maybe the best team here, but the pressures on him have been fantastic; he looked almost a sick man.' The experience was by no means confined to Hidalgo and Bearzot. During his visit to London for the so-called friendly match against England two months previously, Brazil's manager, Claudio Coutinho, had told me: 'It is intolerable. When we lost last week in France my family could hardly leave the house back home in Rio; life was impossible for my ten-year-old son at school. Whatever happens in Argentina, I will not continue afterwards. Why should I accept such conditions when I can retire to a civilized life as a university lecturer?'

Such feelings were echoed by Helmut Schoen, talking to Hugh McIlvanney of the *Observer* shortly before Germany's Second Round encounter with Holland, when he said: 'The World Cups of 1958 and 1962 were garden parties compared with what is involved now, with the pressures that have developed. The increase in pressure seems continuous from one competition to the next. In 1966 it was already terrific, in 1970 it was worse, in 1974 still more terrible and now it is almost completely out of hand. In nearly all countries of the world football is the most popular sport. Today the media bring it to the masses, and bring the feelings and demands of the masses back to those working in the game. Football has become almost a kind of war.'

Wilfried Gerhardt, the German press secretary and Schoen's *alter ego*, who speaks better English than many of the English themselves, added: 'When Helmut shook hands with Bearzot after that game it was not an empty gesture. He was recognizing the bond of fellow sufferers ... even at 62 he stands up to the outrageous requirements of the job better than most. He has low blood pressure, but it is not too serious. Some days he has trouble getting himself going, but a glass of champagne has been prescribed and he finds that no hardship. After that goal-less draw with Italy he looked tired, but Bearzot looked nearly dead, grey and green and awful. I felt sorry for him. I am very close to Helmut and I can see that the periods of introspection he has always needed, those times when he retreats into himself to resolve the questions or the doubts in his mind, are now more frequent and may last longer.'

Schoen went on: 'It is true. When the pitch had to be inspected before the match with Mexico, I could have sent one of my assistants, but I went alone with a driver because I needed to get away and come to terms with my own thoughts. It was an absolute necessity to get away even from the team for an hour or so. At such moments it is inevitable that I should feel a great personal responsibility. Success has many fathers; defeat has only one. Of course there are times when you feel it is all too much and you want to finish but there is, apart from anything else, the matter of the contract and the obligation it imposes. When I try to restore myself after spells of particular pressure I talk to my wife or to a real friend like Wilfried, or at home I take my poodle for walks in the forest. He is a good companion and he always believes my judgements are correct.'

All managers, from the most successful over a long period such as Schoen down to the novices such as Ally MacLeod, are hugely dependent on the quality of the players at their disposal. There were moments in Argentina when it seemed that managers were redundant, as events took their own haphazard course outside the control of the field generals. Coutinho, after six months of intensive preparation, was subjected to selection-by-committee: and the team improved. Ernst Happel

Before and After. Ally MacLeod spreads his arms in would-be victor's salute on first inspection of Cordoba pitch. The electric scoreboard tells its story as Peru celebrate.

was hired as a £70,000 part-timer for the duration of the tournament. His second-in-command Jan Zwartkruis persuaded him to change the team against Austria; and Austria were thrashed. Bearzot, after claiming for two years that Franco Graziani of Torino at centre-forward was the tactical fulcrum of the side and irreplaceable, suddenly replaces Graziani with Paolo Rossi; and Italy prosper. Schoen himself, pressurized by his senior players, plays a full-back, Zimmermann, in midfield; and holds Italy to a draw after struggling against Tunisia. MacLeod finally picks the team which any journalist could have selected for him two months before; and Scotland defeat Holland. Of course the manager is essential, to produce continuity of selection and policy, but it is always likely that personal prejudices may blind him to fluctuations in external circumstances. Which is why, I am personally convinced, even the greatest tactician should work in tandem with an assistant whose judgement he respects: witness Happel and Zwartkruis, Clough and Taylor.

Schoen, of course, has had Jupp Durvall, whose succession when Schoen retired had been accepted as automatic for some years. But it is doubtful how much influence Durvall exerted, how much he shared the load of responsibility. There was widespread speculation in Argentina that Durvall will not survive long, that he is too much of an old-fashioned authoritarian, and the malcontent within the German squad was evident when Bernd Holzenbein stated after the defeat by Austria: 'For six years I kept quiet just to stay in the squad. But it is time someone opened the public's eyes. All you get is discipline; they treat you like children.' While Sepp Maier, their veteran goalkeeper, asserted: 'Only the fact that I want to keep playing stops me speaking my mind. I could tell you things you would not believe.'

The recriminations between manager and team were mutual. A bowed, sad Schoen stated after defeat in his last match: 'I am utterly disappointed, both with the outcome and with the way our team played. I will not criticize players individually, but the defence was very weak. The boys were no good. None of them was up to World Cup standard; I never expected to reach the last four. It is my belief that the team was never better trained, but we did have the bad luck of being unable to field Flohe and Zimmermann, owing to injuries in our last match. In previous championships we would have been able to replace them with others, equally as good.' Exit a man who has won friends and affection around the world during the 16 years of an unparalleled record: World Cup runners-up in 1966, semi-finalists in 1970, winners in 1974, European champions in 1972 and runners-up in 1976.

Yet if the managers at times seemed overpowered by the very events they were directing, one man who triumphantly rose above the emotional blitz was Cesar Luis Menotti. In 1976 he had travelled to Belgrade to study the European finals, but in spite of recognizing the formidable range of qualities which Europe would align against South America two years later, he remained unwaveringly true to his own ideal—an ideal in which the prospects of success seemed about as remote at that time as persuading Tahitians to live in igloos.

Argentina had 48 years' history of producing many of the most gifted, and some of the most villainous, players in the world. In the last 15 years, in particular, their international reputation had been appalling. The incidents are almost too well known to need recounting. In 1966, with possibly the best team in the finals, Argentina had systematically attempted to destroy England illegally in the quarter-final,

only to destroy themselves. The architect of that infamous side, Juan Carlos Lorenzo, had continued to peddle the principles of intimidation and anarchy with Racing of Buenos Aires, Lazio of Italy, Atletico Madrid and ultimately Boca Juniors of Buenos Aires. Menotti resolutely set himself against this demonic tradition, with the conviction in his soul that Argentinian football had something more noble to offer the world.

He stated: 'My country's football needs total reorganization. If we could win the World Cup the way I would like us to, it would inspire others to reassess the way we play the game—our basic philosophy. Perhaps it would stop us placing such reliance on violence and cynicism which are the tools of fear. Argentinian football possesses too much skill to need to be afraid.'

Few believed that Menotti's resolution would survive. Throughout the months leading up to the finals, I half expected any moment to receive one of those terse news agency flashes to announce that he was fired. His supporters, let alone his critics, did not believe he could succeed; off-stage there were continual rumblings from Lorenzo advocating a reversion to the old ways. Menotti held his course, precariously maintaining his policy of playing with wingers, with a midfield which left huge spaces to the rear which others could exploit. Yet it was significant when, following victory in the Final, Menotti listed in order of priority the qualities he

Chain-smoking Cesar Luis Menotti
ponders over Argentina's prospects
during a press conference the day before
the Final.

considered essential in his players: first, intelligence; secondly, a concept of team-work; thirdly, individual skill. For twenty years or so those priorities had often been in reverse.

Enzo Bearzot likewise had conducted a lone crusade to change the face of Italian soccer, which had similarly suffered years of frustration and wasted potential through its caution and intimidation. The high priest of defensiveness had been Helenio Herrera in the fifties and sixties, first with Barcelona and subsequently with Internazionale of Milan. Bearzot was motivated by the same ideals as Menotti. A 50-year-old former wing-half who had captained Torino when Denis Law briefly played there, he knew that Italy's shortcomings were all in the head rather than the feet. It had been a long, slow haul to gain the confidence of his federation as well as his players. In 1976 in New York, before England played Italy in the US Bicentenary tournament, there had been a press conference at the Pierre Hotel to discuss Italy's team. We found ourselves being addressed not by Bearzot, the coach and selector, but Fulvio Bernardini, renowned manager of a former era, retained by the Italian FA as a 'cover' front man.

Why, I asked Dr Franco Carraro, the chairman, should we discuss the team with Bernardini when it was in fact to be selected by Bearzot? The question caused the Italians much embarrassment at the time but was, I think I may modestly claim, at least partially responsible in rationalizing the official attitude to Bearzot's status. After England had defeated Italy 3–2 in the Yankee stadium with a makeshift team—having been two down and the game descending into an all too familiar punch-up—Bearzot had given his players an ultimatum: either they accept his principles, cut out the intimidation and concentrate on positive, attacking formations, or he would quit. Either they wanted to progress or remain what they were, a team of might-have-beens.

159

They accepted his challenge. I admit to being one of those who was fearful that Italy would attempt to kick England to bits in the World Cup qualifying tie in Rome, but by then Bearzot's influence was already beginning to show. Although Italy reverted to type with some ferocious fouls when there was a chance that they would be overrun in the return tie at Wembley, by the time the squad reached Argentina Bearzot's revolution was almost complete: at least within the international squad. Even Benetti, an old leopard who could barely conceal his spots, limited himself to a very occasional flash of the claws, and before Italy faced Argentina in their final match in the first round Bearzot stated: 'It is in our hearts to play the right way, to be entertaining and fair. We want to continue to set a standard that others will be proud to follow.' That night they did so.

Yet as Italy progressed for a while from strength to strength, Bearzot's position was not necessarily secure. He told James Mossop of the *Sunday Express*: 'If I'm not given the chance to continue, whether or not we win the World Cup, then all the work is over. At the moment it is only half complete. I want Italy to be an attacking team. I want to put opponents under pressure. What you are seeing now is the result of three years' effort. All the time I am looking for players of quality and versatility. It does not bother me that Italian league teams still play in the old way. If I see a player of potential I will include him in the national squad.'

The transformation reached a peak, with the reversal of traditional roles, when Italy faced Germany in the Second Round: Germany overcome with caution, Italy the free adventurous spirit. And Bearzot claimed afterwards: 'This match was an acid test for us. It was our greatest satisfaction to see Germany at times only defending and playing without a plan.' Although, suffering I thought more from mental fatigue than anything, Italy's form receded against Holland and Brazil, Bearzot was rewarded by being given a new two-year contract which would lead his country into the 1980 European championship. The final tournament would be in Rome and he would hope for the same emotional support which now reinforced Argentina.

Furrows of strain show on the face of Italy's manager Enzo Bearzot prior to the vital Second Round match against Holland.

Claudio Coutinho had a vision, but it was based on a false premise—that Brazil could reclaim their position as the major power in world football by acquiring the characteristics of Europe. He had misread the condition of Brazil, which was not so much that it lacked the physical commitment and discipline which are such a prominent feature of the European armoury, but that the supply of truly great players which in the past has characterized Brazil's triumphs had temporarily run dry. His attempt to compensate for this with a descent into base, physical expediency possibly, ironically, cost Brazil their fourth championship. Even Bearzot was driven to admit to Jeff Powell of the *Daily Mail* before the clash of Argentina and Brazil in Rosario: 'It seems to have been proved that Coutinho put too much emphasis on physical strength. By insisting on the introduction of men such as Roberto and Dirceu, the officials have restored one of the great qualities of Brazil—skill at speed. Maybe it gives them a chance to draw the match.'

Coutinho, 39-year-old ex-army officer, is a man of some intellect but he had been wrong to suppose, in the Brazilian context, that he could resolve Brazil's present problem by altering its whole credo. Like England, like Argentina, they needed to be true to their natural heritage; once Coutinho was obliged to acknowledge this, Brazil came closer than was widely acknowledged to recapturing the title. Admiral Helenio Nunez had stated: 'The players and directors imposed their points of view on Coutinho and made him change the panorama to save the honour of Brazilian football.' To be fair to Coutinho, he had been undermined by a variety of factors: the loose living of former stars Francisco Marinho and Paulo Cezar which obliged him to leave them out of the squad; the loss of Luis Pererira and Ze Maria with injury; the decline of young Reinaldo; the refusal of Rivelino to co-operate in attack.

Another who mis-read his situation was Ally MacLeod who, like Coutinho, had the most limited experience of international soccer. This was revealed in many statements, notably when he said before the first match against Peru: 'I needed the British Championship matches to try out a few alternatives, but the players had their minds on Argentina.' It was meddling with the teams in those final games, when he should have been playing a settled side, which more than anything sent Scotland into the World Cup disorganized and with their morale at a low ebb. One of the players told Hugh McIlvanney: 'We look disorganized on the field because we are disorganized. For all we achieved in the week we were here before the first match, we might as well have stayed at home. I don't think we worked on one free-kick in that time. Of course it's not as important as the fact that MacLeod had nothing worth-while to say at half-time against Peru, when we were already letting them take over a match that should have been won, surrendering the midfield to them and letting them work their quick one-twos on the edge of our box. After such a performance, I wasn't surprised to find some Scottish punters battering on the sides of our bus and shouting abuse. Coming 7000 miles out here wasn't quite like taking a bus along the road to Hampden, and they have a right to tell us what they think of us.'

MacLeod made more errors than the single false premise that Scotland had the ability to go out and win simply on account of some mythical Celtic chemistry of emotional will-power. All along the rocky route he was making exaggerated

161

claims: that 'no other squad in the whole history of football has been subjected to the sort of pressure Scotland have suffered out here'; that 'my squad has trained harder than any other'; that 'seven or eight of the team just didn't play'. Ron Greenwood, England's manager, who had earlier gone out of his way to support MacLeod, put it succinctly after the 1–1 draw with Iran: 'Let's face it; Scotland did not do their homework.'

Bruce Rioch, the skipper, whose own form jeopardized his claim to a place in the team, by implication condemned his own manager when he said: 'What really took us by surprise was the pace of Peru's wingers. We were amazed. As a professional I can accept the criticism, just as I've accepted praise in the past. But the fact is we did not have enough preparation against foreign opposition.' Lou Macari added: 'The Home Championship was a serious disadvantage for us, the way we played it. We would have been better getting down to the right preparation like other teams.'

Ernst Happel was, throughout the finals, a contradiction. While maintaining a public pretence that Holland were intent on attack—he was most dogmatic about this when I spoke to him three days before the Final, when it was clear from the attitude of some of the players that defensiveness would be half their strategy—his application was closely in keeping with the tactics of his Belgian club, Bruges, who had attempted to throw a blanket over Liverpool in the European Cup final. Happel, an Austrian international half-back with 54 caps, who had fought in the German army on the Russian front, claims to have been the inventor of *catenaccio*: the defensive system of the free man behind a line of markers which was perfected by Italy. He devised it after his club, Rapid of Vienna, went to Brazil in the late forties with one of the best teams in Europe, and were defeated 6–1.

Happel's intentions for the World Cup were clearly revealed when, in a friendly against Austria in Vienna shortly beforehand, he played five men in midfield in a 3–5–2 formation. There is no doubt that his preoccupation with this kind of belt-and-braces job in midfield was modified by the influence of his assistant, Jan Zwartk-

Claudio Coutinho tries to make a point at his press conference, following the removal of his sole powers of selection by Brazil chairman Admiral Helenio Nunes.

ruis. Before the Final, René van der Kerkhof told Rob Hughes of *The Sunday Times*: 'Happel does not spend much time working directly with the players. He picks our teams, decides on the tactics, and passes on the detailed instructions before matches to each of us. He is a great man in football, a strong personality and wise in the game. A man of the same level as the 1974 manager, Rinus Michels, but it is his way to leave most of the day-to-day work with us to Zwartkruis. So it was Zwartkruis who was waiting for us when we went in at half-time against Italy, one goal down and knowing it should have been worse. We had been too conscious that a draw was enough, so we played with too little aggression. We were terrible. Zwartkruis said: 'This is not Holland I have seen. You have not played like Dutchmen.' He made us understand we had 45 minutes to reach the Final. We changed the team—Neeskens stopped marking Rossi and went to midfield. We changed our attitude and took control.'

It was Zwartkruis, for certain, who had influenced the change in attitude which saw Holland switch from defeat against Scotland, at the end of the First Round, to runaway victory over Austria. Yet Brian Glanville of *The Sunday Times* claims that when he asked a Dutch club manager whether Happel or Zwartkruis was truly in charge of the team, he received the reply: 'Neither. It's the players.' I would accept, having spoken to half-a-dozen of the players, that they more than either of the managers took it upon themselves to indulge in the severity of tackling, which was such a feature of their performances against Italy and then Argentina.

Another who set about winning matches more by an attempt to control the opposition than by personal enterprise was Jacek Gmoch, assistant to Kasimierz Gorski in 1974 when Poland took third place. Gmoch, the Computer Man of the World Cup, was more obsessed by dossiers on opposing players than ever was Don Revie, which is perhaps not surprisingly why his team bore a marked resemblance to those of Revie. For six matches Poland played with vast efficiency, a mountain of care, and fewer flashes of inspiration from Lato and Szarmach in attack than made them so attractive in 1974. Kazimierz Deyna, in the final analysis, had a poor World Cup for a player of his exceptional class, even excluding the travesty of his penalty against Argentina. He coaxed matches rather than commanded them. Boniek proved a lively young alternative to the veteran Lubanski, accentuating the fact that, with a front line of Lato, Boniek and Szarmach, Poland should have made more impact than they did. Gmoch's geometry had robbed them of that exciting streak of extravagance.

If Gmoch and Coutinho restricted their teams by wanting talent subordinated to sweat, there were two managers who knew that the only route to any sort of recognition lay through murderous hard work: Majid Chetali of Tunisia and Heshmat Mohajerani of Iran. There can be no doubt that if Scotland had been given half the discipline and organization by MacLeod that Tunisia and Iran exhibited, they would have reached the Second Round and probably the last four. Chetali could not believe his eyes, observing some of the Scots' behaviour, when the two squads shared the same hotel. By solid application, Chetali and Mohajerani squeezed every ounce out of their modest teams, and by so doing reduced the already narrowing gap between Afro/Asia and the game's alleged aristocrats.

CHAPTER TWELVE

Blinkered

The longer the 1978 World Cup continued, the more obvious it was just how much Scotland and England had paid for the confused management of Ally MacLeod and Don Revie. Italy, having profited from Revie's yo-yo direction, at one stage looked the strongest team, with a chance of going all the way to the Final, but then faded. Scotland, when the players finally and unofficially took charge of the team—dispensing with a winger and choosing a middle line of four—defeated Holland, the eventual runners-up. Brazil, third, and Italy, fourth, had both been given a run for their money in recent months by England under the fresh new direction of Ron Greenwood. In the most wide open of all World Cups, the two oldest football nations had missed, possibly, the chance of a lifetime—winning the trophy away from home. What Greenwood had had confirmed is that the right equation with the cream of England's players can bring prestige if not outright victory in Spain—always assuming that England do not fail to qualify for the third time in a row. It is sobering, if not shameful, to recall that England have only twice qualified for the finals in open competition: in 1958 against Denmark and Eire, in 1962 against Portugal and Luxembourg. The continuing development of Greenwood's team in the European championship qualifying games, against Bulgaria, Denmark and the two Irelands, would be critical. The equation, it was clear, should be a balance between the attack of Argentina and the Total Football of Holland. Cesar Menotti, like Sir Alf Ramsey, had been the right man at the right moment but, like Ramsey, will come to reflect on Argentina's moments of undoubted luck.

Scotland, it seemed, learned little from yet another controversial expedition. Although due to meet Austria in Vienna in September, in a European championship group including Belgium, Portugal and Norway, they left no one behind to study the Austrians in their Second Round matches against Holland, Italy and Germany. Two weeks after the Final MacLeod was, astonishingly, given a vote of confidence ... of a sort. The SFA International Committee, meeting in Glasgow and voting on a motion to replace him, decided by 4–3 to retain him, on the casting vote of the chairman, Tom Lauchlan.

On the face of it, MacLeod would have an almost impossible job—even supposing he had acquired some knowledge and a sobering slice of humility from the experiences in Argentina. His relationship with several of the senior players was permanently fractured. From the comments made, and published at the time by members of the SFA, it would be difficult for MacLeod ever to have confidence in them: or they in him. His conduct of the campaign on the field would hardly have inspired confidence among British league managers, or those new young players on whom he would be having to call in the next four years.

The fact that Jock Stein had now been promoted upstairs at Celtic, no longer engaged in the technical day-to-day handling of the league side, would free his vast experience for services to the nation: always supposing that, troubled by a lame leg from a serious car accident, he would still relish the challenge and the responsibility. Yet inevitably the hue and cry would be on again at the first hint of failure for MacLeod in the European ties. Basically a nice, patriotic man, MacLeod would face continuing and possibly intolerable pressures for himself and his family. He might well come to consider that 15 months in the limelight, and the sudden prosperity which attended it, had demanded too high a price in human terms. If MacLeod failed to turn the hairpin corners still awaiting him, if Stein could not be enticed down from Olympus, would the SFA consider, could they dare, the revolutionary step of giving the job to a foreigner . . . or even an Englishman? They could not overlook the fact that Wales had been given considerable stability, continuity and a modicum of success by their quiet, coaching-orientated English manager Mike Smith, ex-Brighton schoolmaster. Wales had been the only British side to qualify for the 1975–6 European quarter-finals: and had they not been robbed by Scotland of a place in Argentina? Whatever MacLeod's future, there would have to be some heart-searching within the SFA in an attempt to correct Scotland's unhappy sequence of World Cup misfortunes.

Great Goal. Two beat five, as Bettega leaps over Tarantini's vain tackle to shoot past Fillol for Italy's 1–0 win. Argentine defenders Olguin, Galvan and Passarella are left stranded by return pass of Rossi (other dark shirt).

It does not read too well: 1954—with Andy Beattie as manager, thrashed 7–0 by Uruguay; 1958—with manager Matt Busby injured, beaten by Paraguay; 1962—under Ian McColl, unlucky to lose qualifying play-off to ultimate finalists Czechoslovakia; 1966—with Jock Stein as stop-gap manager, defeated by Poland at home, Italy away; 1970—under Bobby Brown, qualifying tie thrown away in Hamburg; 1974—Willie Ormond's team squanders goal-advantage against Zaire; 1978—victory over Holland only the second ever in the finals.

The continuing insularity of the English is almost equally alarming. Shortly after the finals, which had been sufficiently attractive to command on three occasions a TV audience of almost half the population, Everton's manager Gordon Lee stated that there had been nothing worthwhile to study in Argentina. Lee's international knowledge, of course, is about on a par with MacLeod's. When Ron Greenwood held a seminar at Bisham Abbey national recreation centre after the finals, it was depressing to find that only half the managers in the First Division bothered to attend. I fear that in this respect the English are the same as the Scots; many believe only what they want to believe. Those who attended the Bisham seminar included young men such as Terry Venables of Crystal Palace upon whose influence the future of the game rests. Greenwood had said before the finals: 'I know what I want to see—the most entertaining, exciting side winning the trophy. I want people to switch off their TV at home and say "That was a great game". I want them to be talking afterwards about the joy of watching it, the beauty of the game.' Here and there, Greenwood got what he wanted; but how could he convince the rest of the game back at home, from Plymouth to Tyneside, to follow suit. For fifteen years Greenwood had been a Pied Piper without a following; he knew that the public, that other managers, coaches and schoolmasters, would only be drawn to his tune if the England team continued to be successful. It is a truly frightening thought how wide an influence, the very future of the game, rests in the private thoughts and ideals of one man.

After every World Cup we all play at picking a World XI, a good parlour game in which our teams never have to take the field and expose themselves ... or us! I was interested that, having nominated my own choice for the World XI and Reserve XI, there were only two players I had not included who were in the team selected by Greenwood: Italy's left-back Cabrini and Holland's winger Rensenbrink. Greenwood chose a front three of Rensenbrink and Italy's left-winger Bettega playing either side of Kempes; whereas I went for a line of Kempes, Rossi (Italy) and Krankl, Europe's leading goal-scorer from Austria. The position for which there was most competition was clearly *libero*, with over half a dozen players of outstanding ability: Tresor (France), Passarella (Argentina), Krol (Holland), Scirea (Italy), Gorgon (Poland), Buchan (Scotland), Obermeyer (Austria), Pirri (Spain), Amaral (Brazil). I chose Tresor, while Greenwood preferred Passarella on account of his greater pace and thrilling excursions into attack. Yet I feel that, in a sound team going all the way to the last four, Buchan would have staked his claim as a reader of the game equal to Bobby Moore.

In goal it was a straight choice between Zoff (Italy) and Fillol (Argentina). After the First Round I would have given it to Zoff, but by the end of the Final, Fillol was undoubtedly the man. The standard of goalkeeping throughout the tournament was exceptionally high, with only Tunisia, France, Mexico and Scotland having keepers of below international standard. The other twelve countries were remarkably well served between the posts, and this factor undoubtedly helped restrict the scoring to 102 goals in the 38 matches, an average of 2·68 a game. After Fillol and Zoff, it would have been an impossible job attempting to take your pick from the rest: Koncilia (Austria), Leao (Brazil), Schrijvers or Jongbloed (Holland), Gujdar (Hungary), Hedjazi (Iran), Quiroga (Peru), Tomaszewski (Poland), Angel (Spain),

Great Save. Dino Zoff (*not in picture*) makes one of the outstanding saves of the finals from this header by Argentine skipper Daniel Passarella (*far left*) from a corner. Others in picture (*left to right*) Bettega, Gallego, Scirea, Gentile, Kempes, Cuccureddu.

Helstrom (Sweden), Maier (West Germany).

There was a shortage of full-backs of quality, with the most obvious candidates being Gentile (Italy), Nelinho (Brazil), Maculewicz (Poland), Vogts (West Germany), Tarantini (Argentina) and Cabrini (Italy)—though I nominated Krol, in his 1974 position at left-back. The choice of central 'stoppers' was as clear-cut as in goal, between Oscar (Brazil) and Bellugi (Italy), though Erny Brandts of Holland is surely a man for the future.

Nor was there much doubt in midfield, with a choice of any three from six: Ardiles (Argentina), Neeskens (Holland), Dirceu (Brazil), Platini (France), Willy van der Kerkhof (Holland) and Benetti (Italy). Deyna (Poland), so elegant and with such vision, was less effective than he should have been; Cubillas (Peru) was brilliant only when he was allowed space. Graeme Souness, belatedly selected for Scotland's last match in which he achieved world-class status, would no doubt have been a candidate for the central midfield position had Scotland survived.

Up front Kempes was the only player in a class of his own. I excluded Rensenbrink because I considered he had had a poor tournament by his own standards, and Ron Greenwood admitted that he had nominated him on his European form. Luque (Argentina) would, I suspect, be less formidable outside the home environment.

167

Torocsik (Hungary) is the one player who, in my opinion, may eventually rise to the level of super-player, if Hungary can maintain their impetus and, more important behind the Iron Curtain, their incentive. Bettega, after a brilliant First Round, seemed to become weary of his responsibilities as the rest of the Italian team fell away. Many coaches will dismiss Peru's wingers Munante and Oblitas as a flash in the pan, but all one can say is, some flash! Causio (Italy), like Rensenbrink, had a slightly disappointing World Cup, while critics of Krankl will say that he is, like Malcolm Macdonald, merely a ferocious left foot. Of Rossi (Italy), so mobile, so opportune, so swift on the turn, we are clearly going to hear a lot more; of Boniek (Poland) too. So my choice was:

World XI: Fillol (Argentina); Gentile (Italy), Oscar (Brazil), Tresor (France), Krol (Holland); Ardiles (Argentina), Neeskens (Holland), Dirceu (Brazil); Krankl (Austria), Rossi (Italy), Kempes (Argentina).
Reserve XI: Zoff (Italy); Nelinho (Brazil), Bellugi (Italy), Passarella (Argentina), Tarantini (Argentina); W. van der Kerkhof (Holland), Benetti (Italy), Platini (France); Munante (Peru), Torocsik (Hungary), Bettega (Italy).

One of the illusions of the World Cup was that many of the 102 goals were scored from outside the penalty area, though in fact this applied to only a fifth—20. The two most outstanding were, of course, Arie Haan's from over 30 yards against Italy, the winner in the Second Round, and Nelinho's equalizer against Italy in the Third Place match. Then there were the free-kicks by Cubillas, Dirceu and Nelinho. But to my mind the three outstanding goals of the finals were scored by Bettega, Gemmill and, inevitably, Kempes. The one with which Italy beat Argentina was a marvellous example of two forwards beating four defenders with a couple of wall passes. It was one of the sweetest moments of the whole exhausting, exhilarating month as Bettega swapped passes with first Antognini, then Rossi, to glide clear of Galvan, Passarella and Tarantini and sweep the ball past Fillol for Argentina's only defeat. Archie Gemmill's, going past three Dutch defenders, putting the ball through Krol's

Poland skipper Kazimierz Deyna hits his penalty shot weakly and Ubaldo Fillol is able to save easily five minutes before half-time, with Argentina leading 1–0. They won 2–0.

legs, and finally sending the goalkeeper the wrong way, was one of those individual once-in-a-lifetime goals which are the stuff of schoolboy fiction; and for a few minutes it enabled us to believe that Scotland could, after all, somehow survive. And the best of Kempes's six, I thought, was the only one scored with his head; it was the first against Poland, as he made a perfectly-timed diagonal run to meet Bertoni's beautifully judged near-post cross.

There was a profusion of memorable saves, and almost half of them seemed to be by Fillol. There were Nasser Hedjazi's saves for Iran from Joe Jordan's free-kick after 20 minutes and from Robertson's header after 81, which deepened Scotland's gloom. There were Quiroga's two saves in a minute from Lato and Deyna; there was Leao's dive at Luque's feet near the end of the Brazil–Argentina draw. Yet I think that the two which, more than any others, actually changed the course of the World Cup were by Fillol and Quiroga against Brazil and Scotland. When Dirceu sent Gil through in the 17th minute of the tribal war in Rosario, and the Brazilian winger shot fiercely from 16 yards into the gap to Fillol's left, it seemed a certain goal. Somehow the Argentinian keeper got down to the ball close to his legs, and in that moment, perhaps, Argentina's name was written on the Cup. The save which destroyed Scotland came after 30 minutes with Peru still trailing to Jordan's goal. It was then that Quiroga got his finger tips to Dalglish's lob out near the edge of the penalty area; from then on the clouds darkened for MacLeod's men.

Should the league system in the First and Second Rounds continue? The absurdity of this year's situation was obvious: that Peru were pointless and had nothing to play for in their final Second Round match with Argentina, yet they held the key to the whole tournament—to the fate of Brazil. The First Round mini-leagues are unavoidable, because it is out of the question to expect squads to travel halfway across the world to play possibly only one match under a knock-out system. Whether the Second Round should in fact revert to a knock-out quarter-final and semi-final, as last used in 1970, is debatable. Both Enzo Bearzot and Claudio Coutinho argued for the knock-out system, Bearzot claiming: 'It is incredible to think that if we had drawn with Holland in our final match in the Second Round, and Germany had won against Austria, we would have been out of the World Cup having won four matches, drawn two and lost none, whereas Germany would have progressed, having won two and drawn four. In 1974 Scotland were knocked out without having been beaten, and West Germany lost to East Germany but still won the Cup.'

Coutinho had a case; Brazil finished third without a defeat; Argentina won the cup, after losing to Italy. Yet would Coutinho and Bearzot be happy with a knock-out system if they lost narrowly in the quarter-final, instead of having two more chances to redeem themselves? Every system has the rub of the green. I would contend that the Second Round league system is certain to project the right teams into the last four, but not necessarily the best *two* into the Final. A good compromise would be for the top two teams in each of the Second Round groups to go into knock-out semi-finals—first in Group A *v* second in Group B and vice-versa—so that the fatuity of goal-difference determining the finalists, as with Brazil in 1978, would be eliminated. However, this would extend an already lengthy tournament by a further two matches and increase the physical demands on the successful teams

What might have been. Brilliant Michel Platini goes down in the penalty area, surrounded by Italian defenders Scirea (8), Tardelli (14) and Zaccarelli (15), as France lose 2–1.

from seven matches to eight. Helmut Schoen had stated in 1974: 'It would be most unwise to increase the number of matches. My team was already almost paralysed by mental and physical fatigue after seven matches; any more would drag them even lower.' So these are the three alternatives: sudden death, perhaps unluckily, in a quarter-final, the lottery of goal-difference, or the burden of more matches. Personally I prefer the old knock-out system, even though still shuddering to this day from the recollection of England's reversal against West Germany at Leon in 1970.

For the record, the leading scorers in 1978 were: Kempes (Argentina) 6; Cubillas (Peru), Rensenbrink (Holland) 5; Krankl (Austria), Luque (Argentina) 4; Roberto (Brazil), Rep (Holland), Rossi (Italy), Rummenigge (W. Germany), Dirceu (Brazil) 3; Bertoni (Argentina), Bettega (Italy), Boniek (Poland), Brandts (Holland), Flohe (W. Germany), Gemmill (Scotland), Haan (Holland), Lato (Poland), Muller D. (W. Germany), Nelinho (Brazil) 2. And the goal averages per match since the Second World War have been:

Date	Matches	Goals	Average
1950	22	88	4·0
1954	26	140	5·4
1958	35	126	3·6
1962	32	89	2·78
1966	32	89	2·78
1970	32	95	2·99
1974	38	97	2·55
1978	38	102	2·68

Results of Previous World Cup Final Competitions

URUGUAY 1930

Group 1		Points		Semi-finals	Final
France	4				
Mexico	1				
Argentina	1	**Argentina**	6		
France	0	Chile	4		
Chile	3	France	2	**Argentina** 6	
Mexico	0	Mexico	0		
Chile	1				**Argentina** 2
France	0				
Argentina	6				
Mexico	3				
Argentina	3			USA 1	
Chile	1				

Group 2					
Yugoslavia	2				
Brazil	1	Yugoslavia	4		
Yugoslavia	4	Brazil	2		
Bolivia	0	Bolivia	0		
Brazil	4				
Bolivia	0			Yugoslavia 1	

Group 3					
Romania	3				
Peru	1	**Uruguay**	4		
Uruguay	1	Romania	2		**Uruguay** 4
Peru	0	Peru	0		
Uruguay	4				
Romania	0			**Uruguay** 6	

Group 4					
USA	3				
Belgium	0				
USA	3	USA	4		
Paraguay	0	Paraguay	2		
Paraguay	1	Belgium	0		
Belgium	0				

ITALY 1934

Eighth-finals	Quarter-finals	Semi-finals	Final
Germany.............. 5	Germany.............. 2		
Belgium.............. 2		Germany.............. 1	
Sweden.............. 3	Sweden.............. 1		
Argentina.............. 2			Czechoslovakia....... 1
Czechoslovakia....... 2	**Czechoslovakia**....... 3		
Romania.............. 1		**Czechoslovakia**....... 3	
Switzerland.............. 3	Switzerland.............. 2		
Netherlands.............. 2			

after extra-time

Austria.............. 3	Austria.............. 2		
France.............. 2		Austria.............. 1	
Hungary.............. 4	Hungary.............. 1		
Egypt.............. 2			**Italy**.............. 2
Italy.............. 7	**Italy**.............. 1–1		
USA.............. 1		**Italy**.............. 0	
Spain.............. 3	Spain.............. 1–0		
Brazil.............. 1			

Third Place Final: Germany 3 Austria 1

FRANCE 1938

Eighth-finals	Quarter-finals	Semi-finals	Final
Hungary.............. 6	**Hungary**.............. 2		
Dutch East Indies....... 0		**Hungary**.............. 5	
Switzerland......... 1–4	Switzerland......... 0		
Germany.......... 1–2			**Hungary**.............. 2
Cuba.............. 3–2	Cuba.............. 0		
Romania.......... 3–1		Sweden.............. 1	
Sweden.......... Bye	Sweden.............. 8		
France.............. 3	France.............. 1		
Belgium.............. 1		**Italy**.............. 2	
Italy.............. 2	**Italy**.............. 3		
Norway.............. 1			**Italy**.............. 4
Czechoslovakia......... 3	Czechoslovakia....... 1–1		
Netherlands.......... 0		Brazil.............. 1	
Brazil.............. 6	Brazil.............. 1–2		
Poland.............. 5			

Third Place Final: Brazil 4 Sweden 2

BRAZIL 1950

Group 1	Points	Final Pool	Points
Brazil . . . . 4⎫			
Mexico . . . . 0⎭			
Yugoslavia . . . . 3⎫			
Switzerland. . . . . 0⎭	**Brazil** 5		
Yugoslavia . . . . 4⎫	Yugoslavia 4		
Mexico . . . . 1⎭	Switzerland. 3		
Brazil . . . . 2⎫	Mexico 0	Uruguay . . . . 2⎫	
Switzerland. . . . . 2⎭		Spain . . . . 2⎭	
Brazil . . . . 2⎫			
Yugoslavia . . . . 0⎭		**Brazil** . . . . 7⎫	
Switzerland. . . . . 2⎫		Sweden . . . . 1⎭	
Mexico . . . . 1⎭			

Group 2			
Spain . . . . 3⎫		Uruguay . . . . 3⎫	**Uruguay** 5
USA. . . . . 1⎭		Sweden . . . . 2⎭	**Brazil** 4
England. . . . . 2⎫			
Chile . . . . 0⎭	Spain 6	Brazil . . . . 6⎫	Sweden 2
USA. . . . . 1⎫	England. 2	Spain . . . . 1⎭	Spain 1
England. . . . . 0⎭	Chile 2		
Spain . . . . 2⎫	USA. 2	Sweden . . . . 3⎫	
Chile . . . . 0⎭		Spain . . . . 1⎭	
Spain . . . . 1⎫			
England. . . . . 0⎭			
Chile . . . . 5⎫		**Uruguay** . . . . 2⎫	
USA. . . . . 2⎭		Brazil . . . . 1⎭	

Group 3			
Sweden . . . . 3⎫			
Italy . . . . 2⎭			
Sweden . . . . 2⎫	Sweden 3		
Paraguay . . . . 2⎭	Italy 2		
Italy . . . . 2⎫	Paraguay 1		
Paraguay . . . . 0⎭			

Group 4			
Uruguay . . . . 8⎫	**Uruguay** . . . . 2⎫		
Bolivia. . . . . 0⎭	Bolivia. . . . . 0⎭		

SWITZERLAND 1954

Group 1	Points	Quarter-finals	Semi-finals	Final

Group 1

Yugoslavia .... 1⎫
France .... 0⎭
Brazil............. 5⎫
Mexico .... 0⎭
France .... 3⎫
Mexico .... 2⎭
Brazil............. 1⎫
Yugoslavia .... 1⎭

Points

Brazil 3
Yugoslavia 3
France........... 2
Mexico.......... 0

Quarter-finals

W. Germany.... 2 ⎫
Yugoslavia .... 0 ⎭

Semi-finals

W. Germany.... 6⎫

Group 2

Hungary .... 9⎫
Korea .... 0⎭
W. Germany .... 4⎫
Turkey .... 1⎭
Hungary .... 8⎫
W. Germany ..... 3⎭
Turkey .... 7⎫
Korea .... 0⎭
Play-off match:
W. Germany ...... 7⎫
Turkey .... 2⎭

Hungary....... 4
W. Germany.... 2
Turkey 2
Korea 0

Hungary........ 4 ⎫
Brazil .... 2 ⎭ Austria .... 1⎭

Final

W. Germany 3

Group 3

Austria .... 1⎫
Scotland .... 0⎭
Uruguay .... 2⎫
Czechoslovakia .... 0⎭
Austria .... 5⎫
Czechoslovakia .... 0⎭
Uruguay......... 7⎫
Scotland .... 0⎭

Uruguay 4
Austria 4
Czechoslovakia ... 0
Scotland 0

Austria .... 7 ⎫
Switzerland ...... 5 ⎭ **Hungary**........ 4⎫

Group 4

England.......... 4⎫
Belgium .... 4⎭
Switzerland ...... 2⎫
Italy .... 1⎭
England.......... 2⎫
Switzerland ...... 0⎭
Italy............. 4⎫
Belgium .... 1⎭
Play-off match:
Switzerland ...... 4⎫
Italy .... 1⎭

England 3
Italy 2
Switzerland 2
Belgium........ 1

Uruguay .... 4 ⎫
England .... 2 ⎭ Uruguay .... 2⎭

Hungary........ 2⎭

Third Place Final: Austria 3 Uruguay 1

174

SWEDEN 1958

Group 1	Points	Quarter-finals	Semi-finals	Final

Group 1

Argentina . . . . 1⎫
W. Germany . . . . . . 3⎭
Czechoslovakia . . . . 2⎫
W. Germany . . . . . 2⎭
Argentina . . . . 1⎫
Czechoslovakia . . . . 6⎭
Northern Ireland . . . 1⎫
Czechoslovakia . . . . 0⎭
Argentina . . . . 3⎫
Northern Ireland . . . 1⎭
W. Germany . . . . . . 2⎫
Northern Ireland . . . 2⎭
Play-off match:
Northern Ireland . . . 2⎫
Czechoslovakia . . . . 1⎭

Points:
W. Germany 4
Northern Ireland . 3
Czechoslovakia . . . 3
Argentina 2

Quarter-finals:
Brazil . . . . 1⎫
Wales . . . . 0⎭

Semi-finals:
Brazil 5

Group 2

France . . . . 7⎫
Paraguay. . . . . 3⎭
Yugoslavia . . . . 1⎫
Scotland . . . . 1⎭
Paraguay. . . . . 3⎫
Scotland . . . . 2⎭
Yugoslavia . . . . 3⎫
France . . . . 2⎭
Paraguay. . . . . 3⎫
Yugoslavia . . . . 3⎭
France . . . . 2⎫
Scotland . . . . 1⎭

Points:
France. 4
Yugoslavia. 4
Paraguay 3
Scotland 1

Quarter-finals:
France. . . . . 4⎫
Northern Ireland . 0⎭

Semi-finals:
France. . . . . 2⎭

Group 3

Sweden . . . . 3⎫
Mexico . . . . 0⎭
Hungary. . . . . 1⎫
Wales . . . . 1⎭
Mexico . . . . 1⎫
Wales . . . . 1⎭
Sweden . . . . 2⎫
Hungary . . . . 1⎭
Mexico . . . . 0⎫
Hungary . . . . 4⎭
Sweden . . . . 0⎫
Wales . . . . 0⎭
Play-off match:
Wales . . . . 2⎫
Hungary . . . . 1⎭

Points:
Sweden 5
Wales 3
Hungary. 3
Mexico. 1

Quarter-finals:
W. Germany . . . . . 1⎫
Yugoslavia. . . . . . . 0⎭

Semi-finals:
W. Germany . . . . . 1⎫

Group 4

England. . . . . 2⎫
USSR . . . . 2⎭
Brazil. . . . . 3⎫
Austria . . . . 0⎭
USSR . . . . 2⎫
Austria . . . . 0⎭
Brazil. . . . . 0⎫
England. . . . . 0⎭
Brazil. . . . . 2⎫
USSR . . . . 0⎭
England. . . . . 2⎫
Austria . . . . 2⎭
Play-off match:
USSR . . . . 1⎫
England. . . . . 0⎭

Points:
Brazil 5
USSR 3
England 3
Austria 1

Quarter-finals:
USSR . . . . 0⎫
Sweden . . . . 2⎭

Semi-finals:
Sweden . . . . 3⎭

Final:
Brazil . . . . 5⎫
Sweden . . . . 2⎭

Third Place Final: France 6 W. Germany 3

Group 1	Points	Quarter-finals	Semi-finals	Final

Group 1

Uruguay 2
Colombia 1
USSR 2
Yugoslavia 0
Uruguay 1
Yugoslavia 3
Colombia 4
USSR 4
Uruguay 1
USSR 2
Colombia 0
Yugoslavia 5

USSR 5
Yugoslavia 4
Uruguay 2
Colombia 1

Brazil 3
England 1

Brazil 4

Group 2

Chile 3
Switzerland 1
W. Germany 0
Italy 0
Chile 2
Italy 0
Switzerland 1
W. Germany 2
W. Germany 2
Chile 0
Switzerland 0
Italy 3

W. Germany 5
Chile 4
Italy 3
Switzerland 0

USSR 1
Chile 2

Brazil 3

Chile 2

Group 3

Brazil 2
Mexico 0
Czechoslovakia . . . 1
Spain 0
Brazil 0
Czechoslovakia 0
Spain 1
Mexico 0
Brazil 2
Spain 1
Mexico 3
Czechoslovakia 1

Brazil 3
Czechoslovakia . 3
Spain 2
Mexico 2

W. Germany 0
Yugoslavia 1

Yugoslavia 1

Czechoslovakia . 1

Group 4

Argentina 1
Bulgaria 0
Hungary 2
England 1
Argentina 1
England 3
Hungary 6
Bulgaria 1
Argentina 0
Hungary 0
Bulgaria 0
England 0

Hungary 5
England 3
Argentina 3
Bulgaria 1

Hungary 0
Czechoslovakia . 1

Czechoslovakia . 3

Third Place Final: Chile 1 Yugoslavia 0

ENGLAND 1966

Group 1		Points		Quarter-finals		Semi-finals		Final	

Group 1

England.......... 0⎫
Uruguay.......... 0⎭
France........... 1⎫   **England** 5   **England** .... 1⎫
Mexico........... 1⎭   Uruguay 4   Argentina....... 0⎭   **England** .... 2⎫
Uruguay.......... 2⎫   Mexico......... 2
France........... 1⎭   France.......... 1
England.......... 2⎫
Mexico .... 0⎭
Mexico .... 0⎫
Uruguay.......... 0⎭
England.......... 2⎫
France .... 0⎭   **England** .... 4⎫

Group 3

Bulgaria .... 0⎫
Brazil............ 2⎭
Hungary .... 1⎫
Portugal .... 3⎭   Portugal........ 6   Portugal........ 5⎫
Brazil............ 1⎫   Hungary........ 4   North Korea.... 3⎭   Portugal......... 1⎭
Hungary .... 3⎭   Brazil 2
Portugal .... 3⎫   Bulgaria 0
Bulgaria .... 0⎭
Portugal .... 3⎫
Brazil............ 1⎭
Hungary .... 3⎫
Bulgaria .... 1⎭   after
                                                                         extra-
                                                                       time

Group 2

W. Germany ..... 5⎫   **W. Germany**.... 5   **W. Germany**.... 4⎫
Switzerland .... 0⎭   Argentina........ 5   Uruguay .... 0⎭   **W. Germany**.... 2⎫
Spain .... 1⎫   Spain........... 2
Argentina .... 2⎭   Switzerland 0
Switzerland .... 1⎫
Spain .... 2⎭
Argentina .... 0⎫
W. Germany ...... 0⎭
Argentina .... 2⎫
Switzerland ...... 0⎭
Spain .... 1⎫   **W. Germany** .... 2⎫
W. Germany ..... 2⎭

Group 4

USSR .... 3⎫
North Korea ..... 0⎭
Chile .... 0⎫   USSR 6   USSR.......... 2⎫
Italy .... 2⎭   North Korea 3   Hungary........ 1⎭   USSR......... 1⎭
North Korea ..... 1⎫   Italy 2
Chile .... 1⎭   Chile........... 1
Italy............. 0⎫
USSR .... 1⎭
Italy............. 0⎫
North Korea ..... 1⎭
Chile .... 1⎫
USSR .... 2⎭

Third Place Final: Portugal 2 USSR 1

177

MEXICO 1970

Group 1		Points		Quarter-finals		Semi-finals		Final
Mexico	0							
USSR	0							
Belgium	3							
El Salvador	0	USSR	5	USSR	0			
USSR	4	Mexico	5			Uruguay	1	
Belgium	1	Belgium	2	Uruguay	1			
Mexico	4	El Salvador	0					
El Salvador	0							
USSR	2							
El Salvador	0							
Mexico	1							
Belgium	0							

Group 4								
Peru	3							
Bulgaria	2							
Morocco	1							
W. Germany	2	W. Germany	6	Brazil	4			
Peru	3	Peru	4			Brazil	3	
Morocco	0	Bulgaria	1	Peru	2			
Bulgaria	2	Morocco	1					
W. Germany	5							
Peru	1							
W. Germany	3							
Morocco	1							
Bulgaria	1							

Italy 1 **Brazil** 4

Group 2								
Uruguay	2							
Israel	0							
Italy	1							
Sweden	0	Italy	4	Italy	4			
Italy	0	Uruguay	3			Italy	4	
Uruguay	0	Sweden	3	Mexico	1			
Israel	1	Israel	2					
Sweden	1							
Uruguay	0							
Sweden	1							
Italy	0							
Israel	0							

Group 3								
England	1							
Romania	0							
Brazil	4	Brazil	6	England	2			
Czechoslovakia	1	England	4			W. Germany	3	
Romania	2	Romania	2	W. Germany	3			
Czechoslovakia	1	Czechoslovakia	0					
Brazil	1							
England	0							
Brazil	3							
Romania	2							
England	1							
Czechoslovakia	0							

MUNICH 1974

Group 1 | Points

W. Germany . . . . . . 1⌋
Chile . . . . 0⌉
GDR . . . . 2⌋
Australia . . . . 0⌉   GDR 5
Chile . . . . 1⌋   W. Germany 4
GDR . . . . 1⌉   Chile 2
W. Germany . . . . . 3⌋   Australia 1
Australia . . . . 0⌉
Australia . . . . 0⌋
Chile . . . . 0⌉
W. Germany . . . . . 0⌋
GDR . . . . 1⌉

Group 2

Brazil . . . . 0⌋
Yugoslavia . . . . 0⌉
Zaire . . . . 0⌋
Scotland . . . . 2⌉   Yugoslavia 4
Yugoslavia . . . . 9⌋   Brazil 4
Zaire . . . . 0⌉   Scotland 4
Scotland . . . . 0⌋   Zaire 0
Brazil . . . . 0⌉
Zaire . . . . 0⌋
Brazil . . . . 3⌉
Scotland . . . . 1⌋
Yugoslavia . . . . 1⌉

Group 3

Uruguay . . . . 0⌋
Netherlands . . . . . . 2⌉
Sweden . . . . 0⌋
Bulgaria . . . . 0⌉   Netherlands 5
Netherlands . . . . . . 0⌋   Sweden 4
Sweden . . . . 0⌉   Bulgaria 2
Bulgaria . . . . 1⌋   Uruguay 1
Uruguay . . . . 1⌉
Bulgaria . . . . 1⌋
Netherlands . . . . . . 4⌉
Sweden . . . . 3⌋
Uruguay . . . . 0⌉

Group 4

Italy . . . . 3⌋
Haiti . . . . 1⌉
Poland . . . . 3⌋
Argentina . . . . 2⌉   Poland 6
Haiti . . . . 0⌋   Argentina 3
Poland . . . . 7⌉   Italy 3
Argentina . . . . 1⌋   Haiti 0
Italy . . . . 1⌉
Argentina . . . . 4⌋
Haiti . . . . 1⌉
Poland . . . . 2⌋
Italy . . . . 1⌉

Group A | Points | | Final

Netherlands . . . . . 4⌉
Argentina . . . . 0⌋
Brazil . . . . 1⌉
GDR . . . . 0⌋
GDR . . . . 0⌉   **Netherlands** . . . . . 6 ⌉
Netherlands . . . . . . 2⌋   Brazil . . . . 4 ⌈ **Netherlands** . . . . . 1 ⌉
Argentina . . . . 1⌉   GDR . . . . 1 ⌋
Brazil . . . . 2⌋   Argentina 1
Netherlands . . . . . . 2⌉
Brazil . . . . 0⌋
Argentina . . . . 1⌉
GDR . . . . 1⌋

Group B | | Points

Yugoslavia . . . . 0⌉
W. Germany . . . . 2⌋
Sweden . . . . 0⌉
Poland . . . . 1⌋
W. Germany . . . . . 4⌉   **W. Germany** . . . . 6 ⌉
Sweden . . . . 2⌋   Poland . . . . 4 ⌈ **W. Germany** . . . . 2 ⌋
Poland . . . . 2⌉   Sweden 2
Yugoslavia . . . . 1⌋   Yugoslavia 0
Sweden . . . . 2⌉
Yugoslavia . . . . 1⌋
Poland . . . . 0⌉
W. Germany . . . . . 1⌋

Third Place Final: Poland 1 Brazil 0

179

The Qualifying Competition

Date	Venue	Match	Results	Referee	Attendance

AFRICA

Concluding Matches

Date	Venue	Match	Results	Referee	Attendance
25. 9.77	Tunis	Tunisia v Nigeria	0:0 (0:0)	J. Carpenter, Ireland Rep.	38,229
8.10.77	Lagos	Nigeria v Egypt	4:0 (1:0)	C. Correia, Portugal	—
21.10.77	Cairo	Egypt v Nigeria	3:1 (2:0)	E. Platopoulos, Greece	90,000
12.11.77	Lagos	Nigeria v Tunisia	0:1 (0:0)	E. Dörflinger, Switzerland	80,000
25.11.77	Cairo	Egypt v Tunisia	3:2 (1:0)	H. Ok, Turkey	42,850
11.12.77	Tunis	Tunisia v Egypt	4:1 (2:0)	G. Menegali, Italy	120,000

Classification:						
1 Tunisia (Qualified)	4	2	1	1	7:4	5
2 Egypt	4	2	0	2	7:11	4
3 Nigeria	4	1	1	2	5:4	3

AMERICA—NORTH AND CENTRAL AND CARIBBEAN

Final Round/All Areas

Date	Venue	Match	Results	Referee	Attendance
8.10.77	Monterrey	Guatemala v Surinam	3:2 (2:1)	M. Wuertz, USA	—
8.10.77	Monterrey	Canada v El Salvador	1:2 (0:1)	L. Pestarino, Argentina	42,000
9.10.77	Mexico City	Mexico v Haiti	4:1 (1:0)	R. Barreto Ruiz, Uruguay	108,000
12.10.77	Mexico City	Canada v Surinam	2:1 (1:1)	L. P. Siles Calderon, Costa Rica	90,000
12.10.77	Mexico City	Mexico v El Salvador	3:1 (1:0)	T. Kibritjian, USA	110,000
12.10.77	Monterrey	Guatemala v Haiti	1:2 (0:2)	L. Pestarino, Argentina	13,465
15.10.77	Monterrey	Mexico v Surinam	8:1 (3:1)	J. L. Valverde Salazar, Costa Rica	52,000
16.10.77	Mexico City	El Salvador v Haiti	0:1 (0:1)	R. Calderon, Cuba	—
16.10.77	Mexico City	Canada v Guatemala	2:1 (2:0)	R. Barreto Ruiz, Uruguay	25,000
19.10.77	Mexico City	Mexico v Guatemala	2:1 (1:1)	L. Pestarino, Argentina	110,000
20.10.77	Monterrey	El Salvador v Surinam	3:2 (1:0)	C. Crockwell, Bermuda	—
20.10.77	Monterrey	Canada v Haiti	1:1 (0:0)	J. L. Valverde Salazar, Costa Rica	30,000
22.10.77	Monterrey	Mexico v Canada	3:1 (2:1)	R. Moses, Netherl. Antilles	55,000
23.10.77	Mexico City	Guatemala v El Salvador	2:2 (0:1)	J. Freundt de la Puente, Dom. Republic	—
23.10.77	Mexico City	Haiti v. Surinam	1:0 (1:0)	C. R. Ortiz Perez, Honduras	—

Classification:						
1 Mexico (Qualified)	5	5	0	0	20:5	10
2 Haiti	5	3	1	1	6:6	7
3 Canada	5	2	1	2	7:8	5
4 El Salvador	5	2	1	2	8:9	5
5 Guatemala	5	1	1	3	8:10	3
6 Surinam	5	0	0	5	6:17	0

AMERICA SOUTH

Group 1 (Brazil, Paraguay, Colombia)

Date	Venue	Match	Results	Referee	Attendance
20.2.77	Bogota	Colombia v Brazil	0:0 (0:0)	M. Comesaña, Argentina	55,439
24.2.77	Bogota	Colombia v Paraguay	0:1 (0:1)	C. A. Orosco Guerrero, Peru	—
6.3.77	Asuncion	Paraguay v Colombia	1:1 (1:0)	R. T. Cerullo, Uruguay	30,154
9.3.77	Rio de Janeiro	Brazil v Colombia	6:0 (4:0)	A. N. Coerezza, Argentina	132,764
13.3.77	Asuncion	Paraguay v Brazil	0:1 (0:0)	L. Pestarino, Argentina	40,490
20.3.77	Rio de Janeiro	Brazil v Paraguay	1:1 (1:0)	R. Barreto Ruiz, Uruguay	94,947

Date	Venue	Match	Results						Referee	Attendance

Group 2 (*Uruguay, Venezuela, Bolivia*)

9.2.77	Caracas	Venezuela *v* Uruguay	1:1 (0:1)	G. Velasquez Ramirez, Colombia	5,000
27.2.77	La Paz	Bolivia *v* Uruguay	1:0 (0:0)	R. Arppi Filho, Brazil	20,306
6.3.77	Caracas	Venezuela *v* Bolivia	1:3 (0:1)	J. Silvagno, Chile	5,034
13.3.77	La Paz	Bolivia *v* Venezuela	2:0 (2:0)	E. Perez Nuñez, Peru	21,217
17.3.77	Montevideo	Uruguay *v* Venezuela	2:0 (1:0)	A. Marques, Brazil	4,383
27.3.77	Montevideo	Uruguay *v* Bolivia	2:2 (1:1)	A. A. Ithurralde, Argentina	7,477

Group 3 (Chile, Peru, Ecuador)

20.2.77	Quito	Ecuador *v* Peru	1:1 (0:1)	A. M. Röhrig, Brazil	—
27.2.77	Guayaquil	Ecuador *v* Chile	0:1 (0:1)	J. E. Romero, Argentina	51,200
6.3.77	Santiago	Chile *v* Peru	1:1 (1:0)	J. Faville Neto, Brazil	67,983
12.3.77	Lima	Peru *v* Ecuador	4:0 (1:0)	L. Barrancos Alvarez, Bolivia	43,319
20.3.77	Santiago	Chile *v* Ecuador	3:0 (2:0)	V. Llobregat, Venezuela	15,571
26.3.77	Lima	Peru *v* Chile	2:0 (0:0)	A. C. Coelho, Brazil	62,000

Group Winners' Tournament

10.7.77	Cali	Brazil *v* Peru	1:0 (0:0)	M. Comesaña, Argentina	50,345
14.7.77	Cali	Brazil *v* Bolivia	8:0 (4:0)	J. Silvagno, Chile	38,037
17.7.77	Cali	Peru *v* Bolivia	5:0 (2:0)	R. Barreto Ruiz, Uruguay	32,511

ASIA/OCEANIA

Concluding Matches

19. 6.77	Hong Kong	Hong Kong *v* Iran	0:2 (0:1)	C. Gussoni, Italy	28,447
26. 6.77	Hong Kong	Hong Kong *v* Korea Rep.	0:1 (0:0)	F. Biwersi, Germany FR	26,952
3. 7.77	Pusan	Korea Rep. *v* Iran	0:0 (0:0)	I. Foote, Scotland	14,882
10. 7.77	Adelaide	Australia *v* Hong Kong	3:0 (1:0)	F. Hungerbühler, Switzerland	14,000
14. 8.77	Melbourne	Australia *v* Iran	0:1 (0:0)	F. Wöhrer, Austria	17,500
27. 8.77	Sydney	Australia *v* Korea Rep.	2:1 (0:1)	J. Keizer, Netherlands	8,719
2.10.77	Hong Kong	Hong Kong *v* Kuwait	1:3 (1:1)	A. Franco Martinez, Spain	25,000
9.10.77	Seoul	Korea Rep. *v* Kuwait	1:0 (0:0)	G. Ciacci, Italy	13,000
16.10.77	Sydney	Australia *v* Kuwait	1:2 (0:1)	M. Vautrot, France	12,015
23.10.77	Seoul	Korea Rep. *v* Australia	0:0 (0:0)	U. Eriksson, Sweden	20,000
28.10.77	Tehran	Iran *v* Kuwait	1:0 (0:0)	C. Thomas, Wales	100,000
30.10.77	Hong Kong	Hong Kong *v* Australia	2:5 (0:3)	A. Ponnet, Belgium	8,000
5.11.77	Kuwait	Kuwait *v* Korea Rep.	2:2 (0:1)	J. Dubach, Switzerland	—
11.11.77	Tehran	Iran *v* Korea Rep.	2:2 (0:1)	P. Partridge, England	85,000

Date	Venue	Match	Results	Referee	Referee	Attendance
12.11.77	Kuwait	Kuwait v Hong Kong	4:0 (3:0)	A. Victor, Luxembourg		25,000
18.11.77	Tehran	Iran v Hong Kong	3:0 (3:0)	M. Raus, Yugoslavia		55,000
19.11.77	Kuwait	Kuwait v Australia	1:0 (0:0)	J. Bucek, Austria		30,000
25.11.77	Tehran	Iran v Australia	1:0 (1:0)	M. Kitabdjian, France		84,000
3.12.77	Kuwait	Kuwait v Iran	1:2 (1:0)	M. Wright, Ireland North		—
4.12.77	Seoul	Korea Rep. v Hong Kong	5:2 (2:0)	H. Aldinger, Germany FR		—

Classification							
	1 Iran (Qualified)	8	6	2	0	12:3	14
	2 Korea Rep.	8	3	4	1	12:8	10
	3 Kuwait	8	4	1	3	13:8	9
	4 Australia	8	3	1	4	11:8	7
	5 Hong Kong	8	0	0	8	5:26	0

EUROPE

Group 1 (Poland, Portugal, Denmark, Cyprus)

Date	Venue	Match	Results	Referee	Attendance
23. 5.76	Limassol	Cyprus v Denmark	1:5 (1:3)	N. M. Doudine, Bulgaria	6,000
16.10.76	Porto	Portugal v Poland	0:2 (0:0)	M. Kitabdjian, France	40,000
27.10.76	Copenhagen	Denmark v Cyprus	5:0 (0:0)	J. Colling, Luxembourg	30,600
31.10.76	Warsaw	Poland v Cyprus	5:0 (3:0)	G. Müncz, Hungary	50,000
17.11.76	Lisbon	Portugal v Denmark	1:0 (0:0)	A. Aouissi, Algeria	30,000
5.12.76	Limassol	Cyprus v Portugal	1:2 (0:1)	C. Ghita, Romania	7,000
1. 5.77	Copenhagen	Denmark v Portugal	1:2 (0:1)	A. Mattson, Finland	46,000
15. 5.77	Limassol	Cyprus v Poland	1:3 (1:2)	M. Ashkenazi, Israel	8,000
21. 9.77	Chorzow	Poland v Denmark	4:1 (2:0)	N. Rainea, Romania	93,000
9.10.77	Copenhagen	Denmark v Portugal	2:4 (1:2)	E. Asim-Zade, USSR	23,300
29.10.77	Chorzow	Poland v Portugal	1:1 (1:0)	W. Eschweiler, Germany FR	80,000
16.11.77	Lisbon	Portugal v Cyprus	4:0 (2:0)	M. Jursa, Czechoslovakia	13,000

Classification:							
	1 Poland (Qualified)	6	5	1	0	17:4	11
	2 Portugal	6	4	1	1	12:6	9
	3 Denmark	6	2	0	4	14:12	4
	4 Cyprus	6	0	0	6	3:24	0

Group 2 (Italy, England, Finland, Luxembourg)

Date	Venue	Match	Results	Referee	Attendance
13. 6.76	Helsinki	Finland v England	1:4 (1:2)	A. Delcourt, Belgium	24,336
22. 9.76	Helsinki	Finland v Luxembourg	7:1 (3:0)	S. I. Thime, Norway	4,555
13.10.76	London	England v Finland	2:1 (1:0)	U. Eriksson, Sweden	92,000
16.10.76	Luxembourg	Luxembourg v Italy	1:4 (0:2)	E. Dörflinger, Switzerland	11,700
17.11.76	Rome	Italy v England	2:0 (1:0)	A. Klein, Israel	70,718
30. 3.77	London	England v Luxembourg	5:0 (1:0)	P. Bonett, Malta	81,000
26. 5.77	Luxembourg	Luxembourg v Finland	0:1 (0:0)	O. Amundsen, Denmark	1,800
8. 6.77	Helsinki	Finland v Italy	0:3 (0:1)	R. Helies, France	17,531
12.10.77	Luxembourg	Luxembourg v England	0:2 (0:1)	A. Jarguz, Poland	10,621
15.10.77	Turin	Italy v Finland	6:1 (3:0)	N. M. Doudine, Bulgaria	68,000
16.11.77	London	England v Italy	2:0 (1:0)	K. Palotai, Hungary	90,000
3.12.77	Rome	Italy v Luxembourg	3:0 (2:0)	D. Maksimovic, Yugoslavia	75,000

Classification:							
	1 Italy (Qualified)	6	5	0	1	18:4	10
	2 England	6	5	0	1	15:4	10
	3 Finland	6	2	0	4	11:16	4
	4 Luxembourg	6	0	0	6	2:22	0

Date	Venue	Match	Results	Referee	Attendance

Group 3 (German DR, Austria, Turkey, Malta)

31.10.76	Izmir	Turkey v Malta	4:0 (1:0)	M. Jursa, Czechoslovakia	68,034
17.11.76	Dresden	German DR v Turkey	1:1 (1:0)	P. Partridge, England	30,000
5.12.76	Valletta	Malta v Austria	0:1 (0:0)	H. Seoudi, Tunisia	7,368
2. 4.77	Valletta	Malta v German DR	0:1 (0:0)	B. Della Bruna, Switzerland	6,279
17. 4.77	Vienna	Austria v Turkey	1:0 (1:0)	V. Jarkov, USSR	60,000
30. 4.77	Salzburg	Austria v Malta	9:0 (5:0)	A. Jarguz, Poland	17,000
24. 9.77	Vienna	Austria v German DR	1:1 (1:1)	T. Reynolds, Wales	72,000
12.10.77	Leipzig	German DR v Austria	1:1 (0:1)	I. Foote, Scotland	95,000
29.10.77	Babelsberg	German DR v Malta	9:0 (3:0)	J. Namdar, Iran	23,000
30.10.77	Izmir	Turkey v Austria	0:1 (0:0)	J. R. Gordon, Scotland	72,000
16.11.77	Izmir	Turkey v German DR	1:2 (0:1)	A. Michelotti, Italy	10,000
27.11.77	Valletta	Malta v Turkey	0:3 (0:2)	M. Larache, Morocco	2,246

Classification:							
	1 *Austria* (Qualified)	6	4	2	0	14:2	10
	2 German DR	6	3	3	0	15:4	9
	3 Turkey	6	2	1	3	9:5	5
	4 Malta	6	0	0	6	0:27	0

Group 4 (Netherlands, Belgium, N. Ireland, Iceland)

5. 9.76	Reykjavik	Iceland v Belgium	0:1 (0:0)	J. Carpenter, Ireland Rep.	9,580
8. 9.76	Reykjavik	Iceland v Netherlands	0:1 (0:1)	P. Mulhall, Ireland Rep.	10,210
13.10.76	Rotterdam	Netherlands v N. Ireland	2:2 (0:1)	A. Franco Martinez, Spain	56,000
10.11.76	Liège	Belgium v N. Ireland	2:0 (1:0)	A. Prokop, German DR	25,081
26. 3.77	Antwerp	Belgium v Netherlands	0:2 (0:1)	S. Gonella, Italy	48,343
11. 6.77	Reykjavik	Iceland v N. Ireland	1:0 (1:0)	R. Glöckner, German DR	10,269
31. 8.77	Nijmegen	Netherlands v Iceland	4:1 (3:0)	M. Hirviniemi, Finland	18,200
3. 9.77	Anderlecht	Belgium v Iceland	4:0 (2:0)	S. I. Thime, Norway	5,807
21. 9.77	Belfast	N. Ireland v Iceland	2:0 (0:0)	H. Lund-Sørensen, Denmark	15,000
12.10.77	Belfast	N. Ireland v Netherlands	0:1 (0:0)	A. J. Da Silva Garrido, Portugal	33,000
26.10.77	Amsterdam	Netherlands v Belgium	1:0 (1:0)	P. Partridge, England	65,000
16.11.77	Belfast	N. Ireland v Belgium	3:0 (1:0)	G. Konrath, France	8,000

Classification:							
	1 *Netherlands* (Qualified)	6	5	1	0	11:3	11
	2 Belgium	6	3	0	3	7:6	6
	3 N. Ireland	6	2	1	3	7:6	5
	4 Iceland	6	1	0	5	2:12	2

Group 5 (Bulgaria, France, Ireland Rep.)

9.10.76	Sofia	Bulgaria v France	2:2 (1:2)	I. Foote, Scotland	45,000
17.11.76	Paris	France v Ireland Rep.	2:0 (0:0)	D. Maksimovic, Yugoslavia	43,417
30. 3.77	Dublin	Ireland Rep. v France	1:0 (1:0)	E. Linemayr, Austria	36,000
1. 6.77	Sofia	Bulgaria v Ireland Rep.	2:1 (1:0)	N. Zlatanos, Greece	35,214
12.10.77	Dublin	Ireland Rep. v Bulgaria	0:0 (0:0)	S. Gonella, Italy	25,000
16.11.77	Paris	France v Bulgaria	3:1 (1:0)	C. Corver, Netherlands	50,000

Classification:							
	1 *France* (Qualified)	4	2	1	1	7:4	5
	2 Bulgaria	4	1	2	1	5:6	4
	3 Ireland Rep.	4	1	1	2	2:4	3

Date	Venue	Match	Results	Referee	Attendance

Group 6 (Sweden, Switzerland, Norway)

Date	Venue	Match	Results	Referee	Attendance
16. 6.76	Solna	Sweden v Norway	2:0 (2:0)	C. Corver, Netherlands	27,800
8. 9.76	Oslo	Norway v Switzerland	1:0 (0:0)	F. Rion, Belgium	15,000
9.10.76	Basle	Switzerland v Sweden	1:2 (1:1)	H. Ok, Turkey	30,000
8. 6.77	Solna	Sweden v Switzerland	2:1 (0:0)	M. Wright, Ireland North	43,799
7. 9.77	Oslo	Norway v Sweden	2:1 (1:0)	A. Prokop, German DR	23,260
30.10.77	Berne	Switzerland v Norway	1:0 (1:0)	V. Lipatov, USSR	11,000

Classification:

1	*Sweden* (Qualified)	4	3	0	1	7:4	6
2	Norway	4	2	0	2	3:4	4
3	Switzerland	4	1	0	3	3:5	2

Group 7 (Scotland, Czechoslovakia, Wales)

Date	Venue	Match	Results	Referee	Attendance
13.10.76	Prague	Czechoslovakia v Scotland	2:0 (0:0)	A. Michelotti, Italy	30,000
17.11.76	Glasgow	Scotland v Wales	1:0 (1:0)	F. Biwersi, Germany FR	65,000
30. 3.77	Wrexham	Wales v Czechoslovakia	3:0 (1:0)	A. J. Da Silva Garrido, Portugal	18,022
21. 9.77	Hampden Park	Scotland v Czechoslovakia	3:1 (2:0)	F. Rion, Belgium	85,000
12.10.77	Liverpool	Wales v Scotland	0:2 (0:0)	R. Wurtz, France	50,850
16.11.77	Prague	Czechoslovakia v Wales	1:0 (1:0)	A. Prokop, German DR	20,000

Classification:

1	*Scotland* (Qualified)	4	3	0	1	6:3	6
2	Czechoslovakia	4	2	0	2	4:6	4
3	Wales	4	1	0	3	3:4	2

Group 8 (Yugoslavia, Spain, Romania)

Date	Venue	Match	Results	Referee	Attendance
10.10.76	Seville	Spain v Yugoslavia	1:0 (0:0)	K. Palotai, Hungary	19,217
16. 4.77	Bucharest	Romania v Spain	1:0 (1:0)	J. R. Gordon, Scotland	18,500
8. 5.77	Zagreb	Yugoslavia v Romania	0:2 (0:2)	M. Ashkenazi, Israel	40,000
26.10.77	Madrid	Spain v Romania	2:0 (0:0)	R. Wurtz, France	40,000
13.11.77	Bucharest	Romania v Yugoslavia	4:6 (3:2)	A. Delcourt, Belgium	35,000
30.11.77	Belgrade	Yugoslavia v Spain	0:1 (0:0)	K. Burns, England	95,000

Classification:

1	*Spain* (Qualified)	4	3	0	1	4:1	6
2	Romania	4	2	0	2	7:8	4
3	Yugoslavia	4	1	0	3	6:8	2

Group 9 (USSR, Hungary, Greece)

Date	Venue	Match	Results	Referee	Attendance
9.10.76	Athens	Greece v Hungary	1:1 (0:0)	F. Wöhrer, Austria	25,000
24. 4.77	Moscow	USSR v Greece	2:0 (1:0)	J. Dubach, Switzerland	50,000
30. 4.77	Budapest	Hungary v USSR	2:1 (1:0)	H. Aldinger, Germany FR	70,000
10. 5.77	Thessaloniki	Greece v USSR	1:0 (0:0)	C. Gussoni, Italy	32,000
18. 5.77	Tbilisi	USSR v Hungary	2:0 (2:0)	J. Taylor, England	70,000
28. 5.77	Budapest	Hungary v Greece	3:0 (2:0)	J. F. Beck, Netherlands	70,000

Classification:

1	*Hungary*	4	2	1	1	6:4	5
2	USSR	4	2	0	2	5:3	4
3	Greece	4	1	1	2	2:6	3

EUROPE/SOUTH AMERICA Play-off

Date	Venue	Match	Results	Referee	Attendance
29.10.77	Budapest	Hungary v Bolivia	6:0 (5:0)	R. Barreto Ruiz, Uruguay	65,000
30.11.77	La Paz	Bolivia v *Hungary*	2:3 (1:2)	C. Corver, Netherlands	—

Qualified for Argentina: *Hungary*

World Cup 1978 Results

First Round

GROUP 1

Italy . . . . (1) 2   **France** . . . . (1) 1 (Mar del
   Rossi, Zaccarelli   Lacombe   Plata)

  Italy: Zoff; Gentile, Bellugi, Scirea, Cabrini; Tardelli, Antognoni (Zaccarelli 45), Benetti; Causio, Rossi, Bettega.

  France: Bertrand-Demanes; Janvion, Rio, Tresor, Bossis; Guillou, Platini, Michel; Dalger, Lacombe (Berdoll 72), Six (Rouyer 76).

Referee: M. Rainea (Romania)

Argentina . . . . (1) 2   **Hungary** . . . . (1) 1 (B. Aires)
   Luque, Bertoni   Csapo

  Argentina: Fillol; Olguin, Galvan, Passarella, Tarantini; Ardiles, Gallego, Valencia (Alonso 75); Houseman (Bertoni 67), Luque, Kempes.

  Hungary: Gujdar; Torok (Martos 46), Kocsis, Kereki, J. Toth; Nyilasi, Pinter, Zombori; Csapo, Torocsik, Nagy.

Referee: A. Garrido (Portugal)

Italy . . . . (2) 3   **Hungary** . . . . (0) 1 (Mar del
   Rossi, Bettega, Benetti   A. Toth (pen.)   Plata)

  Italy: Zoff; Gentile, Bellugi, Scirea, Cabrini (Cuccureddu 79); Tardelli, Benetti, Antognoni; Causio, Rossi, Bettega (Graziani 83).

  Hungary: Meszaros; J. Toth, Kocsis, Kereki, Martos; Pusztai, Pinter, Zombori; Fazekas (Al Toth 46), Csapo, Nagy (Halasz 46).

Referee: R. Barreto (Uruguay)

Argentina . . . . (1) 2   **France** . . . . (0) 1 (B. Aires)
   Passarella (pen.), Luque   Platini

  Argentina: Fillol; Olguin, Galvan, Passarella, Tarantini; Ardiles, Gallego, Valencia (Alonso 64, Ortiz 71), Houseman, Luque, Kempes.

  France: Bertrand-Demanes (Baratelli 58); Battiston, Lopez, Tresor, Bossis; Michel, Platini, Bathenay; Rocheteau, Lacombe, Six.

Referee: J. Dubach (Switzerland)

France . . . . (3) 3   **Hungary** . . . . (1) 1 (Mar del
   Lopez, Berdoll, Rocheteau   Zombori   Plata)

  France: Dropsy; Janvion, Lopez, Tresor, Bracci; Petit, Bathenay, Papi (Platini 45); Rocheteau (Six 75), Berdoll, Rouyer.

  Hungary: Gujdar; Martos, Balint, Kereki, J. Toth; Nyilasi, Pinter, Zombori; Pusztai, Torocsik, Nagy (Csapo 72).

Referee: A. Coelho (Brazil)

Italy . . . . (0) 1   **Argentina** . . . . (0) 0 (B. Aires)
    Bettega

Italy: Zoff; Gentile, Bellugi (Cuccureddu 6), Scirea, Cabrini; Tardelli, Antognoni (Zaccarelli, 45), Benetti; Causio, Rossi, Bettega.

Argentina: Fillol; Olguin, Galvan, Passarella, Tarantini; Ardiles, Gallego, Valencia; Bertoni, Kempes, Ortiz (Houseman 72).

Referee: A. Klein (Israel)

	W	D	L	F	A	Pts
Italy	3	0	0	6	2	6
Argentina	2	0	1	4	3	4
France	1	0	2	5	5	2
Hungary	0	0	3	3	8	0

GROUP 2

West Germany 0   **Poland** . . . . 0 (B. Aires)

West Germany: Maier; Vogts, Russmann, Kaltz, Zimmermann; Bonhof, Flohe, Beer; Abramczik, Fischer, Muller H.

Poland: Tomaszewski; Maculewicz, Gorgon, Zmuda, Szymanowski; Masztaler (Kasperczak 78), Deyna, Nawalka; Lato, Szarmach, Lubanski (Boniek 84).

Referee: A. Coerezza (Argentina)

Tunisia . . . . (0) 3   **Mexico** . . . . (1) 1 (Rosario)
    Kaabi, Gommidh, Dhouib   Vasquez (pen.)

Tunisia: Naili; Dhouib, Kaabi, Jebali, Gommidh; Lahzami (Labidi 88), Rehaien, Akid; Tarak, Dhiab, Aziza (Karoui 70).

Mexico: Reyes; Martinez, Ramos, Tena, Vasquez; Mendizabal (Lugo 67), De La Torre; Cuellar, Rangel, Sanchez, Isiordia.

Referee: J. Gordon (Scotland)

West Germany . . . . (4) 6   **Mexico** . . . . (0) 0 (Cordoba)
    Muller D., Muller H., Flohe (2),
    Rummenigge (2)

West Germany: Maier; Vogts, Russmann, Kaltz, Dietz; Bonhof, Flohe, Muller H.; Rummenigge, Fischer, Muller D.

Mexico: Reyes (Soto 39); Tena, Ramos, Vasquez, Mendizabel; De La Torre, Martinez, Lopez (Lugo 46); Sanchez, Rangel, Cuellar.

Referee: F. Bouzo (Syria)

Poland . . . . (1) 1   **Tunisia** . . . . (0) 0 (Rosario)
    Lato

Poland: Tomaszewski; Maculewicz, Gorgon, Zmuda, Szymanowski; Kasperczak, Deyna, Nawalka; Lato, Szarmach (Iwan 59), Lubanski (Boniek 75).

Tunisia: Naili; Dhouib, Kaabi, Gasmi, Labidi; Gommidh, Lahzami, Rehaien; Akid, Dhiab, Jebali.

Referee: A. Martinez (Spain)

West Germany 0   **Tunisia** . . . . 0 (Cordoba)

West Germany: Maier; Vogts, Russmann, Kaltz, Dietz; Bonhof, Flohe, Muller H.; Rummenigge, Fischer, Muller D.

Tunisia: Naili; Dhouib, Kaabi, Gasmi, Labidi; Gommidh, Lahzami, Rehaien; Akid (Aiza 82), Dhiab, Jebali.

Referee: C. Ovozco (Peru)

Poland . . . . (1) 3   Mexico . . . . (0) 1 (Rosario)
    Boniek (2), Deyna   Rangel
Poland: Tomaszewski; Iwan (Maculewicz 78), Gorgon, Zmuda, Szymanowski; Masztaler, Deyna, Kasperczak; Lato, Boniek (Lubanski 84), Rudy.
  Mexico: Soto; Vasquez, De La Torre, Ortega, Martinez; Gomez, Sanchez, Flores; Cuellar, Rangel, Cardenas.
Referee: J. Namdar (Iran)

	W	D	L	F	A	Pts
Poland	2	1	0	4	1	5
West Germany	1	2	0	6	0	4
Tunisia	1	1	1	3	2	3
Mexico	0	0	3	2	12	0

GROUP 3

Austria . . . . (1) 2   Spain . . . . (1) 1 (B. Aires
    Schachner, Krankl   Ruiz   V.S.)
Austria: Koncilia; Sara, Obermayer, Pezzey, Breitenberger; Hickersberger (Weber 67), Prohaska, Kreuz; Schachner (Pirkner 80), Krankl, Jara.
  Spain: Angel; Marcelino, Migueli, Pirri, De La Cruz; Asensi, San Jose, Cardenosa (Leal 46); Ruiz, Cano, Rexach (Quini 60).
Referee: K. Palotai (Hungary)

Brazil . . . . (1) 1   Sweden . . . . (1) 1 (Mar del
    Reinaldo   Sjoberg   Plata)
Brazil: Leao; Toninho, Oscar, Amaral, Edinho; Cerezo (Dirceu 80), Batista, Rivelino; Gil (Nelinho 68), Zico, Reinaldo.
  Sweden: Hellstrom; Borg, Roy Andersson, Nordqvist, Erlandsson; Tapper, L. Larsson (Edstrom 79), Linderoth; B. Larsson, Sjoberg, Wendt.
Referee: C. Thomas (Wales)

Brazil 0   Spain . . . . 0 (Mar del
                                                                                 Plata)
Brazil: Leao; Nelinho (Gil 69), Oscar, Amaral, Edinho; Cerezo, Batista, Dirceu; Toninho, Reinaldo, Zico (Mendonca 84).
  Spain: Angel; Uria, Olmo, Migueli (Blosca 50), Perez; San Jose, Asensi, Cardenosa; Leal (Guzman 78), Santillana, Juanito.
Referee: S. Gonella (Italy)

Austria . . . . (1) 1   Sweden . . . . (0) 0 (B. Aires
    Krankl   V.S.)
Austria: Koncilia; Sara, Obermayer, Pezzey, Breitenberger; Hickersberger, Prohaska, Kreuz; Jara, Krankl, Kreiger (Weber 71).
  Sweden: Hellstrom; Borg, Roy Andersson, Nordqvist, Erlandsson; Tapper (Torstensson 36), Linderoth (Edstrom 60), B. Larsson; L. Larsson, Sjoberg, Wendt.
Referee: C. Corver (Holland)

Spain . . . . (0) 1   Sweden . . . . (0) 0 (B. Aires
    Asensi   V.S.)
Spain: Angel; Uria, Perez, Olmo (Pirri 46), Blosca; San Jose, Cardenosa, Asensi; Leal, Santillana, Juanito.
  Sweden: Hellstrom; Borg, Roy Andersson, Nordqvist, Erlandsson; L. Larsson, Nordin, B. Larsson; Nilsson, Edstrom (Wendt 59), Sjoberg (Linderoth 66).
Referee: F. Biwersi (West Germany)

Brazil. (1) 1   **Austria**. (0) 0 (Mar del
  Roberto   Plata)
Brazil: Leao; Toninho, Oscar, Amaral, Rodrigues Neto; Cerezo (Chicao 71), Batista, Dirceu, Gil, Roberto, Mendonca (Zico 83).
Austria: Koncilia; Sara, Obermayer, Pezzey, Breitenberger; Hickersberger (Weber 61), Prohaska, Kreuz; Jara, Krankl, Kreiger (Happich 84).
Referee: R. Wurtz (France)

	W	D	L	F	A	Pts
Austria	2	0	1	3	2	4
Brazil	1	2	0	2	1	4
Spain	1	1	1	2	2	3
Sweden	0	1	2	1	3	1

GROUP 4

Peru. (1) 3   **Scotland**. (1) 1 (Cordoba)
  Cueto, Cubillas (2)   Jordan
Peru: Quiroga; Duarte, Manzo, Chumpitaz, Diaz; Cueto (Rojas 82), Velasquez, Cubillas; Munante, La Rosa (Sotil 62), Oblitas.
Scotland: Rough; Kennedy, Forsyth, Burns, Buchan; Rioch (Macari 70), Masson (Gemmill 70), Hartford; Dalglish, Jordan, Johnston.
Referee: U. Ericsson (Sweden)

Holland. (1) 3   **Iran**. (0) 0 (Mendoza)
  Rensenbrink (3) (2 pen.)
Holland: Jongbloed; Suurbier, Krol, Rijsbergen; W. Van der Kerkhof, Jansen, Neeskens, Haan; R. Van der Kerkhof (Nanninga 70), Rep, Rensenbrink.
Iran: Hedjazi; Nazari, Abdollahi, Kazerani, Eskandarian; Parvin, Sadeghi, Nayebagha, Ghasempour; Jahani, Faraki (Rowshan 50).
Referee: A. Archundia (Mexico)

Scotland. (1) 1   **Iran**. (0) 1 (Cordoba)
  Eskandarian (O.G.)   Danaifard
Scotland: Rough; Jardine, Burns, Buchan (Forsyth 56), Donachie; Gemmill, Macari, Hartford; Dalglish (Harper 74), Jordan, Robertson.
Iran: Hedjazi; Nazari, Abdollahi, Kazerani, Eskandarian; Parvin, Ghasempour, Sadeghi, Danaifard (Nayebagha 89); Faraki (Rowshan 84), Jahani.
Referee: Y. N'Diaye (Senegal)

Holland. 0   **Peru**. 0 (Mendoza)
Holland: Jongbloed; Suurbier, Rijsbergen, Krol, Poortvliet; Jansen, W. Van der Kerkhof, Neeskens (Nanninga 68), Haan; R. Van der Kerkhof (Rep 46), Rensenbrink.
Peru: Quiroga; Duarte, Manzo, Chumpitaz, Diaz; Cueto, Velasquez, Cubillas; Munante, La Rosa (Sotil 62), Oblitas.
Referee: A. Prokop (East Germany)

Scotland. (1) 3   **Holland**. (1) 2 (Mendoza)
  Dalglish, Gemmill (2) (1 pen.)   Rensenbrink (pen.), Rep
Scotland: Rough; Kennedy, Forsyth, Buchan, Donachie; Rioch, Gemmill, Souness, Hartford; Dalglish, Jordan.
Holland: Jongbloed; Suurbier, Krol, Rijsbergen (Wildschut 45), Poortvliet; Jansen, W. Van der Kerkhof, Neeskens (Boskamp 8); R. Van der Kerkhof, Rep, Rensenbrink.
Referee: E. Linemayr (Austria)

Peru . . . . (3) 4   Iran . . . . (1) 1   (Cordoba)
    Velasquez, Cubillas (3) (2 pen.)   Rowshan

Peru: Quiroga; Duarte, Manzo (Leguia 67), Chumpitaz, Diaz; Cueto, Velasquez, Cubillas; Munante, La Rosa (Sotil 60), Oblitas.

Iran: Hedjazi; Nazari, Abdollahi, Kazerani, Allahverdi; Parvin, Ghasempour, Sadeghi, Danaifard; Rowshan (Fariba 66), Faraki (Jahani 51).

Referee: A. Jarquz (Poland)

	W	D	L	F	A	Pts
Peru	2	1	0	7	2	5
Holland	1	1	1	5	3	3
Scotland	1	1	1	5	6	3
Iran	0	1	2	2	8	1

Second Round

GROUP A

Italy 0   West Germany 0   (B. Aires)

Italy: Zoff; Gentile, Bellugi, Scirea, Cabrini; Tardelli, Benetti, Antognoni (Zaccarelli 46); Causio, Rossi, Bettega.

West Germany: Maier; Vogts, Russmann, Kaltz, Dietz; Bonhof, Flohe (Beer 68), Zimmermann (Konopka 53); Rummenigge, Fischer, Holzenbein.

Referee: D. Maksimovic (Yugoslavia)

Holland . . . . (3) 5   Austria . . . . (0) 1   (Cordoba)
  Brandts, Rensenbrink (pen.), Rep (2),   Obermayer
  W. Van der Kerkhof

Holland: Schrijvers; Wildschut, Krol, Brandts (Van Kraaij 67), Poortvliet; W. Van der Kerkhof, Jansen, Haan; R. Van der Kerkhof (Schoenaker 60), Rep, Rensenbrink.

Austria: Koncilia; Sara, Obermayer, Pezzey, Breitenberger; Hickersberger, Prohaska, Kreuz; Jara, Krankl, Krieger.

Referee: J. Gordon (Scotland)

Italy . . . . (1) 1   Austria . . . . (0) 0   (B. Aires)
  Rossi

Italy: Zoff; Gentile, Bellugi (Cuccureddu 46), Scirea, Cabrini; Tardelli, Benetti, Zaccarelli; Causio, Rossi, Bettega (Graziani 71).

Austria: Koncilia; Sara, Obermayer, Pezzey, Strasser; Hickersberger, Prohaska, Kreuz; Schachner (Pirkner 63), Krankl, Krieger.

Referee: F. Rion (Belgium)

Holland . . . . (1) 2   West Germany . . . . (1) 2   (Cordoba)
  Haan, R. Van der Kerkhof   Abramczik, Muller D.

Holland: Schrijvers; Wildschut (Nanninga 78), Brandts, Krol, Poortvliet; W. Van der Kerkhof, Jansen, Haan; R. Van der Kerkhof, Rep, Rensenbrink.

West Germany: Maier; Vogts, Russmann, Kaltz, Dietz; Bonhof, Beer, Holzenbein; Abramczik, Muller D., Rummenigge.

Referee: R. Barreto (Uruguay)

Holland . . . . (0) 2   Italy . . . . (1) 1   (B. Aires)
  Brandts, Haan   Brandts

Holland: Schrijvers (Jongbloed 21); Jansen, Brandts, Krol, Poortvliet; W. Van der Kerkhof, Neeskens, Haan; R. Van der Kerkhof, Rep (Van Kraaij 65), Rensenbrink.

Italy: Zoff; Gentile, Cuccureddu, Scirea, Cabrini; Tardelli, Benetti (Graziani 77), Zaccarelli; Causio (C. Sala 46), Rossi, Bettega.

Referee: A. Martinez (Spain)

Austria . . . . (0) 3   West Germany . . . . (1) 2 (Cordoba)
    Vogts, Krankl (2)   Rummenigge, Holzenbein

Austria: Koncilia; Sara, Obermayer, Pezzey, Strasser; Hickersberger, Prohaska, Kreuz; Schachner, Krankl, Krieger.

West Germany: Maier; Vogts, Russmann, Kaltz, Dietz; Bonhof, Beer, Holzenbein; Abramczik, Muller D., Rummenigge.

Referee: A. Klein (Israel)

	W	D	L	F	A	Pts
Holland	2	1	0	9	4	5
Italy	1	1	1	2	2	3
West Germany	0	2	1	4	5	2
Austria	1	0	2	4	8	2

GROUP B

Brazil . . . . (2) 3   Peru . . . . (0) 0 (Mendoza)
    Dirceu (2), Zico (pen.)

Brazil: Leao; Toninho, Oscar, Amaral, Rodrigues Neto; Cerezo (Chicao 76), Batista, Dirceu; Gil (Zico 70), Roberto, Mendonca.

Peru: Quiroga; Duarte, Manzo, Chumpitaz, Diaz (Rojas 11); Cueto, Velasquez, Cubillas; Munante, La Rosa, Oblitas.

Referee: N. Rainea (Romania)

Argentina . . . . (1) 2   Poland . . . . (0) 0 (Rosario)
    Kempes (2)

Argentina: Fillol; Olguin, Galvan, Passarella, Tarantini; Ardiles, Gallego, Valencia (Villa 46); Bertoni, Kempes, Houseman (Ortiz 83).

Poland: Tomaszewski; Maculewicz, Zmuda, Kasperczak, Szymanowski; Masztaler (Mazur 64), Deyna, Nawalka; Lato, Boniek, Szarmach.

Referee: U. Ericsson (Sweden)

Poland . . . . (0) 1   Peru . . . . (0) 0 (Mendoza)
    Szarmach

Poland: Kukla; Maculewicz, Gorgon, Zmuda, Szymanowski; Masztaler (Kasperczak 46), Deyna, Nawalka; Lato, Boniek (Lubanski 86), Szarmach.

Peru: Quiroga; Duarte, Manzo, Chumpitaz, Navarro; Cueto, Quesada, Cubillas; Munante (Rojas 46), La Rosa (Sotil 74), Oblitas.

Referee: P. Partridge (England)

Argentina 0   Brazil . . . . 0 (Rosario)

Argentina: Fillol; Olguin, Galvan, Passarella, Tarantini; Ardiles (Villa 46), Gallego, Kempes; Bertoni, Luque, Ortiz (Alonso 60).

Brazil: Leao; Toninho, Oscar, Amaral, Rodrigues Neto (Edinho 34); Chicao, Batista, Dirceu; Gil, Roberto, Mendonca (Zico 67).

Referee: K. Palotai (Hungary)

Brazil . . . . (1) 3   Poland . . . . (1) 1 (Mendoza)
    Nelinho, Roberto (2)   Lato

Brazil: Leao; Toninho, Oscar, Amaral, Nelinho; Cerezo (Rivelino 77), Batista, Dirceu; Gil, Roberto, Zico (Mendonca 7).

Poland: Kukla; Maculewicz, Gorgon, Zmuda, Szymanowski; Kasperczak (Lubanski 64), Deyna, Nawalka; Lato, Boniek, Szarmach.

Referee: J. Silvagno (Chile)

190

Argentina . . . . (2) 6   **Peru** . . . . (0) 0   (Rosario)
    Kempes (2), Luque (2), Tarantini,
    Houseman
  Argentina: Fillol; Olguin, Galvan, Passarella, Tarantini; Larrosa, Gallego (Oviedo 85), Kempes; Bertoni (Houseman 64), Luque, Ortiz.
  Peru: Quiroga; Duarte, Manzo, Chumpitaz, Quesada; Cueto, Velasquez (Gorriti 51), Cubillas; Munante, Rojas, Oblitas.
Referee: R. Wurtz (France)

	W	D	L	F	A	Pts
Argentina	2	1	0	8	0	5
Brazil	2	1	0	6	1	5
Poland	1	0	2	2	5	2
Peru	0	0	3	0	10	0

THIRD PLACE

Brazil . . . . (0) 2   **Italy** . . . . (1) 1   (B. Aires)
    Nelinho, Dirceu   Causio
  Brazil: Leao; Nelinho, Oscar, Amaral, Rodrigues Neto; Cerezo (Rivelino 64), Batista, Dirceu; Gil (Reinaldo 46), Roberto, Mendonca.
  Italy: Zoff; Gentile, Scirea, Cuccureddu, Cabrini; P. Sala, Antognoni (C. Sala 78), Maldera; Causio, Rossi, Bettega.
Referee: A. Klein (Israel)

Final

Argentina . . . . (1) 3   **Holland** . . . . (0) 1   (B. Aires)
    Kempes (2), Bertoni   Nanninga
                    (after extra-time: 90 minutes, 1–1)
  Argentina: Fillol; Olguin, Galvan, Passarella, Tarantini; Ardiles (Larrosa 65), Gallego, Kempes; Bertoni, Luque, Ortiz (Houseman 74).
  Holland: Jongbloed; Jansen (Suurbier 72), Brandts, Krol, Poortvliet; W. Van der Kerkhof, Neeskens, Haan; R. Van der Kerkhof, Rep (Nanninga 59), Rensenbrink.
Referee: Sergio Gonella (Italy)

APPENDIX FOUR Results Achieved by England Teams Between World Cup 1974 and 1978

Opponents	Result	1	2	3	4	5	6	7	8	9	10	11	Sub
1974-5													
Czechoslovakia (H)	3-0	Clemence	Madeley	Hughes*	Dobson	Watson	Hunter	Bell[2]	Channon[1]	Worthington	Keegan	Francis, G.	… (3)
Portugal (H)	0-0	Clemence	Madeley	Cooper	Brooking	Watson, D.	Hughes*	Bell	Channon	Francis, G.	Clarke	Thomas	Worthington (10)
West Germany (H)	2-0	Clemence	Whitworth	Gillard	Bell[1]	Watson	Todd	Ball*	Channon	Macdonald[1]	Hudson	Keegan	Thomas (8)
Cyprus (H)	5-0	Shilton	Madeley	Beattie	Bell	Watson	Todd	Ball*	Channon	Macdonald[5]	Hudson	Keegan	Hughes (3)
Cyprus (A)	1-0	Clemence	Whitworth	Beattie	Bell	Watson	Todd	Ball*	Channon	Macdonald	Keegan[1]	Thomas	Tueart (11)
N. Ireland (A)	0-0	Clemence	Whitworth	Hughes	Bell	Watson	Todd	Ball*	Viljoen	Macdonald	Keegan	Tueart	Channon (9)
Wales (H)	2-2	Clemence	Whitworth	Gillard	Francis, G.	Watson	Todd	Ball*	Channon	Johnson[2]	Viljoen	Thomas	Little (8)
Scotland (H)	5-1	Clemence	Whitworth	Beattie[1]	Bell[1]	Watson	Todd	Ball*	Channon	Johnson[1]	Francis, G.[1]	Keegan	Thomas (11)
1975-6													
Switzerland (A)	2-1	Clemence	Whitworth	Beattie	Francis, G.*	Watson	Todd	Keegan[1]	Channon[1]	Johnson	Currie	Bell	Macdonald (9)
Czechoslovakia (A)	1-2	Clemence	Madeley	Gillard	Francis, G.*	McFarland	Todd	Keegan	Channon[1]	Macdonald	Clarke	Bell	Watson (5)
Portugal (A)	1-1	Clemence	Whitworth	Beattie	Madeley	Watson	Todd	Keegan	Channon[1]	Macdonald	Francis, G.*	Brooking	Thomas (8); Thomas (4)
Wales (A)	2-1	Clemence	Cherry	Neal	Doyle	Thompson, P.	Mills, M.	Keegan*	Channon	Boyer	Kennedy[1]	Brooking	Clarke (9)
Wales (A)	1-0	Clemence	Clement	Mills	Thompson	Greenhoff, B.	Kennedy	Keegan	Francis, G.*	Pearson	Towers	Taylor[1]	Clement (2); Taylor, P. (8)[1]
N. Ireland (H)	4-0	Clemence	Todd	Mills	Thompson	Greenhoff, B.	Kennedy	Keegan	Channon[2]	Pearson[1]	Francis, G.*[1]	Taylor	Royle (7)
Scotland (A)	1-2	Clemence	Todd	Mills	Thompson	McFarland	Kennedy	Keegan	Channon[1]	Pearson	Francis, G.*	Taylor	Towers (11)
Brazil (A)	0-1	Clemence	Todd	Mills	Thompson	Doyle	Cherry	Keegan	Channon	Pearson	Brooking	Francis, G.*	Doyle (5)
Italy (A)	3-2	Rimmer	Clement	Neal	Thompson[1]	Doyle	Towers	Wilkins, R.	Channon*[2]	Royle	Brooking	Hill	Cherry (9)
Finland (A)	4-1	Clemence	Todd	Mills	Thompson	Madeley	Cherry	Keegan[2]	Channon[1]	Pearson[1]	Brooking	Francis, G.*	Corrigan (1); Mills (3)
1976-7													
Eire (H)	1-1	Clemence	Todd	Cherry	Greenhoff, B.	MacFarland	Madeley	Keegan*	Wilkins, R.	Pearson[1]	Brooking	George	Hill (11)
Finland (H)	2-1	Clemence	Todd	Beattie	Thompson	Greenhoff, B.	Wilkins	Keegan*	Channon	Royle[1]	Brooking	Tueart[1]	Mills (10)
Italy (A)	0-2	Clemence	Clement	Mills	Greenhoff, B.	McFarland	Hughes	Keegan*	Channon	Bowles	Cherry	Brooking	Hill (11)
Netherlands (H)	0-2	Clemence	Clement	Beattie	Doyle	Watson	Madeley	Keegan*	Francis, T.	Greenhoff, B.	Bowles	Brooking	Beattie (2); Pearson (6)
Luxembourg (H)	5-0	Clemence	Gidman	Cherry	Kennedy[1]	Watson	Hughes	Keegan*[1]	Channon[2]	Royle	Francis, T.[1]	Hill	Todd (9)
N. Ireland (A)	2-1	Shilton	Cherry	Mills	Greenhoff, B.	Watson, D.	Todd	Wilkins, R.	Channon*[1]	Mariner	Brooking	Tueart[1]	Mariner (9)
Wales (H)	0-1	Shilton	Neal	Mills	Greenhoff, B.	Watson, D.	Hughes	Keegan*	Channon	Pearson	Brooking	Kennedy	Talbot (7)
Scotland (H)	1-2	Clemence	Neal	Mills	Greenhoff, B.	Watson	Hughes*	Francis, T.	Channon[1]	Pearson	Talbot	Kennedy	Tueart (10)
Brazil (A)	0-0	Clemence	Neal	Cherry	Greenhoff, B.	Watson	Hughes*	Keegan	Francis, T.	Pearson	Wilkins	Talbot	Cherry (4)
Argentina (A)	1-1	Clemence	Neal	Cherry	Greenhoff, B.	Watson	Hughes*	Keegan	Channon	Pearson	Wilkins	Talbot	Tueart (11)
Uruguay (A)	0-0	Clemence	Neal	Cherry	Greenhoff, B.	Watson	Hughes*	Keegan	Channon	Pearson	Wilkins	Talbot	Kennedy (11)
1977-8													
Switzerland (H)	0-0	Clemence	Neal	Cherry	McDermott	Watson	Hughes*	Keegan	Channon	Francis, T.	Kennedy	Callaghan	Kennedy (11)
Luxembourg (A)	2-0	Clemence	Cherry	Hughes*	Watson	Kennedy[1]	Callaghan	McDermott	Wilkins	Mariner[1]	Francis, T.	Hill	Hill (11); Beattie (4); Whymark (7)
Italy (H)	2-0	Clemence	Neal	Cherry	Wilkins	Watson	Hughes*	Keegan[1]	Coppell	Latchford	Brooking[1]	Barnes	Francis, T. (7); Pearson (9)